GOVERNMENT IS GOOD

An Unapologetic Defense of a Vital Institution

Douglas J. Amy
Department of Politics
Mount Holyoke College

First published by Dog Ear Publishing
4010 W. 86th Street, Ste H
Indianapolis, IN 46268
www.dogearpublishing.net

dog ear
PUBLISHING

ISBN: 978-1-4575-0658-1

This paper is acid free.
Printed in the United States of America

FOR SUSAN AND SAM
WHO HAVE KEPT ME SANE ALL THESE YEARS

CONTENTS

Preface

This book is adapted from a website I created several years ago called governmentisgood.com. In one sense, it completes a cycle, because the website originally began as a book manuscript. During the administration of George W. Bush, I searched in vain for a good defense of government against the relentless anti-government rhetoric of the Republicans in power. Finding none, I decided to write my own and eventually ended up with a manuscript. I ultimately decided that publishing that book with an academic press, as I had previously done with my other books, would be a mistake. University presses can afford little advertising and it was unlikely that many people would hear about the book. So I decided to turn it from a book with chapters into a website with articles that would be readily available to the public. I have not regretted that decision, and as of this writing, over 275,000 people have visited governmentisgood.com. I decided to turn the website back into a book because I've had many requests over the last few years to do so. Clearly some people would find it useful to have this information and analysis in book form and I am happy to provide it.

As with any large project like this, I am indebted to many people for their advice and assistance. Doug Campbell, Tom Wartenberg, and Alan Schiffmann looked over early drafts of this material and offered valuable encouragement and suggestions. Many thanks to Judy Greenough who graciously agreed to copyedit every chapter – an invaluable service. George Blackford also provided a lot of support, spotted a number of typos, and made several important suggestions for revisions. Finally, I owe my largest debt to Ed Royce who has been a great friend and a thoughtful companion on this intellectual journey. As always, however, I am ultimately responsible for any mistakes or problems in this book.

INTRODUCTION

Why We Need to Stand Up for Government

Why a book defending government? Because, like many Americans, I have become tired of the government bashing that is constantly coming from the political right. For decades conservatives have been demonizing government and not enough has been done to defend it. Ever since Ronald Reagan declared in 1981 that "Government is not a solution to our problem, government is the problem," Republicans have been waging a political war against this institution. Their core message has been expressed well by Dick Armey, a former Republican House Majority Leader and the author of a Tea Party manifesto. "Markets are smart," says Armey, "Government is dumb."

Conservative politicians have been joined in this anti-government crusade by libertarian thinkers, Tea Party activists, right-wing media pundits, and wealthy corporate lobbies. This powerful political coalition blithely ignores anything good about government and conducts a relentless smear campaign against this institution. As I write this, hardly a day goes by without the political commentators on Fox New ranting about "fascist" programs and "socialist" politicians. Government haters like Rush Limbaugh and Glenn Beck constantly play upon the fears and insecurities of average Americans and encourage them to blame all their problems on big bad government.

This torrent of anti-government rhetoric has been in service of a political program to hobble and reduce government. Make no mistake: the goal of this movement is not merely to eliminate waste or make government more efficient. The ultimate aim is to undo many of the basic government programs that have been in place for decades. Small-government activists want to roll back regulations protecting consumers, workers, and the environment. They want to slash spending on vital safety net programs like Medicare, Medicaid, and Social Security. And they would like to reduce taxes to the point that funding any new government programs becomes extremely difficult.

Consider, for example, the 2008 platform of the Texas Republican Party. It called for "the abolition of federal agencies involved in activities not delegated to the federal government under the original intent of the Constitution." So say goodbye to the Environmental Protection Agency, and the Departments of Energy, Housing and Urban Development, Health and Human Services, Education, Commerce and Labor. The platform also called for a drastic reduction in taxes, the lifeblood of government. Gone would be the personal income tax, the alternative minimum tax, the inheritance tax, the gift tax, the capital gains tax, the corporate income tax, and the payroll tax. In essence, this platform is a recipe for crippling our federal government.

Some had hoped that the election victory of Barack Obama would signal an end to these radical attacks on government. But this has clearly not been the case. In fact, the emergence of the virulently anti-tax and anti-government Tea Party movement has shown that government hating is alive and well in the U.S. And the resurgence of the Republican Party in the 2010 elections was based on a campaign in which nearly every ad harped on how awful government is – a message that apparently still resonates with some Americans.

This book takes on this minimal government movement. It exposes the misconceptions, misleading arguments, and faulty evidence that fuel this smear campaign against government. It describes the disastrous results of anti-government policies like deregulation, which have contributed to problems like the meltdown of the financial system and the massive oil spill in the Gulf of Mexico. It reveals that large majorities of Americans actually want the government to do more, not less, in many areas including energy, health care, poverty, education, and the regulation of big business. Most importantly, this book shows that government is often a powerful force for good in our society. A clear-headed and dispassionate examination of the achievements of government in the United States shows that it plays a unique and crucial role in improving Americans' lives and promoting the public interest.

Government Isn't So Bad

One of the purposes of this book is to show just how one-sided and distorted the right's depiction of government really is, and to set the record straight about this institution. We've all heard the usual complaints of these critics of government: taxes are too high, more government means less liberty, the federal bureaucracy is growing uncontrollably, government regulation undermines economic prosperity, and so on.

I will directly challenge all these criticisms. An objective look of the actual record of government reveals that most of these charges are highly exaggerated, misleading, or simply wrong. Consider, for example, the common charge that the federal bureaucracy is growing at an uncontrollable rate. Simply not true. The facts are these: in 1970, 2,997,000 civilians worked for the federal government; by 2009, that figure had grown to – or rather been reduced to – 2,804,000. In 1970, federal bureaucrats made up 3.8% of total U.S. workers, while in 2009 they made up a mere 2.0%. So much for the ever-growing federal bureaucracy.

Most of the other traditional right-wing criticisms of government are off the mark as well. This book shows that Americans are *not* hugely overtaxed, that big government does *not* inevitably impinge on individual freedoms, and that government is *not* the natural enemy of business. In the end, much of what we think we know about what is wrong with government – and what conservatives keep telling us – is simply mistaken.

Government is Actually Good

The other main purpose of this book is to make the case that government – despite its flaws – plays a valuable and indispensable role in promoting the public good. In short, government is good. Now I am *not* saying that everything that government does is good, or that every administration is good. That would be ridiculous. But I am saying that the institution of democratic government is a good thing and that on balance it plays a very positive role in the lives of all Americans.

Indeed, it is not an exaggeration to say that a good portion of the improvement in the quality of Americans' lives during the last 100 years has been due to the efforts of our federal, state, and local governments. Consider, for instance, the wide variety of essential functions that government performs in our society. Things like providing roads and sewers and other crucial infrastructure facilities, preventing economic depressions, eliminating horrible diseases like polio and smallpox, ensuring drinkable water and breathable air, dispensing justice, providing retirement security, preventing business abuses, sponsoring stunning scientific breakthroughs, feeding the hungry, protecting our bank deposits, recalling unsafe products, educating our children, reducing workplace injuries and deaths, responding to disasters and emergencies, preventing crime, protecting civil liberties, rescuing endangered species, ensuring the safety of drugs, guarding our national security, caring for the elderly, and so on.

Seen this way, it is clear that the supportive role that government plays in all our lives is large and indispensable. We are usually told that the high quality of life enjoyed by so many people in the United States is due to the abundance created in the private sector, but in fact it is also due to the many activities of the public sector. The good life as we know it in the United States literally could not exist without the constant assistance and protection we all get from an extensive network of government laws and programs.

Democratic government is actually one of the greatest institutional inventions of modern Western civilization. It allows us to pool our resources and to act collectively to address the serious social, economic, and environmental problems that we are unable to deal with as individuals. The public sector is also how we provide for essential human needs that are neglected by the market – such as clean air and water, safe workplaces, and economic security. What's more, government serves as an essential instrument of moral action – a way for us to rectify injustices, eliminate suffering, and care for each other. In short, democratic government is one of the main ways we work together to pursue the common good and make the world a better place.

Many Americans seem to intuitively understand and value the crucial role that government programs play in society. While conservatives maintain that most people want to see government cut back, polls show that the opposite is true. Less than 10% of Americans want to see the government spend less in areas like education, environmental protection, healthcare, crime prevention, childcare subsidies, and Social Security. In fact a majority of Americans want the government to do more in all of these areas.

Government Does Have Its Problems

To say that government is good is not to deny that it has its problems. There are incidents of shameful waste, some regulations are poorly designed, and some politicians abuse their power. Such problems certainly need to be addressed. More disturbing is the fact that our government is clearly not as democratic and accountable as it should be. Money plays too big a role in politics, and special interests have way too much political power. Well-funded lobbies routinely get their way in Congress, while the voices of average Americans go unheard. Several chapters in this book detail this "deficit of democracy" and discuss how it might be fixed. We do need to improve government, but we don't need to radically reduce it.

We also need to put these problems with government into perspective. Whatever drawbacks this institution has right now are far outweighed by the enormous benefits that we all enjoy from a vast array of public sector programs. On the whole, despite its flaws, government does a lot of good for all of us.

What is at Stake in the Battle over Government

Why is it so crucial to set the record straight about government? Why is it important for Americans to realize that their local, state, and federal governments are in fact acting as powerful forces for good in our society? Because the negative images of government that are being constantly promoted by conservatives have had widespread and damaging political repercussions. These distorted views of government have been used to fuel and justify the conservative campaign to substantially reduce government – to undermine important social programs and rollback regulations that are supposed to protect consumers, investors, workers, and the environment.

In recent years, Americans have become all too aware of what is at stake in this battle over government. The disastrous results of pushing for smaller government – especially the efforts to reduce the regulation of businesses – have become obvious to all of us. Deregulation of the financial sector cost Americans billions of dollars in investments due to the mortgage loan crisis and the resulting meltdown of the financial system. Also, thousands of Americans have gotten sick because of lax and under-funded food inspection programs – thanks again to Republican hostility to regulation. And it is impossible to ignore one of the largest ecological disasters in the nation's history, brought on in large part by a lack of effective government oversight of oil drilling operations in the Gulf of Mexico. The human costs of this oil spill were in the hundreds of billions of dollars, and the ecological costs will be enormous as well.

These well-known examples of the disastrous results of the attack on government are merely the tip of the iceberg. There are literally thousands of other cases of how cutbacks on government programs have led to increasing problems and suffering for the public. Consider just one example: the deregulation of rat poison. In 1998, the Environmental Protection Agency mandated child-proofing of rat poisons that were manufactured in candy-like pastel pellets. It required that the pellets have a bitter taste and a bright dye. But some manufacturers protested, and in the spirit of limiting government and getting it off the back of business, the Bush EPA rescinded those requirements in 2001.

By 2004, poisons centers were reporting that 50,000 children a year were requiring treatment for ingesting rat poisons – three times as many as when the childproofing requirements were in effect.

We must also consider the long list of problems caused by cutbacks in state and local programs. Our children's education is suffering as thousands of teachers are being laid off, class sizes are ballooning, and textbooks are becoming older and scarcer. Vital police and firefighting services are being reduced. Bridges and roads are falling into disrepair. State colleges are become less affordable to poor and working class students. There have also been large cuts in health care programs, food programs, libraries and park budgets, and state aid to the elderly and disabled. Many Americans have seen the quality of life in their communities suffer because of these efforts to reduce government.

We Need a Better Defense of Government

Until now, those who have been attacking government have been doing a much better job than the few who have been trying to defend it. Republicans have been waging their anti-government campaign on two fronts. First has been the attack on specific government programs, from welfare and Medicaid to environmental protection and business regulation. Second, and perhaps more important, has been the effort to delegitimize government itself – to convince Americans that government is a bad thing that should be limited whenever possible.

Unfortunately, many centrist and liberal politicians have been fighting back on only one front. They tried, during the Bush administration, to defend particular public sector programs from attack, including Social Security and environmental protection. And during the Obama administration, they have pushed through several critically needed new programs, such as health care reform. But most liberals have still not been aggressively promoting the idea that *government itself* is valuable and beneficial. They have not been making the positive case for a healthier and more active public sector.

Actually, it has been worse than that. Beginning in the 1980s, some Democrats beat a retreat away from the notion that government is good. They routinely reinforced anti-government stereotypes by focusing on its negative aspects, such as complaining about government waste. Many also supported damaging tax cuts and ill-considered deregulation efforts. And some Democratic candidates even joined Republicans in running against Washington and "big government" in their election campaigns. Consider the words uttered by Bill Clinton in his 1996 State of The Union Address: "We know big government does not have all the answers. We know there's not a program for every problem. ... The era of big government is over." These kinds of statements inadvertently added legitimacy to the right-wing crusade against government. One conservative journal, the *Weekly Standard*, was so excited about Clinton's statement that they declared on their front cover "We've Won!"

Clearly many centrist and liberal lawmakers understand the valuable and indispensable role that government plays in our society, but many seem to believe that if they too jump on the anti-government band-wagon, this will take the issue away from the conservatives. But this strategy has utterly failed. It has only added fuel to the anti-government fire that Republicans have been stoking for years. Far from abandoning this issue, the right has only pressed harder in their efforts to delegitimize government and reduce liberal programs.

It is important to see that this Democratic Party retreat represents an enormous change from the more positive attitude toward government – even big government – that was common during large parts of the twentieth century. Then, many politicians and members of the public embraced *big* government as the only thing that could counterbalance the power of *big* business, prevail over the *big* foreign threats of fascism and communism, complete *big* national projects like the interstate highway system, and solve *big* societal problems like economic depressions, racism, and environmental pollution.

Americans need to recognize that government can still play this kind of vital role in our society. Government is *not* the problem; it is actually the only *solution* to most of the pressing problems we face as a nation – including infrastructure decay, persistent unemployment, rising health care costs, and global warming. As this book shows, if we want an America that is prosperous, healthy, secure, well-educated, just, compassionate, and unpolluted, we need a strong, active, and well-funded public sector.

How this Book is Organized

Part I: Why Government is Good. The first section of the book describes how government acts as a force for good in society. One chapter chronicles a day in the life of an average middle-class American and identifies the myriad and often overlooked ways that government laws and programs improve our lives. Other chapters describe the forgotten achievements of government; how government is the only way to effectively promote public values like justice, equality and security; how public sector policies and institutions protect and enhance our freedoms; how a free market economy would be impossible without the elaborate legal and regulatory infrastructure provided by government; and why we need more – not less – government.

Part II: The War on Government. This section of the book chronicles the unrelenting assault on government being waged by conservative forces in this country. Chapters describe how cuts in social programs and rollbacks of regulations have harmed the health, safety, and welfare of millions of Americans and how these assaults have taken place on many fronts – in Congress, the administrative branch, and the federal courts, as well as on the state and local level. Also addressed: how the right's radical anti-government agenda is out of touch with the views and priorities of most Americans, who is funding this anti-government movement, and what the real truth is about government debt and deficits.

Part III: How to Revitalize Democracy and Government. There are, in fact, some problems with American government, and we need to address these if we are to restore Americans' faith in this institution. Right now, the main problem with our government is that it is not accountable and responsive enough to the public. We have a deficit of democracy – with special interests too often winning out over the public interest. Chapters in this section describe this problem and how we can fix it. There are several reforms – including public financing of elections – that could help our government live up to its democratic ideals. The final chapter discusses how we can begin to build a pro-government political movement, including ways to "reframe" the way we think and talk about government and strategies for building a pro-government coalition in this country.

PART I

WHY GOVERNMENT IS GOOD

CHAPTER 1

A Day in Your Life

Ask yourself this question: "What has government done for me lately?" If you are like most Americans, you will probably answer: "Not much." Many people feel like they pay a lot in taxes but don't really get anything back from government. Surveys show that 52% of Americans believe that "government programs have not really helped me and my family."[1] But let's see if that is really true. Let's examine a typical day in the life of an average middle-class American and try to identify some of the ways that government improves that person's life during that 24-hour period.

> **6:30 a.m.** You are awakened by your clock radio. You know it is actually 6:30 because the National Institute of Standards and Technology keeps the official time. And you can listen to your favorite radio station only because the Federal Communications Commission brings organization and coherence to our vast telecommunications system. It ensures, for example, that radio stations do not overlap and that stations signals are not interfered with by the numerous other devices – cell phones, satellite television, wireless computers, etc. – whose signals crowd our nation's airwaves.
>
> **6:35 a.m.** Like 17 million other Americans, you have asthma. But as you get out of bed you notice that you are breathing freely this morning. This is thanks in part to government clean air laws that reduce the air pollution that would otherwise greatly worsen your condition.
>
> **6:38 a.m.** You go into the kitchen for breakfast. You pour some water into your coffeemaker. You simply take for granted that this water is safe to drink. But in fact you count on your city water department to constantly monitor the quality of your water and to immediately take measures to correct any potential problems with this vital resource.

6:39 a.m. You flip the switch on the coffee maker. There is no short in the outlet or in the electrical line and there is no resulting fire in your house. Why? Because when your house was being built, the electrical system had to be inspected to make sure it was properly installed – a service provided by your local government. And it was installed by an electrician who was licensed by your state government to ensure his competence and your safety.

6:45 a.m. You sit down to breakfast with your family. You are having eggs – a food that brings with it the possibility of salmonella poisoning, a serious food-borne illness affecting tens of thousands of Americans every year. But the chance of you getting sick from these eggs has now been greatly reduced by a recently passed series of strict federal rules that apply to egg producers.

7:00 a.m. You go into your newly renovated bathroom – one of a number of amenities that you enjoy in your house. But the fact that you can legally own your own house is something made possible by government. Think about this: "ownership" and "private property" are not things that exist in nature. These are legal constructs: things created by laws that are passed and enforced by government. You couldn't even buy your home without a system of commercial laws concerning contracts and a government that ensures that sales contracts are enforced. So the fact that you live in your own home is, in part, a benefit of government and the rule of law.

7:01 a.m. Government also helps you own your house in more than the legal sense. On a more practical level, the federal government actually gives you money every year to help pay for your house. It's called a mortgage interest tax deduction and it is one of the larger benefit programs run by the federal government – amounting to over $60 billion dollars a year. You can also deduct any real estate taxes you pay. These largely overlooked subsidy programs have enabled millions of people to buy their first home or to move up to a larger home than they could afford otherwise.

7:02 a.m. Back in the bathroom. You use the toilet and flush it. Your local government then takes care of transporting this waste, treating it, and disposing of it in an environmentally responsible manner – all without a second thought by you.

7:20 a.m. As you are getting dressed, a glance outside the window shows some ominous clouds. You check the weather on your TV. All these weather forecasts are made possible by information gathered and analyzed by the National Weather Service, a government agency. Every day, on your behalf, it takes in 190,000 weather observations from surface stations, 2,700 from ships, 115,000 from aircraft, 18,000 from buoys, 250,000 from balloons, and 140 million from satellites – all just to help you plan what to wear and make sure you don't get stuck in a snow storm. And oh yes, this agency may save your life with its hurricane and tornado warnings.

7:30 a.m. Before you leave home, you take your pills to control your high blood pressure. But how do you know that this medicine is safe or effective? Without the testing required by the Food and Drug Administration, you wouldn't. And without the vigilance of the FDA, you could easily fall victim to unscrupulous marketers of unsafe and worthless medicines.

7:45 a.m. You put a couple of letters in your mailbox. For less than the price of a cup of coffee, a government employee will come to your house, pick up the letters, and have them delivered in a few days to someone on the other side of the country. A pretty good deal.

7:50 a.m. You and your child walk across the lawn to your car and arrive without getting dog poop on your shoes. A small but welcome achievement that is made possible now by a local law that requires people to clean up after their pets. Also, the reason your neighborhood is not plagued by stray cats and dogs is that your local Animal Control officer is on the job dealing with this constant problem.

7:52 a.m. You help your young child into your car and you pull out of your driveway. You have now entered an experience that is improved by government in almost more ways that you can count. Driving your car is inherently dangerous. But it is made immensely safer by government laws and regulations, such as those mandating child safety seats and the use of seat belts – rules that have saved tens of thousands of lives. Driving down the street is also made much safer by a local government that enforces traffic laws and discourages people from driving too fast or driving drunk. Most state governments also minimize your risk of being run into by someone driving on bald tires or with faulty brakes by requiring regular inspections of all vehicles. And state driver's license examinations ensure that all drivers are at least minimally competent and can actually see the road. In addition, if you are hit by another car, the potentially disastrous costs of an accident are covered because the government requires that all drivers to have auto insurance. In fact, without this extensive network of government laws and regulations covering automobiles and driving, it would be foolish for us to ever venture out on the road.

8:15 a.m. You drop your child off at day-care. It took a long search to find a good program and it is an expensive one, but it is worth it so you can feel confident that your child is in a safe, nurturing, and stimulating environment while you are at work. One of the reasons you can afford this program is the $3,000 child care tax credit you get from the federal government every year. Equally important, your child benefits from the fact that most state governments now enforce day-care requirements for group size, ratios of children per staff member, teacher training, nutrition, health, safety, and space requirements.

8:35 a.m. Your trip on the freeway is much safer due to federal restrictions on the number of hours that truck drivers can operate their vehicles without resting. Thousands of people die every year from truck-related traffic accidents, but it would be much worse without these regulations that keep sleepy truck drivers off the road.

8:55 a.m. You arrive at work and take the elevator. You just assume that the elevator is safe; and it is, thanks in part to the annual elevator inspections conducted by your state government. It is probably nothing you will appreciate until the next time the elevator breaks down with you inside, and that makes you think a bit more about the reliability of elevators.

9:00 a.m. While at work, your rights and wellbeing are constantly protected by a wide-ranging network of federal and state laws. The Occupation Safety and Health Act works to protect you from unsafe and unhealthy work conditions. Federal law protects you from workplace discrimination based on race, gender, religion, national origin, or disability. State laws may also require your employer to purchase worker's compensation insurance so that you are covered in case you are injured on the job

Noon. For lunch you have your usual sandwich and microwaveable cup of soup. But why did you choose that particular soup? Perhaps because it was low in salt and fat. But how do you know that? Because the government requires all food packaging to have a truthful and easily readable panel on the label that supplies you with the nutritional information necessary to make a good choice. Food companies tell you what *they* want you to know about their products, but the Food and Drug Administration's labeling requirements tell you what *you* need to know to eat in a healthy way.

How do you know the lettuce in your sandwich is not laced with unhealthy doses of pesticides? Because the Department of Agriculture has developed and is enforcing uniform standards for pesticide residue on raw foods.

Microwave ovens are potentially very dangerous machines, but you can use this one with confidence because of detailed government regulations that limit the maximum amount of radiation leakage and mandate two different safety interlocks that prevent its operation with the door ajar or open.

12:45 p.m. After lunch, you walk to a nearby ATM and get some cash out of your account – and your money is actually there. That wasn't always true during the economic depression of the 1930s when many banks failed. But your money is safe — as it was during the recent financial and banking crisis — because the government guarantees your deposits. In addition, those pieces of paper you put in your wallet are only worth something thanks to the federal government. Our monetary system is entirely a government creation, and the value of money is only maintained because the government regulates the money supply and protects it from counterfeiters. Quite an important service really.

1:00 p.m. Back at work you hear rumors about a new downsizing plan being talked about by management – a fairly typical occurrence in these days of heightened national and international corporate competition. You know your job is one that could be lost, but you also know that you will be eligible for state-mandated unemployment insurance should that happen. This is just another way that government helps you to cope with the economic risks and uncertainties of a modern economy.

3:00 p.m. On a break, you call your elderly mother in the hospital to check on how she is recovering from her broken hip. Thanks to Medicare, her medical expenses are covered and she does not have to worry about this becoming a financial disaster for her. Thanks to the federal Family and Medical Leave act, you will also have the right to take several days off to tend to your mother when she comes home from the hospital.

3:10 p.m. You call to arrange for a physical therapist to work with your mother when she comes out of the hospital, and again this is paid for by Medicare. And you can be reasonably confident that she will get good therapy because your state Department of Health has a program of examining and licensing these therapists in order to ensure the quality of their work.

5:00 p.m. You leave work—thanks to the government-mandated 40-hour workweek. Labor Department regulations prevent your company from making you work past 5:00 unless it pays you overtime.

5:15 p.m. You stop at a local gas station to fill up. The very fact that this oil company offers this gas to you for sale is dependent on the existence of certain government laws. This company would not do business in your town without a legal system that assures them that you will pay for any gas you pump into your car. This economic exchange – like buying your house – would not be taking place without a system of statutory and common law that protects private property and regulates sales transactions. This simple sale is covered by Article Two of the Uniform Commercial Code – dozens of pages of laws that regulate every phase of a transaction for the sale of goods and provide remedies for problems that may arise.

5:15 p.m. You pump 15 gallons of 87 octane gas into your car and pay for it. But how do you know that you really got 15 gallons, and not 14½? And that the gas was actually 87 octane? This is only ensured by the presence of that little sticker on the gas pump that shows that a worker from your city's Division of Weights and Measures has inspected the pump and the gas. These public employees make sure that you get what you pay for – from a pound of sliced turkey breast to a carat of diamond – by constantly testing and inspecting all commercial meters and scales, and by verifying the accuracy of checkout scanners. This is a crucial service, since more than half of the income of the average family is used to purchase necessities bought by weight or measure or scanned at a checkout station.

5:15 p.m. How do you know the price you are paying for this gasoline is a fair and competitive one? In many states, the Department of Attorney General has been responsible for finding and prosecuting cases of price manipulation and price fixing by oil companies and distributors.

5:30 p.m. As you drive home, you notice the tree-lined streets and the nice houses in your neighborhood – generally a pretty good place to live. Thanks again to government. Without zoning rules, you might have an auto body shop or a fast-food outlet move in next door. Or worse yet, a fertilizer plant or a toxic waste site. But there are no noxious smells in the air, no excessive and dangerous traffic on your street – thanks to your government. Pleasant and livable neighborhoods are only possible with extensive government planning and zoning regulation.

5:35 p.m. As you approach your house, you see your child coming down the sidewalk. The government-provided sidewalk. The sidewalk that allows your child to walk to the neighbor's house down the street to play with a friend without the risk of being hit by a car.

5:45 p.m. You go for a jog in your local public park.

6:30 p.m. You take your family out for dinner at a local pizza restaurant. You enjoy a good meal and no one gets sick from E. coli or other food-borne illnesses. This is in large part because your local government conducts regular inspections of all food establishments to protect the health of customers.

7:30 p.m. Back at your house. You settle in for a quiet evening at home – one that is undisturbed by those annoying telemarketers calling you up to try to sell you something. This is because you have signed up with a state or federal no-call registry – a government service now enjoyed by over 60 million Americans.

8:00 p.m. You do a quick check of your e-mail – just one of the many services you enjoy over the internet every day. We all tend to think of the internet as the product of those talented and imaginative entrepreneurs in the high-tech companies. But the internet actually began with government programs that created ARPANET and later NSFNET, early computer networking systems that developed the software and networking infrastructure that form the foundations of today's internet. The government also helped to fund research that led to web browsers like Internet Explorer and search engines like Google.

11:00 p.m. You go to bed. During your sleep, you are protected by a smoke detector that your city requires to be installed in every residence. Maybe you would have bought one of these yourself, but this law helps to ensure that everyone is protected from the dangers of fire.

4:00 a.m. You are asleep in your comfy bed. Unlike that time you stayed in a small inn in Costa Rica, where you were woken up regularly at 4 in the morning by the roosters crowing in the neighborhood. By law, no one can keep roosters in your neighborhood and so you remain in blissful slumber.

Government: The Illusion and the Reality

So goes your typical day as an average middle-class American – *if* you happen to be paying attention to all the different ways that government laws and programs help you lead a better life. For most of us, thinking about our day this way is a real eye-opener. We like to see ourselves as rugged individualists, leading our lives without any help from anyone, especially government. But this is an illusion. As we have just seen, the reality is completely different. We are constantly benefiting from a variety of government laws and programs. Federal, state, and local government employees are literally working around the clock to make our lives better in innumerable ways. Ironically, even those conservatives who complain that they don't want government "interfering" in their lives depend heavily and repeatedly on government throughout their day. And the examples described earlier are only a small sample of the many ways that government programs improve our lives. They do not even include many of the most important services of government, such as preventing economic depressions, catching criminals, caring for our fragile ecosystem, dispensing justice, thwarting terrorist attacks, and eradicating deadly diseases. A detailed description of all the various ways that our lives are improved by the activities of local, state, and federal governments could easily take up hundreds of pages.

Many conservative critics of government like to portray it as a malevolent force whose extensive network of laws and regulations are increasingly invading our lives in harmful ways. They have it half right: government policies do affect our everyday lives in many ways, but these efforts are usually beneficial. For most of us, most of the time, government is not some faceless bureaucrat who is constantly ordering us around; it is more like a guardian angel: an invisible benevolent being that accompanies us throughout their day, easing us through potential difficulties and protecting us from impending harms. Admittedly, the angel analogy is a bit exaggerated, but the underlying truth is not: government has an extensive and overwhelmingly positive effect on our everyday lives.

Why We are in Denial About the Value of Government

So why are most people in denial about the beneficial roles that government plays in their lives? There are several answers. First, most Americans have become so used to the benefits of government that they simply take them for granted. Benefits that are provided reliably for long periods of time – such as clean water and a stable currency system – tend to fade into the background and to not be considered benefits at all. They disappear from our consciousness.

Our failure to notice or appreciate what government does for us also has to do with the unique and peculiar nature of many government benefits. The benefits we get from paying our taxes are usually not immediate, and they are often not particularly tangible either. They can be remote and elusive. This is easy to see if we contrast government benefits with the benefits we receive from exchanges in the marketplace. When we go to the store, we hand over our money and immediately get something very concrete in return – a candy bar, a blouse, some groceries. This kind of exchange is very satisfying; we see what we get for our money right away.

Not so with many of the exchanges we have with our governments. We shell out money for our taxes, but what we gain in return is frequently delayed or remote. For instance, we pay our local government to treat our sewage, but the environmental payoffs may not be immediately obvious to us. When we later go fishing or swimming in our local lake or river – waters whose purity depends upon adequate sewage treatment – we probably do not see this enjoyable experience as a result of our sewer tax. When benefits are remote like this, it is hard to make the connections between them and the taxes we pay. It is unlikely, for example, that we associate sending our check to the IRS with getting reliable weather forecasts every morning, or with the purchase of a flack vest that saves a police officer's life in Los Angeles, or with badly needed emergency aid that goes to a hurricane victim in Florida.

Government benefits are also different because they are often less tangible than the goods we get from a store. These benefits frequently take the form not of the presence of something, but of the absence of something. Think of it this way: much of the job of government in our lives is to ensure that bad things don't happen to us. We pay taxes so that our homes don't get burgled, and our food doesn't make us sick, our banks don't fail, and our bridges don't collapse. In other words, often when people in government are doing their job right – *nothing happens.* No wonder no one notices. So while we really do get a lot for with our taxes, we often get it in a form that is largely invisible to us.

This is one of the reasons why we too easily fall for the illusion that government is doing nothing for us.

The Conservative Campaign Against Government

There is, however, another much more disturbing reason that most of us mistakenly believe that government doesn't do much for us: it's because this is what we are being constantly told. One of the most consistent political messages promoted by conservative pundits and politicians in this country is that our governments are essentially thieves – that they take our taxes but rarely give us back anything of value. The political right is continually telling us that we benefit little from public programs. Here's how Dick Armey, former Republican House Majority Leader, used to drive this point home: "I don't want to give the impression that most government programs are designed, even ostensibly, to help families with the needs of everyday life. Most government programs don't even pretend to do that, and very few American families would notice their disappearance."[2]

This idea that government programs do not benefit the average American is simply one part of a larger smear campaign against government being waged by the right-wing in the country. During the last 30 years, conservatives have spent a great deal of time and money trying to convince Americans that government is bad. They have relentlessly promoted a series of negative stereotypes about government, invoking ominous images of "Big Brother" and the "Taxman." They have blindly ignored everything that is right with government and aggressively advanced a vision of government as a dark force in society. We have been continually told that government is inefficient, ineffective, corrupt, oppressive, overly expensive, and bad for business. The core message has been clear: government doesn't help us, it hurts us; it doesn't solve problems, it *is* the problem. This claim that "government is bad" has been a central political theme in virtually every Republican election campaign during the last three decades. Americans have always been somewhat suspicious of government, but this tendency has been greatly exacerbated and exaggerated by a steady diet of anti-government rhetoric coming from the political right.

The media often go along with the conservative smear campaign against government – sometime intentionally, sometimes not. Explicitly right-wing media outlets like Fox News are full of daily diatribes against big government. Conservative commentators lambaste "wasteful" social programs, "ridiculous" regulations, and the "stupid" liberals who support these things. Even the more neutral mainstream news outlets inadvertently convey an almost entirely negative view of government to the public. It is not news when government works well, only when it fails. So news stories focus on policy blunders, government waste, and corrupt politicians. When is the last time that you heard something positive about government in the media – something about how government is working to improve people's lives?

In this context, it is hardly surprising that most of us mistakenly believe that government programs do little to benefit us – that is what we are being constantly told. Every day we are hearing about what is wrong with government, so it is inevitable that we tend to develop an incomplete, distorted, and negative view of the public sector. But it is time to set the record straight about this much-maligned public institution. That is the purpose of this book.

---

1. Meg Bostrum, *By, or for, the People: A Meta-Analysis of Public Opinion of Government* (New York: Demos, March 1, 2005) p. 34.
2. Dick Armey, *The Freedom Revolution* (New York: Regnery Publishers, 1995), p. 293.

CHAPTER 2

The Forgotten Achievements of Government

One of the most persistent myths about American government is that it has a poor record of achievement. Conservatives and libertarians have constantly promoted the idea that government fails more often than it succeeds. They have been telling Americans for years that government is an incompetent institution that has achieved little of real value in society. As one conservative critic put it: "The more important question is not why government is so big ... but why with few exceptions, it fails in even its simplest tasks."[1] Another critic, Charles Murray, puts it even more bluntly: "The reality of daily life is that, by and large, the things the government does tend to be ugly, rude, slovenly – and not to work."[2] Or consider the bold challenge uttered by Rush Limbaugh on one of his radio shows: "With the exception of the military, I defy you to name one government program that has worked and alleviated the problem it was created to solve. Hhhmmmmmmmm? I'm waiting. . . . Time's up."[3]

The Stereotype: Government as Bungling and Inept

Many of us have bought into this image of government as a bungler – a bunch of bureaucrats that can't do anything right. Ask most Americans and they will tell you: if you want something messed up, have the government do it. We've all heard the jokes:

> Q: How many government bureaucrats does it take to screw in a light bulb?
> A: Two. One to assure everyone that everything possible is being done while the other screws the bulb into the water faucet.
> Q: How many government workers does it take to screw in a light bulb?
> A: Two. One to screw it in and one to screw it up.

This popular view of government as a low-achieving screw-up is echoed in many surveys as well. When asked, "When the government in Washington decides to solve a problem, how much confidence do you have that the problem will be solved?" only four percent of Americans said "a lot." Sixty-four percent said "none at all" or "just a little." Of these, more than a three out of four said the reason was "government is incompetent" not that "those problems are often difficult to solve."[4] Surveys also show that a large majority of citizens (70%) believe that "government creates more problems than it solves."[5] Clearly, for many Americans, government is the Inspector Clouseau of institutions.

But how accurate is this popular image of the government as a bumbling fool? Actually, this is largely a stereotype – one based primarily on myth and selective anecdotal evidence. Of course anyone can cite a number of failed government policies – such as the war on drugs or public housing programs. But it is wrong to leap from this kind of anecdotal evidence to the conclusion that government as a whole is inherently incompetent. The reality is this: most government programs are successful most of the time. By and large, the public sector does a good job providing clean water to drink, keeping the peace, sending out Social Security checks, reducing workplace injuries, ensuring aircraft safety, feeding the hungry, putting out fires, protecting consumers, and so on.

Once we begin to look at the actual performance of major government programs, we see that the vast majority of them have produced substantial improvement in the problem areas that they are addressing – they have produced successful results. This is not the conventional wisdom, but it is what the evidence shows if you bother to look at it. Let's consider some of that evidence.

An Initial List of Government Achievements[6]

Let's start by taking up Rush Limbaugh's challenge: can we name any government programs that have worked? Actually, that is quite easy to do. What follows is a short list of some of the federal government's greatest accomplishments. These are policy programs that have not only worked, but have been very successful and have greatly improved the quality of life of most Americans.

- **Regulation of the Business Cycle.** Until the financial crisis that began in 2008, most of us had forgotten how dependent we are on the federal government to prevent economic depressions.

Since the 1930s, the government has used a variety of monetary and fiscal policies to limit the natural boom and bust cycles of the economy. Before government took on this responsibility, severe depressions were a routine and recurring problem in this country – occurring in 1819, 1837, 1857, 1873, 1893, 1907 and 1929. Thanks to government intervention, we have been able to avoid the enormous amount of human suffering caused by these massive economic meltdowns – the widespread joblessness, the destitution, the rampant hunger, the disease, the riots, the hopelessness and the despair. By any measure, eliminating these depressions and this misery has been one of the greatest – and often unheralded – achievements of our federal government.

- **Public Health Programs.** A variety of programs run by the National Institutes of Health, the Centers for Disease Control and Prevention, and state and local Public Health departments have greatly improved the health of most Americans. For example, the scourges of polio, cholera, and smallpox have been effectively eradicated from this country – a huge achievement. And vaccination programs have reduced by 95% our risks of contracting potentially debilitating diseases like hepatitis B, measles, mumps, tetanus, rubella, and diphtheria. Federal funds spent on buying and distributing these vaccines have saved countless lives and the billions of dollars it would cost to treat these illnesses. In addition, the dedicated scientists who work for the CDC are all that stand between Americans and a potentially catastrophic epidemic imported from abroad. The most likely and worrisome threat is from a new and deadly strain of bird flu. The last deadly flu epidemic to hit the United States, in 1918, killed over 675,000 people in a matter of months.
- **The Interstate Highway System.** Started by the Eisenhower administration in the 1950s, this system now forms the backbone of long-distance travel and commerce in the United States. It makes up less than 1% of our highways, but carries almost a quarter of all roadway traffic. It has also allowed millions of Americans to move out of big cities and live in more pleasant suburban and small town environments. In addition, the interstate system has the benefit of being considerably safer than the old two-lane highways it replaced – saving hundreds of thousands of lives. Even some conservatives have been forced to admit the success of this building program, with George Will calling it "the most successful public works program in the history of the world." It's hard to imagine the U.S. without this

interstate highway system, and this system would not exist at all if it weren't for the government.

- **Federal Deposit Insurance.** Another government program we've taken totally for granted until recently is federal protection of our bank deposits. In bad economic times, banks are inherently vulnerable to destructive "runs" – where worried depositors all seek to take out their money at the same time. Before the FDIC, in the depression of the 1930s, over 5,000 banks went bust and millions of Americans lost their savings. The main reason we had no disastrous runs on banks (and money market funds) during the financial panic of 2008 was that government was there to guarantee those deposits.
- **Social Security and Medicare.** Without these two government programs, growing old would be hell for many Americans. Before Social Security and Medicare, millions of the elderly were doomed to spend their retirement years in poverty and illness. Social Security has cut the rate of poverty for the elderly by over half – from 29% in 1966 to 10% today. Not surprisingly, financial columnist Jane Bryant Quinn has described Social Security as "arguably the U.S. government's greatest success." Medicare has also been incredibly successful. It has doubled the number of the elderly covered by health insurance, so that 99% now enjoy that benefit. Without this form of "socialized" medicine, 15 million of our neediest citizens would be going without many vital medical services and many would have to choose between food and medicine. Older Americans are now living 20% longer, thanks in part to this effective program. These two programs have done more than anything else to relieve the pain and suffering of our elderly population.
- **GI Bill** Without this program, the middle class as we know it would not exist. The GI Bill provided government funds for 16 million World War II and Korean veterans to attend college. It allowed my father to become the first one in his family to graduate college, to become an engineer, and to go on to build a middle-class life for our family. Historian David Kennedy has remarked that "GI Bill beneficiaries changed the face of higher education, dramatically raised the educational level and hence the productivity of the workforce, and in the process unimaginably altered their own lives."[7]
- **Federal Housing Authority.** The middle class housing building and buying boom in the United States was initially financed by cheap GI Bill housing loans and by Federal Housing Authority

insurance of conventional home loans. In 1945, only 44% of Americans owned their own home. But thanks in large part to the FHA program that lowered interest rates and down payments, 63% of Americans owned a home by 1968. These homes have become a multi-generational source of wealth for tens of millions of Americans. The FHA still insures over $50 billion a year in mortgages, and remains especially important for low-income house buyers.

- **Consumer Protection.** In reaction to increasing public pressure in the early 1970s, government began to pass legislation to protect consumers from shoddy and dangerous products. The Consumer Product Safety Commission remains the key agency enforcing these laws. The need it fills is still a vital one – products kill over 20,000 consumers a year and injure over 25 million more. It would be far worse if the CPSC did not recall hundreds of products every year. It is estimated that its activities produce $10 billion in savings on the health care bills, property damage, and other costs associated with these defective products.
- **Anti-Discrimination Policies.** Since the 1960s, policies like the Civil Rights Act and Title IX have chalked up impressive gains in decreasing discrimination against minorities and women. Racial segregation in hotels, restaurants and other public facilities has been eliminated. Housing discrimination and workplace discrimination, while not completely eradicated, have been substantially reduced. College enrollment for minorities has greatly increased, jumping 48% during the 1990s alone. In terms of gender, workplace discrimination and sexual harassment have decreased and record numbers of women are now attending colleges and graduate schools. There is still room for improvement – particularly in the area of equal wages – but it is clear that these policies have made substantial progress in eliminating racist and sexist practices that had existed for hundreds of years.
- **Clean Water and Clean Air Programs.** America's water and air are significantly cleaner than they were in the 1960s, thanks to federal legislation. The levels of four of the six air pollutants covered by the Clean Air Act – nitrogen dioxide, smog, sulfur dioxide, and lead – have been reduced dramatically, by an average of 53%. The quality of the air has significantly increased in virtually every metropolitan area in the U.S. The Clean Water act has been similarly successful. When it was passed in 1972, only one-third of the nation's waterways were safe enough for

fishing or swimming. Today that has doubled to two-thirds. And while only 85 million Americans were served by sewage treatment plants in 1972, that figure has now risen to 170 million.

- **Workplace Safety**. Businesses love to complain about the rules of the Occupational Safety and Health Administration and sometimes its policies have been a bit overboard – but it has clearly been very effective in greatly increasing the level of protection for American workers. In 1970, the year before the creation of OSHA, 22,000,000 people were injured on the job and 14,000 died from job-related injuries. Since then, OSHA has helped to cut occupational injury and illness rates by 40 percent. Even more important, between 1980 and 2002, workplace deaths fell from 7.5 per 100,000 workers to 4.0. Particularly impressive has been its success against brown lung disease among textile workers, which has been virtually eliminated.
- **The Military.** Even Rush Limbaugh, who has never met a government program that he likes, admits that the U.S. military is a great success story. Although debates continue to rage over how the military should be used, there is complete agreement that our Army, Navy, and Air Force are the most effective military organizations in the world today. We have the best trained and the best equipped armed forces, and they have an unparalleled ability to effectively project military force – as was demonstrated in the two recent Gulf wars. In the case of the military, the government has clearly done an exemplary job of creating a well-working and effective organization.
- **The West.** Although few Americans think about this, much of the Western United States as we know it today is the creation of various federal programs. It has been that way from the very beginning, starting with government-sponsored explorations of the West in the early and mid-19th century. It continued with the federal government providing the money and troops for the depressingly efficient program of "Indian removal." The government also sold public land to settlers for low prices and sometimes even gave it away. The railroads, which spurred so much growth in the West, would not have been built without massive subsidies from the federal government. And today, much of the farming in many Western areas is made possible by federal water projects, substantial parts of the ranching are subsidized by the artificially low grazing fees on federal property, and much of the mining is made more profitable by dirt cheap access to federal land. Cities like Los Angeles and Las Vegas

would dry up and blow away without the federally funded dam and canal projects that provide water to those arid regions. So it is ironic that while anti-big government sentiment is very strong in parts of this region, the West literally would not and could not exist as it does today without the sustained help of the federal government.

- **National Weather Service.** This government agency not only makes your life more convenient by forecasting your daily weather, it also helps to ensure the safety of planes in the air and ships at sea and it has saved countless lives with its hurricane and tornado warnings. It also just keeps getting better. It's predictions of hurricane paths has improved by fifty percent during the past 15 years; and its forecasts of weather 72 hours in advance is now as reliable as 36-hour forecasts 25 years ago.
- **Poverty Policies.** This may seem counter-intuitive. Everybody knows that poverty policy is the classic example of government failure. How could it possibly be considered a success when the poverty rate is essentially the same as it was thirty years ago? The answer is that most of the policies aimed at the poor in the U.S. were never intended to get them out of poverty. They were only intended to alleviate the suffering of the poor – and studies have shown that they have been very successful in doing this.[8] For example, food stamps have worked to greatly reduce hunger and malnutrition among the poor. The poor are much healthier and have more access to medical treatment thanks to Medicaid. And rent subsidies have allowed many of the poor to move out of places with leaking roofs, inadequate heat, and faulty plumbing. These three programs form the backbone of our anti-poverty efforts – their combined budgets are eight times larger than that for welfare – and in terms of achieving their stated goals, these programs have to be considered impressive government successes.
- **Student Financial Aid Programs.** College is getting increasingly expensive and more and more students require financial help to attend. The federal grants, loans, and work study money provided by the Department of Education form the largest source of college financial assistance, providing billions of dollars in funding each year. These programs have worked to remove financial barriers for students and thus create more equal opportunity in higher education. They have been a major factor in producing the rapid increases in college enrollment seen in the last 50 years, and they have also contributed to the increasing class and racial diversity of the college population.

- **Food and Drug Safety Programs**. The federal government enforces extensive rules to protect the public from tainted food and directly regulates both the meat and poultry industries. It also plays a key role in ensuring the safe use of pesticides on agricultural products, both from here and abroad. Federal authorities are also on the frontlines in combating new threats to our food system, such as mad-cow disease. In addition, the Food and Drug Administration ensures that the drugs we take are pure and effective – an enormously complicated enterprise. Every year the FDA identifies almost 3,000 products that are unfit for consumption and ensures their withdrawal from the marketplace. Americans are undoubtedly safer and healthier thanks to these government programs.
- **Funding Basic Science Research**. Most research on basic scientific topics – in physics, biology, chemistry, etc. – does not have immediate commercial applications and so this work is highly dependent on government funding. Federal funds pay for 80% of the basic science research in this country, through laboratory facilities in universities and in government agencies such as the National Institutes for Health. For this reason, the government deserves a great deal of credit for the important scientific and technological breakthroughs produced by these efforts. In just one area – biomedical science – basic research has provided the foundation to develop new diagnostic technologies, such as nuclear magnetic resonance machines, and new treatments for cancer, diabetes, and many other diseases. It is revealing that nearly half of the most important medical treatments in the field of cardiovascular-pulmonary medicine have their origins in basic research attempting to unravel the mysteries of the lungs, heart, and muscles – work done by scientists not working in this specific disease area.[9] Beyond such practical payoffs, government-funded basic research has also made important progress in answering many of the most profound questions that have baffled humanity for centuries: What is the nature of matter and energy – and the nature of reality itself? How did the universe begin? How will it end? Are we alone in the universe? What is the nature of life – and how did it begin? The achievements of basic science in the United States have been many and stunning – and these are achievements of government as well.

Pretty impressive – and this list could go on much further. Other clearly effective programs and policies would include our National

Parks, the Voting Rights Act, Rural Electrification, AmeriCorps and the Peace Corps, the Cooperative Extension Service, the Federal Aviation Administration, and the National Crime Information Center. And again, these are just the accomplishments of government on the federal level – they don't count the thousands of other successful public sector endeavors on the state and local level.

All of these programs have worked exceptionally well and have made substantial progress in dealing with the problems they are addressing. And many of these problems have not been easy ones to tackle. Regulating the economy, controlling diseases, dismantling segregation, and protecting the environment have all been inherently difficult and complex endeavors, which only makes these achievements of government even more impressive.

A More Comprehensive Look at the Evidence

But while such lists of achievements can go a long way toward invalidating the popular notion that government is inherently incompetent, there is even better evidence available. Ideally, the best evidence would be a comprehensive evaluation of how government is doing in addressing our major societal problems – one that looked at both our successes and our failures in these areas. Surprisingly, this kind of study has rarely been attempted – undoubtedly because it is a very daunting task. But fortunately, a study in this vein was conducted in the 1990s by Derek Bok, a former president of Harvard. In *State of the Nation*, Bok set out to evaluate how American society was doing – whether things were generally getting better or worse in this country.[10] To do this, he first identified a wide ranging set of societal goals that most Americans agreed upon – such as a growing economy, high quality health care at a reasonable cost, personal freedom, reduction of poverty, a high per capital income, clean air, equal opportunity in hiring, lower crime rates, retirement security, and so on. He eventually identified seventy five of these goals which he divided into five categories: prosperity, quality of life, opportunity, personal security, and values. For our purposes, much of what is interesting about these goals is that almost all of them are the subject of one or more government programs. This means that we can use progress or lack of progress in these areas as a rough indicator of the effectiveness of these programs. Bok established generally how much progress we've made in furthering these goals between 1960 and 1990 – rating the situation in each of these areas as "improved," "about the same," or "worse." In the end, Bok found that the country had improved in the vast majority of these areas – more than two-thirds. These areas of improvement included:

Amount of air pollution
Average retirement income
Equality of opportunity
Extent of pre-natal care
Life expectancy
Per capita income
Percent of home ownership
Public spending onthe arts
Equality of education for minorities
Rates of accidental death at work
High school and college graduates
Technical quality of health care
Amount of water pollution
Percent of elderly in poverty
Voting rights
Housing discrimination
People with health insurance
Worker productivity
Number of scientists
Infant mortality
Discrimination in hiring
Incidence of poverty
Degree of legal freedom
Availability of child care

Of course there were some areas of disappointment as well – but far fewer. In five of the seventy five areas we are doing about the same – controlling inflation and unemployment, student achievements in math and reading, and protecting workers from arbitrary discharge. Bok found outright failures – where we were in fact worse off – in less than a quarter of the areas he studied. These included: incidents of homicide and rape, success in solving crimes, rate of productivity increase, cost of health care, percent of children born out of wedlock, affordability for renters, voting rates, drug use, percent of income given to charities, workers with representation, and concentration of poverty in urban neighborhoods

Overall, however, the results of this study clearly show that Americans were much better off in 1990 than in 1960. Of course, a few things have changed in these areas since Bok's study in 1990 – some for better and some for worse. For example, crime rates have gone down substantially, while schools have grown more racially segregated than before. But by and large, Bok's main point remains: there has been improvement in most areas that Americans say they care about and much of the credit for these successes must go to government. As Bok concluded:

> During the past thirty-five years, our society has made substantial progress in most of the fields surveyed. In almost all of these advances, government actions have played a prominent role, whether it be in cleaning up the environment, expanding personal freedom, extending health care to the poor and elderly, reducing poverty, or increasing opportunities for women and minorities. Federal policies have clearly had a hand in America's greatest domestic achievements...[11]

To acknowledge the successes of government does not mean that we have to be satisfied with them. As I point out in another chapter, "Why We Need More Government," American government could certainly do more to address problems like environmental pollution, rising health care costs, poverty, and so on. Despite our achievements, there is clearly room for improvement in many government programs.

But the basic point here is this: there is simply no credible support for the government bashers' contention that most government activities are ineffective and that policies usually make things worse rather than better. Exactly the opposite is the case. Faced with this kind of evidence, to continue to believe that government is incompetent is not simply mistaken – it is so disconnected from the real world that it seems to border on the delusional.

Attacking Programs that Work

Conservatives are not only in denial about the impressive record of government policy successes, they have actually attacked many of the programs responsible for these achievements. As detailed in Part II of this book, anti-government forces have been systematically trying to tear down social programs and rollback regulations. Many of the successful programs mentioned earlier have already been undermined. When Republicans were in control of Congress during the administration of George W. Bush, they cut back spending for vital infrastructure facilities, lessened enforcement of clean air laws, cut spending for basic scientific research, weakened consumer protection regulations, and cut back on student financial aid.

Particularly troublesome were efforts to undermine Social Security, a successful program that is fully solvent for at least several more decades. Conservatives tried to institute a privatization plan that would have allowed some of the money that goes toward Social Security to be invested by individuals themselves in the stock and bond markets. They claimed this was necessary because the program was fiscally unstable in the long run. But their privatization plan would have done nothing to address that problem. Besides, many economists and government analysts have pointed out that the problems facing this program are decades in the future and can be fixed with quite modest reforms.[12] More importantly, the Republican plan would have had several detrimental effects. The government would have had to borrow at least a trillion dollars to fund this scheme, greatly increasing public debt, which is already soaring. It also would have cost workers a great deal more in the commissions and fees they would have to pay to brokers and mutual fund companies – amounting to billions of dollars that would have been skimmed off the top of the retirement system. Finally, and most importantly, this privatization plan would have put workers' savings much more at risk in volatile financial markets. When the stock market plunged in 2008, many retirees who saw their IRAs melting away were very glad to still have the stable income coming from Social Security.

What the Right Really Hates: Successful Programs

Such vociferous attacks on successful government programs like Social Security reveal one of the dirty little secrets of anti-government conservatives and libertarians: they hate successful government programs even more than unsuccessful ones. Government programs that work contradict the conservatives' contention that government is bad and always screws things up. Worse, successful programs may actually encourage people to view the government and their taxes in a more positive light. So it is the very success of a program like Social Security that invites attack by conservatives. As Paul Krugman has explained, government haters "are not sincerely concerned about the possibility that the system will someday fail; they're disturbed by the system's historic successes. For Social Security is a government program that works, a demonstration that a modest amount of taxing and spending can make people's lives better and more secure. And that's why the right wants to destroy it."[13]

Some of this same perverted political logic was at work in the defeat of Clinton's universal health plan in the early 1990s. Some conservatives opposed it because they thought it was too expensive and wouldn't work. But others opposed it precisely because they were afraid it would work. As Grover Norquist has explained, many on the right feared that if the plan passed, it would be a big step down the road toward a more generous government on the European model. They were afraid this would generate much more public support of government and much less support for Republicans who wanted to reduce government. In Norquist's words, the conservative opponents were motivated by "sheer terror of Clinton's health care plan. The goal was to stop the government seizure of the health care industry. Had the Democrats taken over health care, I think we would have become a social democracy and we could have never undone it. We wouldn't have won in '94 ..."[14]

More recently, many people were disturbed when Rush Limbaugh said in a much publicized speech, "I hope Obama fails." This is simply another example of how the political right fears the success of government programs. If Obama's efforts to revive the economy succeed, and he is able to make health care more accessible and affordable, this would demonstrate that government programs can work. This realization might lead to public demands for even more active government – a conservative nightmare. So for Limbaugh it is better that the government fails, even if that means that public must suffer the consequences.

Clearly part of the conservative plan has been to not let government be too successful. They also hope that less successful government will undermine confidence in government and lead to increased support of government cuts. How this strategy works is easiest to see on the local level. Consider the situation in the small town I live in, which is probably typical of many areas in this country. There is a state-imposed restriction on the rate at which local property taxes can be raised – a favorite policy of tax haters and government bashers. But town expenses are rising higher than this restricted rate, which means that the town budget has had to be cut for many years in a row. Any fat has been cut out of the budget long ago, so the city government has been forced to fire some firefighters, decrease road maintenance, lay-off teachers, and so on. As budget cuts have led to decreased services and/or a lower quality of service, citizen complaints about local government have risen. This situation is very ironic: the myth of inefficient and ineffective government has contributed to tax cuts and caps, which in turn actually make government less able to do its job, which simply reinforces the idea that government is inept and inefficient.

Or consider what happened to FEMA – the Federal Emergency Management Agency. Before the administration of George W. Bush, FEMA had amassed an admirable record in responding to emergencies and was considered to be a federal government success story. But under Bush, the agency was downsized because it was seen as an example of an oversized federal bureaucracy.[15] An incompetent political crony was appointed as administrator. Its budget was cut and the agency was folded into the Department of Homeland Security, where its mission was re-oriented toward fighting acts of terrorism. Given this kind of mistreatment, it is hardly surprising that FEMA's response to Hurricane Katrina was slow and incompetent. And of course this incompetence was then used by conservatives to impugn the abilities of federal bureaucracies.

The more conservatives have been able to cut taxes and programs, the more debilitated the public sector has become, and the more disillusioned the public has become about government performance. This is then seized on by government bashers to justify further cuts in taxes and government. It is a negative feedback loop that works to the advantage of those who want to hobble government. Interestingly, just the opposite seems to be the case in other advanced democracies, especially many of those in Europe. Hatred of government and taxes is much less common there, in part because governments are more expansive in the programs they offer their citizens. Since people can see more benefits coming from government – efficient and clean public transportation, free colleges, universal health care, child allowances for every family, substantial retirement benefits – they are much less resentful and more appreciative of government. So in these countries there is a positive feedback loop: the more government does for people, the more people support the government and are willing to pay higher taxes. This suggests that the problem in the U.S. is not that government does too much, but that it doesn't do enough.

Resisting the Siren Song of Government Haters

The right-wing attack on useful government programs is one reason why it is important to set the record straight about how successful government has really been in this country. The image of government as an inherently incompetent institution has been one of the best rhetorical weapons in the war on public sector programs. Republicans have been relentless in taking advantage of this negative stereotype to mobilize public support for cutting taxes and programs. This ineptness theme has also been particularly useful in right-wing efforts to oppose any new policies that would expand the responsibilities of government. As Milton Esman has pointed out, the political right has figured out that "the most effective case they can muster to discredit and defeat a measure they oppose is to argue that it would increase the scope of the federal government and the role of bureaucrats. The merits of the proposal seem almost incidental."[16]

All conservatives have to say is, "Do you want the government to now be in charge of (fill in the blank)?" and many people will say "No" because they know that the government will screw it up. This tactic was especially effective in the effort to defeat President Clinton's attempt to enact universal health insurance in the 1990s. As one marketing expert concluded at the time, the Republicans essentially won the battle once they succeeded in defining the issue as whether we want a "government-run" health care system.[17] Who would want incompetent government bureaucrats in charge of their health care?

In the 2010 battle over health care reform, Republicans and conservative Democrats trotted out this same argument and used it to defeat the effort to adopt a government-run, single-payer health plan. They even shot down the more modest proposal to have a "public option" to compete with private insurance – an approach highly favored in public polls. The end result: a watered-down bill that kept private business in charge of health care.

The fact is, government-run health care programs like Medicare are among the most efficient and effective health care programs in this country. But few people seem to know this. Consider this. During the 2010 elections, Rep. Robert Inglis held a town meeting. He reported that one man warned him to "keep your government hands off my Medicare!" "I had to politely explain," said Inglis, "that, 'Actually, sir, your health care is being provided by the government.' But he wasn't having any of it." This story says a lot about how brainwashed some Americans have become about government incompetence. Apparently, a program as useful and effective as Medicare could not possibly be a creature of government.

Fortunately, however, there are reasons to believe that people can see through this anti-government rhetoric and recognize that many government programs are actually very successful. For example, surveys show that if Americans pause to consider how public agencies actually do their job, and if they have some experience with those agencies, then they can get beyond their knee-jerk skepticism about government effectiveness. A poll done by the Pew Trust found that 82% of recipients of Social Security actually had a favorable view of that agency – even though only 44% expressed a favorable view of government. Similarly, 80% of airline passengers had a favorable view of the Federal Aviation Administration, while only 46% had a positive view of government.[18] So while the negative myths of government hold considerable sway when we think of government in the abstract, when we look at specific programs and agencies, reality can break through and we can make a more accurate assessment of their worth and effectiveness.

Again, all of this is not to say that American government is perfect – that is hardly the case. It has had its fair share of ineffective policies and failed programs – Prohibition and the Vietnam War being two of the most spectacular historical examples of grand failures. But every kind of organization fails at times. Take the business community. Large corporations – like Circuit City and Linens 'n Things – can go bankrupt, and 80% of all new small businesses go under within five years. And yet few of us would leap to the conclusion that business people are an incompetent bunch of losers. We need to cut the same kind of slack for government.

Americans must stop being taken in by the siren song of government haters who insist that government makes a mess of everything it does. We need to acknowledge that government has repeatedly taken on difficult and complex problems and made substantial progress toward solving them, and in doing so it has bettered our lives in innumerable ways. Recognizing this impressive record of achievement is important if we are to build public support for a more active government – one that takes on the serious social, economic, and environmental problems we face as a society today.

---

1. Phillip K Howard, *Death of Common Sense : How Law is Suffocating America* (New York: Warner Books, 1996), p. 9._
2. Charles Murray, *What It Means to Be a Libertarian* (New York: Broadway Books, 1997) p. 147.
3. Limbaugh quoted in Al Franken, *Rush Limbaugh is a Big Fat Idiot* (New York: Dell Publishing, 1996), p. 10.
4. Jacob Weisberg, *In Defense of Government* (New York: Scribner, 1996), p. 32.
5. Derek Bok, *The Trouble with Government* (Cambridge, MA: Harvard University Press, 2002) p. 43.
6. Many of these government successes were adapted from Paul C. Light's, *Government's Greatest Achievements: From Civil Rights to Homeland Security* (Washington, DC: Brookings Institution, 2002).
7. Quoted in Cass R. Sunstein, *The Second Bill of Rights* (New York: Basic Books, 2004) p. 15.
8. Susan Mayar and Christopher Jencks, "War On Poverty: No Apologies, Please" *New York Times*, November 9, 1995, op-ed page.
9. National Institute of General Medical Science, "Why Do Basic Research?" (http://www.nigms.nih.gov/news/science_ed/whydo.html#payoff), June 29, 2006
10. Derek Bok, *The State of the Nation* (Cambridge, MA: Harvard University Press, 1996).
11. Bok, *State of the Nation*, p. 405.
12. Paul Krugman, "Inventing a Crisis" *New York Times*, December 7, 2004, p. A31.
13. Ibid.
14. Rick Henderson and Steven Hayward, "Happy Warrior," *Reason Online*, http://reason.com/9702/fe.int.norquist.shtml, Dec. 7, 2004.
15. Ibid.

16. Milton J. Esman, *Government Works: Why Americans Need the Feds* (Ithaca, NY, Cornell University Press, 2000) p. 6.
17. Thomas Scarlett, "Killing Health Care Reform", *Campaigns & Elections*, October/Nov. 1994, p. 6.
18. Cited in Charles T. Goodsell, *The Case for Bureaucracy: A Public Administration Polemic*, 4th Edition (Washington, DC: Chatham House, 2003), p. 29.

CHAPTER 3

Doing Good Through Government

In America, we often think of being moral and doing "good works" as things we do in our private lives. For example, when we think of institutions that are doing good works, we tend to think of organizations like churches and charities that operate privately. Giving blood or volunteering at our local soup kitchen are the kinds of things that come to mind when we want to help others in our community—when we want to be responsible and moral people.

But if you really think about it, the institutions that do the most "good works" in our society are not churches or charities; they are our local, state, and federal governments. These governments do an enormous amount to feed the hungry, heal the sick, take care of the old, protect the young, and so on. In fact the good created by these governments far exceeds all the good accomplished by churches and charities in our society. When we think about some of the greatest moral achievements in our history, it is often the American people acting through their government that brought them about. It is government that abolished slavery and ended child labor. It is government that has saved millions of lives through public health programs to eradicate diseases. It is government that has drastically reduced poverty among the elderly. It is the government that is saving us all from the widespread suffering and despair caused by economic depressions.

On any measure, the good works accomplished by government have far eclipsed those of churches and other charities. And this makes sense, because the resources of these private institutions are very limited compared to the resources wielded by government. So while my local soup kitchen feeds dozens of people a week, it is the federal food stamp program that is primarily responsible for greatly reducing hunger among the thousands of poor in our community. On the surface, it seems that charities may spend large amounts on helping the needy in our society – after all, Americans give about $240 billion to philanthropic organizations annually. But this figure is misleading. Most of the money raised by charities and non-profit organizations does not in fact go to those in need. Most of it goes to programs and facilities – like the YMCA, art museums, colleges, medical research, public television stations, churches, etc. – that primarily serve the middle and upper class people who donate the money. Only about 10% or $24 billion goes to fund human service programs for the needy. And only half of that amount – about $12 billion – goes to services for low-income families.[1]

In contrast, the federal government alone spends over $200 billion a year on programs aimed at poor and low-income families, including welfare, food stamps, Medicaid, and housing subsidies. Moreover, government also funds much of the anti-poverty and anti-hunger work done by charitable groups and non-profit human service organizations. Catholic Charities USA, which provides emergency food and shelter to the poor, gets 65% of its budget from the government.[2] So it is clearly the government that is carrying the bulk of the load in caring for the neediest people in our society. Private charities and non-profits simply do not have the means to deal adequately with poverty, homelessness, hunger or virtually any of the serious problems that are causing suffering in our society.

So while most of us do not think of it this way, government is actually one of the main ways that we act as good people in the world. Our contributions to government in the form of taxes go to fund a wide variety of programs and services that have eliminated enormous amounts of suffering and vastly improved millions of people's lives. Democratic government is in part a manifestation of our desire to be responsible moral people, and it is the primary institutional mechanism that we use to make the world a better place.

Government as our Main Instrument of Compassion

One of the best examples of government as a moral instrument is the way we use it to express compassion and caring toward one another. One of our highest moral responsibilities is to try to allay the suffering of our fellow human beings. The most obvious examples of this kind of public compassion are, of course, social programs. Programs like Medicare, Medicaid, food stamps, welfare, unemployment, and disaster relief are some of the major ways that we as a society express compassion for each other. They are the way we try to relieve the suffering of old age, illness, poverty, and natural disasters. Sometimes we support social insurance programs like unemployment relief for selfish reasons, because we ourselves might need to use them at some time. But often we also support them even if we know that we probably won't need them – because we care about the people that do.

Of course social programs are not the only way we use government to come to the aid of our fellow citizens. We also use the regulatory process. We pass rules that lower injuries at the workplace, keep unsafe products off the market, and ensure that medicines actually work. Such regulations are necessary to protect all of us from the risks and harms caused by unfettered corporations and market forces. Environmental regulations allow us to extend this protective process beyond the human community and act as caretakers for the earth and all of its creatures.

Even many conservatives acknowledge that compassion is an important goal of public policy. When he first ran for office, George W. Bush repeatedly called himself a "compassionate conservative" – a clear admission that this virtue has a great deal of public appeal. The problem of course is that, once in office, President Bush consistently championed cuts in many social programs that helped the needy, such as Medicaid, food stamps, and the low-income fuel assistance program. He also rolled back workplace safety rules and neglected enforcement of regulations to protect the environment. These actions raised serious questions about how truly committed to compassion Bush really was. Can you be compassionate if you consistently undermine the use some of the main tools of compassion in our society – social programs and regulatory rules? It would be like a doctor who claims to care for her patients and yet steadfastly refuses to use antibiotics and painkillers in their treatment.

Caring for each other through government is a noble endeavor and an expression of the best of what is in us. And so if we really believe in compassion, if we really believe that we have an ethical obligation to be "our brother's keeper," then we must also support an active and well-funded public sector that serves as one of our main means for acting in this moral way.

Markets versus Governments as Moral Instruments

But if we are going to say that government is an important instrument for moral action, shouldn't we also say that the market is too? After all, the market does do an enormous amount of good by providing the products and services that we all need – and in this way it has certainly made the world a better place for many. Doesn't that make the market a moral tool as well? Not really. As any economist will tell you, markets are not the realm of moral behavior; they are the realm of self-interested behavior. Economists firmly believe that markets do work in the public interest, but they see that as an indirect effect of people acting in their own private interest. In unregulated markets, people are often encouraged to act selfishly to maximize their own well-being – by paying the lowest price, charging the highest price, getting the biggest salaries, or putting their rivals out of business. People are not obligated to take into account moral considerations, such as what is best for society or what is the right thing to do.

For example, consider the different ways that markets and governments respond in the aftermath of a disaster like an earthquake or flood. Governments and charities rush in with aid to those suffering in the affected areas – a moral response. But the natural response of economic markets is to price gouge. The shortages of such things as food, water, ice, and building materials caused by such disasters means that the demand for these things are very high and merchants can charge prices much higher than normal.

This does not mean that markets are bad or that they are immoral – that is not true either. Markets are simply amoral – that is, morality is not relevant consideration and so sometimes the results of market processes are good and sometime they are bad. That is why it is morally dangerous to rely on markets to produce the public good. While markets are incredibly useful and productive institutions, they are only moral insofar as they are structured to serve moral purposes for society. And that is why we need government as a way to pursue our moral goals – so that we can do the right thing when the market fails to do so. Government can subsidize the building of low-cost housing when the private sector fails to meet that need, or provide health insurance to those who can't afford it. In contrast to markets, the aim of governments is usually to do the right thing for the public – to do what it is the public interest. This is what makes government the primary site of moral action in our society.

This is not to suggest that democratic governments always do the right thing. We and our government have certainly made clearly immoral decisions in the past – such as when public policies supported slavery or the removal of Indians from their native lands. And there is certainly heated disagreement today over whether our state governments are pursuing the right policies in terms of abortion or gay marriage. But what is important to see is that democratic government is an ongoing moral enterprise – a public search for the right thing to do. It is a process of constantly re-imagining and re-inventing what it means to live in a good society.[3] We can certainly deny the morality of specific policies, but what we cannot and should not deny is that government is the main place in which we as a society collectively debate moral issues and where we have to decide the right course of action. Of course government sometimes fails to do the right thing, but that doesn't mean that it still isn't engaged in a moral endeavor.

Government and the Higher Values of Life

Michael Lerner is an author, rabbi, and editor of the magazine Tikkun. In his book, *The Left Hand of God*, he makes an eloquent argument for how politics can and should be a means for pursuing our desire to be compassionate and caring human beings. He believes that many Americans are experiencing a spiritual crisis – that they find themselves living lives where "feelings of emptiness, disconnection from others, and isolation have become common."[4] He traces much of this problem to our capitalist culture, which promotes a view of life informed mostly by selfishness and materialism. We spend most of our working lives in business organizations, he points out, where competitive individualism and greed are the highest values and where we pursue our own interests, often at the expense of others' interests. Our participation in the market economy often seems to be mostly about acquiring money and things.

Many people, Lerner argues, want more than this from life – they want lives where they can express their higher values and where they can feel a real connection to their fellow human beings. Some people seek this kind of more meaningful life in private spiritual quests, but Lerner suggests that we should be seeking it through the public sphere as well. He calls for the pursuit of "a meaning-oriented approach to politics." An approach that has as its focus "the yearning of human beings for a world of love and caring, for genuine connection and mutual recognition, for kindness and generosity, for connection to the common good, to the sacred, and to a transcendent purpose for our lives."[5] Political activity, he suggests, can allow us to pursue our most cherished values in a way that we cannot in our private lives or in the market.

This view of politics (and government) as a way of expressing our most humane instincts can seem naïve at first. Many people tend to see government as the realm where special interests groups try to get as much as they can for themselves – an activity motivated by selfishness and greed. There is obviously some truth to this. But that is not all of what government is about. It is also about people trying to help their fellow human beings and trying to promote what is good for all. That is why many people get involved in politics in the first place.

One of the reasons that so many Americans reacted so enthusiastically to Barack Obama's campaign for president was that he tapped into this idea that government can be an expression of our higher values – that it can be a force for good in the world. He revived the liberal idea that it is virtuous and meaningful to work through government to solve people's problems and improve people's lives, and many voters responded strongly to this hopeful message.

Limiting Government Limits our Ability to Do the Right Thing

If modern democratic government and its programs are often a reflection of our best selves – our most decent selves – then right-wing attempts to drastically cut taxes and shrink the public sector can only serve to diminish our ability to act as responsible moral beings. The more we Americans accept the conservative vision of government as "bad," and the more we go along with their attempts to weaken this institution, the more we weaken our ability to make the world a better place. If we want to care for each other and do as much as we can to alleviate human suffering, then we need to acknowledge that government is often the best way to achieve those goals.

---

1. Barbara M. Blank, *It Takes a Nation* (Princeton, NJ: Princeton University Press, 1997), p. 202.
2. Blank, p. 203.
3. Thanks to Michael Lipsky at Demos for making this point to me.
4. Michael Lerner, *The Left Hand of God: Taking Back Our Country from the Religious Right* (San Francisco: HarperSanFrancisco, 2006) p. 56.
5. Lerner, p. 158.

CHAPTER 4

Government as the Champion of Justice, Equality, Freedom, and Security

Do you believe in justice? That our civil liberties should be protected? That all citizens should all be treated as equals? You would probably answer, "Of course!" But do you also realize that if you are an avid supporter of public values like "justice," "liberty" and "equality," then you should also be an avid supporter of government? Government is often the *only* institution that can make these kinds of core political values a reality. In fact, without an active and healthy public sector, these kinds of public values would be in very short supply. Take justice, for instance. It is not usually something provided by the marketplace or created by the actions of individuals. More often it is something that can only be provided and sustained in the public sphere by the actions of government organizations like the courts and the legislatures. If we want a just society, we must work through government to get it.

This argument – that government is an essential mechanism for realizing vital public values – is an important one in making the case for government. Government is good not simply because it provides us as individuals with certain services and benefits (such as the ones described in the earlier chapter "A Day in Your Life") but also because it is the main way to promote important values that are good for us as a whole – values that are in the public interest. This view of government as the insurer of core democratic values is one that goes back to the very beginning of our national political institutions. Consider, for example, the political sentiments expressed by the founding fathers in the preamble to the U.S. Constitution:

> We the People of the United States, in Order to form a more perfect Union, establish Justice, insure domestic Tranquility, provide for the common defense, promote the general Welfare,

> and secure the Blessings of Liberty to ourselves and our Posterity, do ordain and establish this Constitution for the United States of America.

From the outset, the American government was primarily seen as an indispensable means of establishing and promoting certain universally recognized public values, such as justice, tranquility, and liberty. And today, as citizens, we need to recognize in government what the founding fathers saw in it: that it is the only institution we can rely on to nourish and protect these kinds of values in our society.

Many people actually share this value-oriented vision of government. They get involved in politics and the governing process not because they want something for themselves but because they want to promote certain democratic values – such as equality or freedom – that they feel are important. They have a vision of what the good society is and they try to use government to make that vision a reality. They vote for candidates and lobby the government not simply to line their own pockets but in order to encourage government to do what is right for society as a whole. Many people participate in the democratic process because they want to promote principles and values that they believe are in the public interest. For many people in the National Rifle Association, for example, it is not just about owning their own shotgun, it is about liberty. And for many in the Civil Rights movement it was not about using the same restaurants as whites, it was about equality.

To really appreciate the unique role that government plays in promoting these basic political principles, we need to take a more careful look at some of these key values and see how they can be ensured only by government and how they are embodied in particular policies and programs. Let's start with justice and fairness.

Justice and Fairness

"Life isn't fair" is a favorite saying among conservatives. And the often unspoken corollary is, "So get used to it." But most people do not want to get used to it. In fact, the desire for fairness is as American as apple pie – it is in our blood. We get riled up when people are not treated fairly and we think something should be done about it. And more often than not the place that people turn to try to right these wrongs – to make life fairer for themselves and others – is government. Government is the main provider of justice and fairness in American society. Many government policies and government institutions are explicitly designed to promote these important public values.

The most obvious manifestation of this is the criminal and civil justice system. It is the primary way we as a society ensure that criminals are punished and that wrongs are righted. This kind of legal justice is not something that can be reliably provided by the private sector. We would not want, for instance, for there to be a market in legal justice. We would not want this justice to be something provided to the highest bidder. In fact, those times when our current justice system does take on the characteristics of a market – such as when the rich are able to get off because they can afford to hire the most talented and expensive lawyers – are exactly the times when we think the justice system has broken down. Justice should not be for sale, it must be available to all people equally, and only government can provide that.

Nor can we rely on people acting outside of the law, either individually or in private groups, to provide justice in our society. All too often the result of this kind of approach is the revenge killing, the lynch mob, or the drive-by gang shooting. Justice administered outside of government and outside of the law is almost always arbitrary, inappropriate, violent, and out of control. For justice to be true justice it must be ordered by law and administered by the government.

It is revealing that even libertarians and other anti-government ideologues admit that the criminal and civil justice systems are parts of government that are absolutely necessary and cannot be done away with. They argue that running the police, the courts, and prisons are legitimate public endeavors that must be maintained even in a minimal version of government. But there is hardly anything "minimal" about the extent and costs of this justice system. It is hardly "small" government at all. The caseloads in our courts are enormous. Over 338,000 civil and criminal case filings were made in federal district courts in 2008. State courts handled nearly 28 times as many civil cases and 82 times as many criminal cases as did the federal system – with their case filings totaling over 12 million.[1] Of course the vast majority of these cases were settled and did not come to trial, but these numbers give us a good idea of the enormous workload being put on our court system.

The legal justice system is also hardly "minimal" if we look at how many people it employs and how much money it cost the taxpayers. In 2006, 2.4 million people were employed in the justice systems administered at the federal, state, county, and city level. These include the police, prosecutors, judges and other staff in the judicial system, and those working in corrections facilities. And 2006, the nation spent a total of $214 billion on criminal and civil justice services.[2] In short, government endeavors to establish and maintain a criminal and civil justice system are neither simple nor cheap, they are massive and very expensive. They require a healthy and adequately funded government.

Consider what happened in 2003 when anti-government activists successfully lead a campaign to stop a desperately needed state tax increase in Alabama. Part of what suffered as a consequence was the administration of justice. Alabama already was spending too little on its justice system, and its state prisons were a disgrace. The state allocated only half of what the rest of the country allocated per prisoner and the prison system housed twice as many prisoners than it should. With the failure of the tax increase, 5,000 inmates had to be let out of the prisons before finishing their sentences. The lack of tax revenue meant that other parts of the criminal justice system were also undermined. Funds for the courts were cut by 10 percent, which meant laying off 400 employees. This included probation officers who were needed to keep track of recently released prisoners. And finally, public safety spending had to be cut by 18 percent, including state troopers. This meant that there were only seven troopers to patrol all of the state roads between midnight and 6 a.m. The lesson here? You get what you pay for in a criminal justice system and if you want to reduce taxes you should be prepared to live in a less safe society.

Social and Economic Justice

It is important to see that the government is not only the sole source of legal justice, it is also where people usually go to promote social and economic justice as well. Americans have a strong moral sense that people should be treated fairly and that people should get what they deserve – irrespective of their class, race, gender or age. And again, the mechanism of government is usually the only way that this kind of social fairness and justice can be effectively promoted. Many government policies – from minimum wage laws to anti-discrimination rules– exist primarily to ensure that Americans are treated fairly.

There is little in the private market that promotes economic or social justice. For example, the market does not ensure that people will be treated fairly as employees or as consumers. Some businesses will treat their employees and customers fairly, but some will not. Some will exploit their workers and hire and fire them arbitrarily. Some will not give their customers a fair value for their money. You can complain to the Better Business Bureau, but it is unlikely to have any real effect. So most people turn to the government and the government has responded with a variety of laws that are designed to ensure that people are treated fairly by businesses. One of the most obvious manifestations of this is anti-discrimination laws. Firms cannot hire and fire people based on their race, gender, or age. Nor can they deny a service or product to someone on the same unfair basis. We also have a variety of consumer protection laws – like lemon laws – that work to ensure that consumers get a fair shake from businesses. We also have anti-trust laws to prevent companies from creating monopolies and oligopolies that can then use price-fixing to charge consumers unfair prices. Since fairness is not an inherent attribute of markets, government is needed to inject that value into economic relationships.

Interestingly, however, businesses also rely on government to ensure that *they* are treated fairly. "Fair competition" between companies is a basic requirement of an efficient and productive market economy. But fair competition does not come naturally to the marketplace; it must be created and enforced by a variety of government policies. Left to themselves, many businesses would not treat their competition fairly. They would dump goods on the market at below cost to drive their competition out of business. They would try to restrict their competitors' access to vital goods and services. And then there are the blatantly criminal activities that some businesses would use to eliminate fair competition. In countries like Russia, with poorly funded and poorly functioning public sectors, organized crime plays a significant role in the economy and stifles competition with threats, beatings, kidnappings, and murder. Far from wanting to be left alone by government, most corporations rely on various government agencies and regulations to ensure that their competitors do not have an unfair advantage over them.

The government has also intervened to ensure economic fairness in other ways. Most people would probably agree that it is unfair for businesses to exploit workers and pay them slave wages that nobody could possible live on. People deserve a fair day's pay for a fair day's work. That is exactly why we have minimum wage laws – to ensure that everyone gets a semblance of fair pay for the work they do. This kind of commitment to economic fairness also underlies the Earned Income Tax Credit program of the federal government. Supporters of this law – both Republicans and Democrats – believe that if people are willing to work hard and not rely on welfare, then it is not fair for them to live in poverty. So the EITC utilizes tax credits to subsidize the income of low-income families by several thousand dollars a year. This program has proved to be one of the most successful policies in lifting families out of poverty in the U.S.

Many other government policies are necessary to ensure that life is fairer and that people actually get what they deserve out of life. The whole idea of Social Security is that it would be intolerably unfair for people to work hard all their lives and then be forced to either not retire at all or to live in destitution in their old age. There will always be, of course, some unfairness in life. But this doesn't mean we must accept it or not try to eradicate it whenever we can – that is part of our moral responsibility. We can make life much fairer than it naturally is, but we must usually employ the institutions of government to make it so. So while conservatives are right that "Life isn't fair," it would be more accurate to change that saying to "Life, without government, isn't fair."

Security

"Security" is sometimes not thought of as a democratic value in the same way as more obvious things like "justice" or "freedom." But creating a safe and secure society and protecting people against major threats to their welfare are important functions of democratic governments. This was clear even to the creators of the Constitution, who listed "insure domestic Tranquility," and "provide for the common defense" as central reasons for establishing our democratic government. They understood that an ordered, peaceful, and secure society is not possible without the constant action of government.

From the beginning, our democratic government was primarily concerned with our physical security – ensuring that the country was immune from outside attack, that citizens were safe from criminals, and that they were protected from threats like fire. But as our society has evolved, new threats to the welfare of ourselves and our families have emerged, and people have been able to use democratic government to help deal with these risks and create a more secure society. Citizens have organized themselves into lobbies and political movements that have demanded that the government lessen the serious risks associated with such things as economic depressions, excessive inflation, loss of a job, dangerous workplaces, environmental pollution, lack of health insurance, retirement insecurity, dangerous products, serious illnesses or disability, terrorism, bank failures, investment fraud, earthquakes and other natural disasters, and so on.

All of these things are worth worrying about because they can inflict major harm to our families and us – some can even ruin our lives. Modern governments and many of their policy programs have developed in large part to manage and minimize these kinds of serious risks to our well-being.[3] Of course, we can do some things individually to try to minimize some of our risks. We can drive carefully; we can avoid smoking, we can eat more healthily; we can try to save more money, and so on. But for many of these risks, there is little we can do alone to effectively avoid or manage them. Such things as job loss, cancer, environmental pollution, terrorism, crime, industrial obsolescence, and economic downturns are basically out of our control as individuals. So we must act collectively to try to manage these risks – and that is where government comes in. In many cases, government programs are the only way to make our lives more secure. And the benefits of these programs go beyond merely minimizing these risks, they also allow us to be free of the constant anxiety and fear that would plague us if these risks were not managed effectively.

Government efforts to manage risks and increase our societal security basically take two forms: policies that share and reallocate risks, and policies that lessen risk. Risk-sharing policies usually take the form of social insurance programs that spread the risk around to a large number of people. Most of what we think of as social welfare programs – Social Security, Medicare, and so on – are in fact social insurance programs design to redistribute risks. It is no coincidence that we call these programs a "social safety net" – they are designed to allow us to live our lives with the knowledge that the government is there to catch us if we fall. So we all contribute to the Medicare program, and when we get old and sick, that program is there to take care of us – even if we don't have the money to pay for that care ourselves. Social Security is not only there to give us some retirement security, but it also helps those who become disabled and unable to work. Even programs like food stamps and welfare, which may seem like redistributive programs aimed exclusive at the poor, do in fact have a broad social insurance dimension to them. Many Americans are only a job loss, a divorce, or a serious illness away from poverty. In fact, studies show that over fifty percent of Americans will become poor at some point in their life, so poverty programs actually act as a safety net for large numbers of citizens.[4]

Governments also try to actually *reduce* risk rather than just spread it around, and this usually involves some kind of regulatory policy. Environmental policies lower the risk that we will be poisoned by the air we breathe or the water we drink. Consumer regulations protect us from unscrupulous businesses that would cheat us or sell us dangerous products. Other rules minimize the workplace dangers and diseases. Governments also engage in regulating the larger economic system itself. Capitalist economic systems are prone to a whole host of malfunctions, from runaway inflation to prolonged depressions. The economic crisis that began in 2008 is only one of the latest examples of these problems. Modern governments use monetary and fiscal policy to keep in check these serious threats to our economic well-being. For example, the Federal Reserve board regulates interest rates to make sure that the economy is not growing too quickly or too slowly. And government can increase its spending to stimulate a stalled economy. Without this kind of macro-economic regulation by government, our welfare would be constantly threatened by these serious economic problems.

Even before the financial system meltdown, it has become clear that Americans are now living in a time of increased economic risks. People's incomes have become less secure as wages stagnate, part-time jobs proliferate, and income inequality increases. Globalization has made many more jobs less secure and put more companies themselves at risk of going under. More and more companies are defaulting on their pension arrangements with their employees. More businesses are also not offering health insurance or are making their workers pay more for it. Ironically, as these risks increase, anti-government activists seem more interested in getting the government out of the risk management business. While in office, President Bush trumpeted his plan for an "ownership society" in which people would take much more individual responsibility for such things as their retirement and health care arrangements – all in the name of increasing their "freedom" and reducing their reliance on government. His plan to privatize part of Social Security and have people risk part of their retirement funds in the stock market was one primary example of this approach. But as James Surowieki has written in the *New Yorker*, this approach would have only resulted in making people much less economically secure:

> The ownership society promises freedom, but at the price of a huge shift in risk, away from government and society and onto individual citizens. Social Security, Medicare, insurance – these are basically collective risk-sharing mechanisms. Rather than let each person run the risk of ending up destitute or sick, these programs pool the risk. Because the risk is shared, it can be managed, and people can be guaranteed a minimally acceptable outcome. In Bush's brave new world, that guarantee will be eliminated.[5]

Conservatives are often very inconsistent – if not hypocritical – in their view of whether government should be providing security. On the one hand, they are often critical of government efforts, like social programs and regulations, which try to manage and reduce risks for our families and us. But on the other hand, they are obsessed with *national* security and are willing to spend hundreds of billions of dollars on that. They also support dozens of laws and programs that serve to minimize risks for companies and markets. For example, corporations are shielded by limited liability laws in every state. Bankruptcy laws also play a major role in protecting corporations from financial risks. Regulations that stabilize the money supply also work to minimize risks for businesses. So for conservatives, strong government action to protect us against foreign threats and to reduce the financial risks to business is highly desirable. They only oppose government risk management when it involves policies that protect the public.

During the last 100 years, government has emerged as the major way that we as a society increase our security and manage the uncertainties of modern life, and so any systematic attempt to cripple or reduce government will inevitably tend to make us less safe, less secure, and increase our burden of worry and anxiety. To the extent that we see security as an important public value, then, we must also value government and the government programs that help us to collectively shelter ourselves from the dangers and threats we all face.

Equality

Equality is another basic American value. It has been a part of American political culture ever since the Declaration of Independence observed that "all men are created equal," which at the time was a very radical and revolutionary idea. Today, as back then, Americans deeply believe that no one is inherently better than anyone else – that we all deserve equal respect and equal treatment no matter who we are. But once again, this is a value that can really only be promoted by government. The equality fostered by government takes several forms. One is legal equality, which was a central concern of the founding fathers and a major focus of many of the amendments in the Bill of Rights. In a democracy, we are all equal before the law. We have the same legal rights and protections – we have the right to a lawyer, a jury trial, property rights, and so on. We have all become so used to these rights of equal legal treatment that we sometimes forget that they only exist because our democratic government mandates and enforces them.

Democratic government also promotes political equality. What separates democracy from other political systems is the idea that all citizens should have the same amount of power. Rich or poor, male or female, black or white – we should all have an equal say over what government does. Instead of rule by those who have the most power or the most money, the ideal of democracy is that we all deserve to share power equally. Government attempts to make this ideal a reality by conducting free and fair elections. In elections, everyone has exactly the same amount of political power – one vote. It is one of the rare situations in life when we all have the same power. This is intended to give everyone an equal chance to determine who will run the government. In practice, of course, other forms of power – such as campaign contributions – also have an influence over who wins elections. But that is exactly why there has been great pressure to enact campaign finance reform – so that the power of special interest money can be limited or eliminated in elections. The campaign finance reform movement aims to make sure that it is the vote – the only power that is allocated equally to all – that finally determines who rules in our government.

Government is also the only societal institution that is in a position to promote another kind of equality – economic equality. There is, of course, a great deal of disagreement in this country over what degree of economic equality is desirable. How much poverty is acceptable in the richest society in the world? Should we try to create more equal economic outcomes, or simply try to ensure equal opportunity? Can we have true equality of opportunity in a society with vast differences in wealth and income – in a society where some grow up in neighborhoods plagued by violence, drugs, and inferior schools? But while we debate these questions about economic equality, what is not debatable is that only government can create more of it. The market obviously does not do this – it is in fact responsible for the growing disparities in wealth and income that we have been experiencing over the last several decades. But government can use a variety of policies to lessen these economic inequalities. Minimum wage policies are, for instance, an effort to raise up those on the bottom rungs of the economic ladder and create more economic equality. The Earned Income Tax credit is another policy mechanism for boosting the earnings of low income Americans. To the extent, then, that we want to address economic need and promote more economic equality, we have no choice but to turn to government.

Freedoms and Rights

When most people think of the defining characteristics of a democratic society – those that separate them from non-democratic societies – the first thing they usually think of are individual rights and liberties.

A democratic society is a free society – with freedom of speech, freedom of religion, property rights, the right to a lawyer and a jury, the right to vote, and all the other protections we enjoy as individuals. But what we often forget is that these crucial rights and freedoms are enacted and protected by government. They are created in our state and federal constitutions, and our courts are the watchdogs that we use that prevent our rights and liberties from being violated. (For a more elaborate version of this argument, see the chapter, "Government as the Primary Protector of our Rights and Liberties.")

Once again, there is virtually nothing in the private sector that protects these vital liberties. In fact, it is the propensity for private individuals and organizations to create oppressive and intolerable conditions for people that has led to a demand for a steady expansion of the rights and freedoms of individuals in America. Workers have organized and pressured the government to ensure their right to strike and their right to labor in a safe workplace. Environmentalist groups have fought numerous political battles to establish and protect our rights to breathe clean air and drink pure water. Women, the elderly, the disabled, and minorities have lobbied to free themselves from discrimination and segregation in the private sector. All of these groups have worked through government to increase their rights and liberties, and these are only guaranteed through various government policies programs that are created and maintained by various governments.

In short, we rely heavily on government to create and nurture the vital liberties that we have come to enjoy as part of our life in this democracy of ours. This fact, however, is lost on anti-government conservatives. In their view, government is actually the primary threat to our liberties and that is one of the main reasons it must be reduced to a minimum. (For a detailed rebuttal of this allegation, see the chapter "More Government Does Not Mean Less Freedom.") I will not repeat the arguments of that chapter here, but simply point out that while democratic government can at times threaten our freedoms, it more often functions to protect and expand the freedoms and rights of average Americans.

Conclusion

The overall point is this: to the extent that we cherish important public values like justice and equality, we need a public sector strong enough and well-funded enough to make these things a reality. Conversely, attacks that weaken government also weaken it as a force for good in our society. They are attacks not simply on specific programs but on core American values. When a Republican Congress limits the use of class action suits, this limits our access to justice. And a refusal to raise the lagging minimum wage is a denial of fairness to low-income workers. If anti-government zealots succeed in their efforts to cut taxes, restrict social spending, and roll back regulations, we will then have a society that is less just, more unequal, less secure, and more unfair. In short, a less decent and less civilized society. Is this the kind of world we want to live in?

1."Workload of the Federal Courts Grew in Fiscal Year 2008." http://www.sconet.state.oh.us/PIO/news/2009/fedCourts_040109.asp. See also, Brian J. Ostrom, et al., "Examining Trial Trends In State Courts: 1976-2002," *Journal of Empirical Legal Studies*, Volume 1, Issue 3, 755-782, November 2004.

2. Figures from Bureau of Justice Statistics, "Nation Spends $167 Billion On Criminal And Civil Justice Services," May 2, 2009. http://www.ojp.usdoj.gov/bjs/pub/eande.htm

3. See David A. Moss, *When All Else Fails: Government as the Ultimate Risk Manager* (Cambridge: Harvard University Press, 2004).

4. Mark Robert Rank, *One Nation, Underprivileged: Why American Poverty Affects Us All* (Oxford: Oxford University Press, 2004), p. 93.

5. James Surowieki, "The Risk Society," *The New Yorker*, Nov. 15, 2004, p. 40.

CHAPTER 5

Taxes are Good

Are taxes bad? If you've been listening to conservatives for the last several decades, you would certainly think so. Virtually every Republican candidate for office in recent memory has run on an anti-tax platform – arguing that Americans are overtaxed, that taxes hurt economic growth, etc. And it is this hatred of taxes that helped propel the passage of hundreds of billions of dollars of tax cuts during the administration of George W. Bush.

This anti-tax campaign strikes a real emotional chord in some Americans and it has been one of the most effective rallying cries of anti-government conservatives. It taps into a taxophobia that is deeply ingrained in American political culture and that manifests itself in the activities of over 800 local and state anti-tax groups. These tax-haters have also been playing a large part in organizing the grassroots Tea Party movement.

But conservatives are dead wrong about taxes. Taxes are not bad.

Taxes are good.

The argument *for* taxes is a very straightforward one: if government is on balance a very positive force in society, then taxes are good. If what we have seen in earlier chapters in this book is true – that government programs help us all in myriad ways every day, that most government programs are working effectively to solve our social problems, and that government is the only way to promote important values like justice and economic security – then the taxes needed to support these government activities should be seen as a positive good. To put it another way, you can't support the things the government does – like caring for the elderly, establishing justice, providing public education, fighting terrorism, and protecting the environment – and still maintain that the taxes that support those things are bad. Taxes are the lifeblood of government and so if government is basically good, then so are taxes.

So instead of seeing paying taxes as analogous to being mugged by the government, we ought to think of these payments more like the tithing that many people do in their churches and synagogues. Most people see these regular donations as a charitable contribution to the good works being done by these religious organizations – and they certainly don't resent these contributions. But if the government is also an institution dedicated in large part to doing good works – to promoting the public interest – then we should not resent our taxes contributing to those governmental activities. In fact, we should feel good about all the good our tax dollars are doing – just as we feel good about all the good our religious donations do. Of course it could be argued that there is a big difference here – that giving money to churches is voluntary and we are required to pay taxes. But in practice, many religious organizations require members who can afford it to contribute regularly – payments that are really more like mandatory dues than purely voluntary donations. In any case, the point is that contributing toward an organization that is promoting the public good should not be seen as a bad thing.

But of course anti-government conservatives have been very successful at "framing" taxes in a negative way. As linguist George Lakoff has explained, part of their strategy has involved a careful choice of the words they use to talk about taxes.

> Conservatives have worked for decades to establish the metaphors of taxation as a burden, an affliction, and an unfair punishment – all of which require "relief." ... And on the day that George W. Bush took office, the words *tax relief* started appearing in White House communiqués to the press and in official speeches and reports by conservatives. ...The word *relief* evokes a frame in which there is a blameless Afflicted Person who we identify with and who has some Affliction, some pain or harm that is imposed by some external Cause-of-pain. Relief is the taking away of the pain or harm, and it is brought about by some Reliever-of-pain. ... The term *tax relief* evokes all of this and more. Taxes, in this phrase, are the Affliction (the Crime), proponents of taxes are the Causes-of Affliction (the Villains), the taxpayer is the Afflicted Victim, and the proponents of "tax relief" are the Heroes who deserve the taxpayers' gratitude. Every time the phrase tax relief is used and heard or read by millions of people, the more this view of taxation as an affliction and conservatives as heroes gets reinforced.[1]

As Lakoff explains, the Democrats have inadvertently played into this process of demonizing taxes whenever they supported tax cuts and used the term "tax relief." In 2004, for example, in John Kerry's campaign for president, he talked often about enacting tax relief for the middle class, instead of for the rich. In his 2008 campaign, Barak Obama also thought it was necessary to offer tax cuts to the lower and middle classes, and he then went on to include billions of dollars of this kind of "tax relief" in his first budget. And while Kerry and Obama probably thought their proposals were progressive, they ended up reinforcing a very regressive conservative message that taxes are an unfair burden on most Americans.

Lakoff argues that we need to promote a very different view of taxes—one that uses a very different kind of metaphor. The metaphor he suggests is that of taxes as "dues".

> Taxes are our dues — we pay our dues to be Americans and enjoy the benefits of American society. Taxes are what we pay to live in a civilized society that is democratic, offers opportunity, and has a huge infrastructure available to all citizens. This incredible infrastructure has been paid for by previous taxpayers. Roads and highways, the Internet, the broadcast airwaves, our public education system, our power grid — every day we all use this vast infrastructure. Our dues maintain it.[2]
>
> It is about being a member, a part of the community. People pay a membership fee to join a gym, the local YMCA, or a club for which they get to use the basketball courts, the swimming pool, and the golf course. They did not pay for these facilities with their own memberships. They were built and paid for by other members, and all the current members maintain them with their dues. It is the same thing with our country — being a member in good standing of a remarkable nation. Americans pay their dues.

This idea of taxes as dues is not original to Lakoff. It is an idea that has often been expressed, but has not been promoted with the same ferocity or persistence of the taxes-as-affliction metaphor. Franklin Delano Roosevelt once remarked that "Taxes, after all, are dues that we pay for the privileges of membership in an organized society." And Oliver Wendell Holmes, Jr. expressed a similar sentiment when he said that "I like to pay taxes. With them I buy civilization."

The Disconnect Between Taxes and Programs

One of the reasons that some Americans do not have this more positive view of taxes is that they seem to ignore the basic connection between taxes and the beneficial programs they fund. What else could explain the fact that polls repeatedly reveal that many people support tax cuts while at the same time they support increasing government spending in many areas? Naturally, anti-government and anti-tax advocates like to encourage this sense of disconnection between taxes and programs. That is why, for example, when conservatives talk about tax cuts, they rarely talk about the programs cuts that must necessarily follow. They focus on how money will be returned to tax payers, not how money will be taken away from needed government programs. To listen to them, tax cuts are all gains and no pain.

This sense of disconnection is also helped along greatly by the political illusion that was discussed in the chapter "A Day in Your Life:" that the benefits of many government programs are elusive and are often easy to ignore or take for granted. Unlike marketplace transactions, where what we get for our money is immediate and tangible – what we get for our taxes is often delayed and less tangible. When we draw clean water from our taps, we rarely stop to make the connection between this and the taxes we pay to ensure the purity of this vital resource. Also, many of the benefits that come to us from our taxes take the form of things that do not happen to us – like not getting mugged or not breathing dirty air – and these we hardly notice at all.

Anti-government conservatives and libertarians are very good at taking advantage of the fact that while what government does for us often seems elusive, the taxes we pay to government are all too real to most people. Consider, for example, the strategy employed by Arnold Schwarzenegger when he was running for governor of California. In his campaign, he complained loudly about how overtaxed Californians were: "From the time they get up in the morning and flush the toilet, they are taxed. When they go get a coffee, they are taxed. When they get in their car, they are taxed. When they go to the gas station they are taxed. When they go to lunch, they are taxed. This goes on all day long. Tax. Tax. Tax. Tax. Tax."[3] This is true – and it helped Schwarzenegger get elected – but it is a misleading half-truth. He leaves out the rest of the story: that we are also constantly benefiting from government programs throughout our day. He deliberately ignores the connection between taxes and the programs they fund. We may be taxed when we flush the toilet, but what we get is the efficient and easy way to dispose of our waste in a manner that does not poison our water or spread disease. We may be taxed when we buy a cup of coffee, but our taxes help pay for inspections of coffee houses and restaurants that ensure that their food and drinks are fit for human consumption. We may be taxed when we pay for gas, but what we get is the interstate highway system that many of us so frequently use. So the reality is really this: Tax. Benefit. Tax. Benefit. Tax. Benefit. Tax. Benefit. While government may be constantly taking from us in the form of taxes, it is also constantly giving back to us in the form of the various programs that improve our daily lives.

Government bashers like Schwarzenegger can only succeed in making taxes seem onerous and unfair by completely ignoring what we get in return. This tactic may be bogus, but it has been a raging success. Conservatives have been winning this ideological fight in the United States in part because they have convinced most Americans to see themselves primarily as "taxpayers" not "beneficiaries." In their rhetoric, they make sure to constantly refer to people as "taxpayers." This is another attempt to frame the issue in a way that encourages us to think of government as bad – as a burden on us. "Taxpayers" is not a neutral term at all, but one loaded with powerful political meaning. It unconsciously reinforces a view of citizen/government relations being one-way – from our wallets to its coffers. A recent poll revealed that 28% of Americans agreed with the statement: "I don't like paying taxes because the government doesn't do anything for people like me."[4] And as long as people continue to see themselves only as taxpayers and not beneficiaries, as long as they ignore the connection between our taxes and what they get back from government, they will be ripe for the picking by those who want to weaken government.

Why Highly Taxed Europeans are Not in Revolt

Here's a questions that has vexed conservatives for decades: Why isn't there a huge tax revolt in Europe? Citizens in most European countries pay much higher taxes than we do in the United States, but virtually no substantial tax revolt movements exist in these countries. They should be marching in the streets by the millions demanding large tax cuts – but they aren't. Why is that the case? The answer probably has much to do with the fact that people in Europe can recognize more easily the inherent connection between the taxes they pay and the benefits they receive. The benefits of government programs in these countries are much more obvious than they are in the United States – and so the taxes that pay for them are not resented as much. The European social welfare state is so much more extensive than what we have in the U.S. that it is impossible for citizens to not notice all the valuable things they are getting for their taxes.

T.R. Reid, in his book *The United States of Europe*, tells a story which illustrates this point very well. He lived in Great Britain for years, and at first he was stunned by the 17.5% tax that was added to virtually every purchase he made. "I kept wondering: Why do the Brits put up with a tax that high?" He came to understand the answer to this question when his youngest daughter had to go to the emergency room with a severely infected ear. After a wait of fifteen minutes, his daughter was seen and given effective treatment. Grateful, he went to pay the bill only to have the nurse proudly announce to him that "There won't be a bill to pay. We do it a bit differently here. In the National Health Service, we don't charge for medical treatment." And suddenly he "got it" about the taxes:

> Had the same minor medical crisis occurred in American, we would surely have received the same level of professional treatment. But we would have received something else along with it: a wad of bills. Having had a similar experience in emergency wards in the United States, I would expect that treatment like we got at St. Mary's in London would have brought bills of about $200 from the hospital, another $150 or so from the doctor, and another $100 from some lab technician. And I would likely have faced a three-month battle with an insurance company trying to get the bills paid. In Britain, there was no need to argue with the insurance company over the bill, because there was no bill (and consequently, no insurance company). As we left the hospital, my wife said quietly, "Now I see why we pay that 17.5 percent."[5]

And beside universal health care, the typical European also gets a lot more for their taxes – including a free university education, paid maternity and paternity leaves for everyone, clean and efficient public transportation, retirement security for all, and so on. So ironically, the reason many people in the U.S. hate taxes more than Europeans may be because we pay so little in them and get comparatively so little for them in return. If we paid more taxes like the Europeans do, and then got many more important and obvious social and economic benefits, we would probably see the connections between taxes and government benefits more clearly – and so resent our taxes less. Strange but true.

Addressing Criticisms of Taxes

In the battle over Americans' hearts and minds concerning taxes, only one side is really fighting. Virtually no one is promoting the more positive and constructive view of taxes. Many Democratic politicians wouldn't be caught dead advocating tax increases. So the political effort is all on the other side, with a continual and vociferous conservative assault on taxes – one that typically goes unanswered. But we need to take a more careful look at how this assault is mounted. We need to look more critically at the main reasons the anti-government forces offer for why taxes are bad and tax cuts are good.

In a nutshell, these are the main conservative complaints:

- Americans are greatly overtaxed and their tax burden is continually rising.
- Most of our taxes don't go to programs that help average Americans, but to foreign aid and welfare.
- Taxes are bad for the economy because they hinder productivity and economic growth.
- We would all be better off if we could keep more of the money we now pay in taxes.

There is nothing surprising here. In fact, these points are repeated so often by tax critics that most of us are very familiar with them and we often readily accept them as fact. And if they did happen to be true, they would be a pretty damning indictment of taxes and a powerful rationale for cutting them. But in reality these typically conservative criticisms about taxes are at best confused and misleading, and in most cases simply not true at all.

American's Are Not Overtaxed

Saying that taxes are good does not necessarily mean that all levels of taxation are good. Taxes could certainly be too high and prove to be too much of a burden on taxpayers. And this is exactly what anti-government crusaders like to argue. They maintain that Americans are horribly overtaxed and it is getting worse all the time. For example, when the Republicans took over Congress in the 1990s, David Keating of the National Taxpayers Union described our taxes problems this way: "If we don't seize on this revolutionary moment to rein in taxes and rein in entitlements, we could be looking at a government headed for financial oblivion…and a populace that is so over-taxed and so desperate that we could be talking about real revolutions."[6] This kind of anti-tax rhetoric is used to fan the fires of resentment against government – particularly the federal government and its income tax. And there is resentment aplenty, with many Americans feeling fed up with being "sucked dry" by the government tax collectors.

But many people greatly exaggerate the tax burden in this country. Here is a quick quiz: Guess what percentage of Americans pay over 20% of their household income in federal income taxes? Polls show that most Americans put that figure at 38%. But the real figure is shockingly lower: less than 1%. According to the Congressional Joint Committee on Taxation, over 85% of us pay less than 10% of our income in federal income taxes. The average middle-class family now pays less than 5% of their income in federal income taxes – a historical low. How is this possible? Because many people are too poor to pay income tax, and many of the rest of us have deductions and credits that reduce our effective tax rate to much less than the official tax rate for our income group. In any case, the point is most of us tend to wildly overestimate how much everyone is paying in taxes.

Also, even a cursory examination of the facts shows that Americans are taxed relatively lightly compared to most other Western countries, and that our tax burden has not been skyrocketing at all. Table 1 makes it clear that Americans carry much less of a tax burden than the citizens in virtually every comparable Western European country. We pay the lowest taxes as a portion of Gross Domestic Product than any of these nations – usually by a very large amount. For example, we would have to increase tax revenues by almost 60 percent to match those of France, and by 40 percent to catch up with the Dutch. So it makes little sense to maintain that we are overtaxed in this country.

Table 1: Total Tax Revenue as a Percentage of GDP: 2009

Country	**Taxes as % of GDP**
Denmark	48.2
Sweden	46.4
Italy	43.5
Belgium	43.2
Austria	42.8
France	41.9
Iceland	41.4
Netherlands	39.1
Germany	37.0
United Kingdom	34.3
Canada	31.1
Spain	30.7
Switzerland	30.3
United States	**24.0**

Source: *Revenue Statistics 1965-2009*, OECD 2010.

Nor is it true that our taxes have been increasing at a precipitous rate. To see this we merely need to consider how tax revenues as a percentage of GDP have changed over the last several decades. This is a good measure because it takes into account economic growth and inflation, and so it gives us a much broader and more accurate picture of how much government is receiving in taxes. These figures, as shown in Table 2, indicate that the government take has changed relatively little in the last 40 years – either on the federal or the state and local level. In fact, we've had a remarkably stable rate of taxation. In 1970, total government receipts were 28.3% of the GDP while in 2007 they still only amount to 29.2%. In contrast, many other Western nations had substantial increases in their taxes during this same period. Between 1975 and 2003, Austria went from 37.4% to 43% and Italy from 26.1% to 43.4%, for instance.[7] In any case, the figures for the U.S. show that conservative claims of an increasingly greedy government taking more and more money out of our pockets in taxes are simply false. Given these facts – that we are not overtaxed and our taxes are not mushrooming – the so-called "Tax Revolt" movement begins to make less and less sense

Table 2: Government Receipts as a Percentage of GDP: 1970-2007

	1970	1980	1990	2007
State & Local Govt. Receipts	9.3	8.8	9.7	10.4
Federal Government Receipts	19.0	19.0	18.0	18.8
Total Government Receipts	28.3	27.8	27.7	29.2

Source: U.S. Government, *Budget for the Fiscal Year 2009, Historical Tables, 2008.*

Most of Your Tax Money Doesn't Go to Others

Anti-government conservatives build up a lot of public resentment about taxes by suggesting that most of our tax money goes to help people other than ourselves – that it is redistributed to programs like welfare and food stamps that primarily help the poor and minorities. According to them, the government takes your money and then spends it on other people while you are left to struggle to make ends meet, pay your medical bills, send your kids to college, and so on. This argument is sometimes a thinly veiled attempt to mobilize opposition to government by fanning people's racial and class resentments. But more importantly, it is simply not true. Most people have wildly exaggerated ideas about how much of their tax money is going to "others" in the form of welfare or foreign aid. When the public was asked to name the two largest parts of the federal budget, the leading responses were foreign aid (41%) and welfare (40%) – ahead of other choices like Social Security, defense, and health.[8] This is highly delusional. Spending on foreign aid and welfare actually amounts to *less than 3%* of the federal budget.

What we have here, then, is another common negative stereotype about government perpetuated by the right. The idea that the government spends most of our tax dollars on "them" rather than on "us" is simply not rooted in reality. Studies have also shown that the vast majority of government dollars, which come from taxes on the middle and upper classes, are spent on benefits for the middle and upper classes, not the poor. Consider, for example, the federal money handed out in social welfare spending. In a typical year, the government spends over three times the amount of money for programs that everybody benefits from – like Social Security and Medicare – than it spends for programs aimed at the poor, such as Medicaid, welfare, and food stamps.[9]

Here is another quick quiz: What is the dollar value of the benefits from federal programs that the average middle-class wage earner receives? $1,000? $5,000? A 2007 study by the Tax Foundation found that it was over $10,000.[10] And that figure does not include any benefits from such so-called "public goods" programs as environmental protection and public-health efforts. Include those and the value of federal programs rises to over $16,000 a year. And if we add in the benefits from state and local programs, the total amounts to over $27,000. So there is no question that we are all getting back a great deal in government benefits for the taxes we pay.

Taxes Are Not Hurting the Economy

Another very common criticism of taxes by conservatives is that taxes hurt the economy and that cutting them will increase economic growth. This was the argument used repeatedly by Republicans in Congress and the Bush administration as they passed a number of massive tax cuts. Conservatives are certainly correct that in principle taxation could be so high – say a 75% income tax on everyone – that it would stifle economic growth and any incentive that people have to work harder. But our current taxes are nowhere near this extreme, so the question is not whether taxes could hurt the economy, but whether our current taxes are hurting the economy.

The conservative case for our taxes hurting the economy is very straightforward. The argument is that taxes on various forms of income are a drag on worker productivity and consumer savings, and thus ultimately on economic growth. So the higher these taxes are, the more it slows the economy down. Conversely, if we cut these taxes, then people would have more incentive to work hard and save, and this would give a long term boost to the economy. Sounds logical enough. But it is wrong. There is little evidence to support this contention and plenty that contradicts it. Consider for example, the effect of tax changes on worker productivity. From 1950 to 1963, when the top individual income tax rate averaged 91.1%, productivity growth was 3.5%. From 1964 to 1980, when taxes were cut and the top income rate fell to 71.2 %, productivity did not go up as conservatives predicted, but actually went down a bit to 2.2%. And in fact, as shown in Table 3, the long-term statistics concerning tax rates and productivity show that as tax rates have fallen from the 1950s to the early 1990s, productivity fell as well. And when the tax rate went up in the later 1990s, productivity actually rose. This does not mean, of course, that tax cuts discourage worker productivity or that tax rises encourage it; but only that productivity depends on a large number of factors besides taxes. As we have seen in recent years, for example, technological changes like increases in computer use have a much more significant impact on productivity than tax rates do. But in any case, the point is that the tax-bashers are simply wrong about how tax cuts will boost worker productivity. Strike one for their side.

Table 3: Top Income Tax Rate and Productivity Growth in the United States 1950-2002.

	Top Average Income Tax Rate	Average Annual Productivity Growth Rate
1950-1963	91.1%	3.5%
1964-1980	71.2%	2.2%
1981-1986	53.2%	2.1%
1987-1992	30.8%	1.7%
1993-2002	39.5%	2.1%

Source: U.S. Bureau of Labor Statistics (2003).

Conservatives are also wrong about the effects of tax cuts on investment and savings. The boost to investment predicted by conservatives after the tax cuts during the Reagan administration never took place. Between 1979 and 1989, the average rate of investment was 2.5%. From 1989 to 2000, it rose significantly to an average of 5.9%. But this was after George H. W. Bush and Bill Clinton both raised federal taxes. There is also little evidence that the Reagan tax cuts boosted savings either. Savings rates fell from 8.8% of personal disposable income in 1981 to 6.0 percent in 1986.[11] Moreover, two economists who did a comprehensive survey in 1996 of the economic literature on the effects of tax cuts on savings concluded: "Virtually no empirical study suggests a large saving response by households to changes in after-tax return."[12] Strike two for tax cutters.

But what about the over-all beneficial effects of tax cuts on economic growth? Again, history is a good guide. From 1981 to 1985, after the tax cuts of the Reagan administration, the economy did grow at a good rate – averaging 2.6% a year. But between 1976 and 1980, when the tax rates were higher, it grew even faster – averaging 3.2%. Similarly, after taxes were raised by Bush and Clinton, economic growth actually picked up and averaged 3.2% between 1989 and 2000.[13] So there is clearly not a strong relationship between tax rates and growth in this country. Strike three – they're out.

Comparing the U.S. to other countries brings little solace to tax cutters either. They like to think that our growing economy outpaces those of other advanced democracies in large part because of our lower tax burden. But the research doesn't bear any of this out. Consider the results of a study that compared tax levels and economic growth rates between 1970 and 2000 for a large number of countries.[14] It did find that Denmark and Sweden, which had much higher taxes than the U.S., also did worse in terms of average growth – about 1.6% versus about 2.3% for the U.S. But how do anti-tax advocates explain Finland and Norway, which had taxes almost 50% greater than we did, but actually enjoyed higher rates of growth? In fact, the overall results of the study indicated very little correlation between taxes and economic growth – with the U.S., Italy, Canada, the United Kingdom, Germany, Belgium, France and the Netherlands having relatively similar rates of growth, but widely varying tax levels – from 27% to 42% of GDP. International comparisons, then, contradict rather than support the conservative contentions that we need to cut taxes to ensure economic growth or that high taxes hurt the economy. Clearly a country can have high taxes and strong economic growth as well. Strike four.

One economic analyst, Anna Bernasek of *The New York Times*, examined a wide variety of academic studies on the relationships between tax rates on productivity, savings, and growth. She concluded that the "notion that taxes are bad for the economy is just that: a notion not backed by strong evidence. And the costs of ignoring experience in favor of hope can be high: mounting deficits, decaying infrastructure, inadequate investment in public education and research. So the next time some proponent of tax reform promises king-size economic benefits, there is reason to be skeptical."[15]

Are We Better Off Paying Less Taxes?

There is another common anti-tax argument offered by conservatives. It is a reliable old standby: Tax cuts are good because they put more money in your pocket. It is an appeal based on pure greed and selfishness. This argument is not based on any sense of what is in the public interest, only what is in your own private interest. But it can very seductive to some Americans. And anti-tax advocates do not hesitate to play this selfishness card. Consider, for example, the way Grover Norquist of Americans for Tax Reform explains the benefits of tax cuts: "When the government doesn't take as much of your money next year as it did last year, we have more money. The government has a lower tax rate, and depending on economic growth, may have more or less money, but we, the people, have more money. So it is a good thing for us to have lower taxes."[16]

But here is the question: are we really better off as individuals in the long run if we were to pay much lower taxes? Naturally, most people would *feel* better off with a few more thousand dollars to spend. But what Norquist leaves out, and hopes Americans don't notice either, is the essential connection between tax dollars and government programs. When the government returns tax money to individuals, it must also necessarily begin to curtail important government programs that benefit us all. Tax cuts on the scale envisioned by small government advocates can't help but cut deeply into the dozens of vital government service and benefits detailed in earlier chapters. Loss of these collective benefits means that we would probably not be better off at all. Do you really believe that you would be better off if you had 27 more dollars in your pocket – the amount the average American spends to fund the Environmental Protection Agency – and had to forego all those agency's programs to ensure clean air and clean water and to deal with environmental threats like toxic waste, oil spills, mercury and lead contamination, radioactive waste, pesticide poisoning, ozone depletion, and global warming?

The reality is that in modern societies, we simply face too many serious problems and risks that we cannot deal with effectively as individuals. Having a few more thousand dollars in our pockets will not help us to deal effectively with a deteriorating public school system, police and fire department layoffs, unclean air or polluted water, unsafe food, being laid off from our jobs, threats from terrorist organizations, and so on. These kinds of problems can only be addressed collectively – through collective institutions like government that allow us to pool our resources and efforts to most effectively address these threats to our well-being.

Let's focus for a moment on one particular problem: the economic insecurity felt by a growing number of Americans. We have increasing trouble paying for health care and health insurance. Many of us are unsure whether and how we can pay for our kids to go to college. Being laid off means economic disaster for most families. Personal bankruptcies have been growing dramatically. Many Americans are also very uncertain about whether they will have enough money to live a decent life in retirement, and wonder who will take care of them in their old age. And many of these problems are greatly intensified when we have a severe recession — like the one that began in 2008. But the point is that even in "good times," life for many Americans is full of persistent and serious economic worries.

Conservatives realize this situation all too well and have been relentless in their efforts to exploit these economic insecurities to support their campaign to reduce taxes and government. Their message is very seductive: Couldn't we all use more money in our paychecks to meet our pressing economic needs? They also like to suggest that high taxes are much of the reason for our economic insecurities. As Rep. Dick Armey has argued, the reason that "education and health care are difficult to afford is because the government itself makes us poorer through high taxes."[17]

But here again the government bashers have it exactly wrong. The cause of people's economic insecurities is not government taxes. Virtually all of these insecurities are coming from changes in the economy. Globalization contributes to stagnating wages. Mergers and downsizing threaten many people's job security. Many corporations can no longer afford to provide health care benefits or retirement plans for their employees. And so on. Not only are taxes not causing these insecurities, they can actually be a large part of the solutions to many of these problems. The most viable approach to many of these economic worries is again not to try to go it alone, but to support an expansion of government programs to address them directly. As we've seen, one of the main functions of modern government is to pool collective resources (taxes) to provide social insurance against many of the economic risks we all face – such as losing our job, or retiring, or facing a major illness. The better – and better funded – these programs are, the less economic worries we have.

Again, looking at Europe is instructive here. Europeans are more secure economically because they have more extensive programs to protect them from the many economic risks of modern life. They have universal health care, extensive unemployment insurance programs, generous government pensions, and free or very low-cost higher education. So instead of leaving everyone on their own to face these economic difficulties – they pool their tax resources and solve these problems for all citizens. Certainly this costs more in taxes, but the economic security that is enjoyed by everyone is priceless.

This is another reason why Europeans are not revolting against their high taxes. In Europe, taxes are not seen as a threat to people's economic security – they are seen as providing that security. Europeans do not feel like they cannot afford to pay those high taxes, rather they feel that they cannot afford to *not* pay them – and thus risk losing the crucial economic safety net that their social programs give them. To over-simplify only a bit: for Europeans, more taxes mean more economic security. It is a very different attitude toward taxes than we have here – but it is one we might learn a great deal from.

Seeing Government as "Them," Not "Us"

The anti-tax arguments of conservatives and libertarians also rely heavily on denying the connection between the people and their government. They do not want us to see public money as "our" money being spent for "our" benefit. Grover Norquist, for instance, rankles when people refer to the government as "we." When the interviewer Terry Gross pointed out to him that "The Bush tax cuts would cost us about $1.1 trillion over the next 10 years, and we're going to be hundreds of billions of dollars in debt." He responded by saying: "Well, there's a very interesting use of the word 'we.' Every time you use the word 'we,' you meant the government, and I tend to use the word 'we' to mean the American people and to speak of the government as the government." [18]

For anti-government advocates this is a crucial distinction. They don't want people seeing government as "we." In terms of taxes, they want people to see the government as "them" taking money from "us." It is this same rhetorical point that President George W. Bush expressed when he was pushing for one of his tax refunds: "It is not the government's money," he said. "It is *your* money." But isn't the government's money in a very real sense "our" money too? Aren't government programs "our" programs? Al Gore, when he was running for president, certainly thought so. Responding to Bush's tax cut proposals, he argued: "Their theory is that's going to be good for the country, and they say it's your money. Well, it is your money. But it's your Medicare, it's your Social Security, it's your environment, it's your school system, it's your country."[19]

In a working democracy, government is supposed to be "us," and its spending policies are supposed to generally reflect "our" collective will. Granted this process works imperfectly and sometimes special interests win out over the public interest in budget battles. But the basic idea underlying democratic government is that it is a reflection and representation of us. This gives us a very different perspective on taxes. As Benjamin Barber has explained:

> The money does not belong to the government, it belongs to us. But the government belongs to us too. 'It' does not steal from "us," we pool resources so we can act on behalf of the commonweal – the weal (well-being) common to us. … Taxes are not tithes imposed by tyrants; they are self-imposed duties that permit our government to discharge our common purposes. … To cry "Give Americans back their hard-earned tax dollars!" is a disingenuous way of saying "To hell with establishing justice, promoting welfare and securing liberty!" It is nothing more than a cynical bribe to get people to give up on one another and to go it alone.[20]

The Real Problems with Taxes

All of this has been a defense of taxation and an argument that taxes play a very positive and beneficial role in our society. But this is not to say that there are no problems with taxes in this country. Of course there are – but they are not the problems that conservatives usually cite, like that we are overtaxed or that taxes are strangling the economy. In fact, if you ask the American people, their main complaint about taxes is something quite different. Pollsters have found that "What most bothers the public about taxes is the feeling that some in America are not paying their fair share. They believe that middle and lower income people pay too much while the wealthy and corporations pay too little."[21] So some of the real questions surrounding taxes involve how fair they are, and how much of the tax burden should be shouldered by various economic classes. There are other issues as well: Are there better and worse ways to collect taxes? Should we be relying more on regressive taxes like sales taxes and less on more progressive approaches like income taxes? Should we continue the substantial tax breaks given to the middle and upper classes, such as the home mortgage interest deduction? All of these are valid and ongoing controversies about taxes in our society. But the important point here is that while these questions of what makes for a fair and effective tax system are valid issues for debate, the legitimacy of taxes themselves is not.

Reasons for Hope

Americans need to come to their senses about taxes. We need to reject taxophobia and stop falling for conservative arguments about how taxes are bad. We need to recognize that taxes are necessary and beneficial – that they are indeed the dues that we pay to live in a modern, functioning society with all the government benefits to which we have become accustomed. We need to appreciate that there is a very real connection between the taxes we pay and the vital services and programs offered by our state, local, and federal governments – and that cutting taxes the way many conservatives propose will inevitably undermine the viability of these programs and harm the public interest.

Embracing a more realistic view of the value of taxes is especially important if we want to make progress on a number of important fronts. If we want to make health care more accessible, improve education, combat global warming, etc., we need more money to do so – which means tax increases. The trillions of dollars that were spent on the Iraq War and the economic bailout have produced record budget deficits that cannot be sustained. So there is no more free lunch. If citizens want more out of their government, they must be willing to pay for it.

Fortunately, there are reasons to hope that Americans are coming around to a more positive view of taxes. Polls show that the number of Americans who believe that taxes are too high has been dropping over the last several years and is now at its lowest level since the 1960s.[22] Much more importantly, they also see taxes as an important part of their contribution to a democratic society. 81% of Americans agree with the statement: "I don't mind paying taxes because my taxes are part of my contribution to society as a citizen of the United States." Another 84% also say "I don't mind paying taxes because my taxes contribute to making sure we have public schools, clean streets, public safety, national defense, and a cleaner environment." And even 74% say that that "I don't mind paying taxes because I want government to play a strong role in helping people when in need."[23] We need to actively promote and build on these kinds of pro-tax sentiments. We need to go on the political offensive on the issue of taxes and make it clearer that in many cases paying more taxes makes us better off, not worse off.

Thankfully, a number of Americans have already begun to fight tax cuts and even support tax increases. In my own town, a majority of residents have voted several times in the last decade to raise their own taxes to pay for such things as a new fire station and a badly needed renovation of our high school. Many Americans are also now saying that they are willing to have their taxes increased – if the money goes to important programs like education and environmental protection. It is also encouraging that during the ongoing fiscal crisis in the states, thirty-three state legislatures have made the brave choice to raise taxes to ensure the continuation of vital services. And in a few of these states, even some Republican politicians have acknowledged the necessity of boosting revenues and have gone along with these tax increases – a testimony to the fact that common sense can triumph over blind political ideology. All of these things suggest that while anti-government crusaders may still be able to fool some of the people all of the time with their rhetoric about the evil of taxes, they are not able to fool all of the people all of the time.

---

1. George Lakeoff, "Simple Framing," Rockridge Institute, August 25, 2006, http://www.rockridgeinstitute.org/projects/strategic/simple_framing
2. George Lakeoff, "Progressive Frame for Taxes," Rockridge Institute, August 25, 2006, http://www.rockridgeinstitute.org/research/rockridge/taxation
3. Larry Kudrow, "Terminating Any Doubt," *National Review Online*, http://www.nationalreview.com/kudlow/kudlow082103.asp
4. Meg Bostrum, *By, or for, the People: A Meta-Analysis of Public Opinion of Government* (New York: Demos, March 1, 2005) p. 27.
5. T. R. Reid, *The United States of Europe* (New York: Penguin Press, 2004) p. 145.
6. People for the American Way, "National Taxpayers Union, August 25, 2006. http://www.pfaw.org/pfaw/general/default.aspx?oid=10235
7. *Revenue Statistics 1965-2003*, OECD 2004, p. 18.

8. Kaiser Family Foundation, "National Survey of Public Knowledge of Welfare Reform and the Federal Budget," http://www.kff.org/kaiserpolls/1001-welftbl.cfm. June 23, 2006
9. Mimi Abramovitz, "Everyone is Still on Welfare: The Role of Redistribution in Social Policy," *Social Work*, Volume 46, No. 4, p. 299.
10. Andrew Chamberlain and Gerald Prante, "Who Pays Taxes and Who Receives Government Spending? An Analysis of Federal State and Local Tax and Spending Distributions, 1991-2004." http://www.taxfoundation.org/files/wp1.pdf
11. All of these figures are from John O. Fox, *If Americans Really Understood the Income Tax* (Boulder Colorado:Westview Press, 2001) p. 170.
12. Fox, p. 169.
13. Fox, p. 166.
14. Joel Slemrod and Jon Bakija, *Taxing Ourselves, 3rd Edition: A Citizen's Guide to the Debate over Taxes* (Cambridge, MA: MIT Press, 2004), p. 119.
15. Anna Bernasek, "Do Taxes Thwart Growth? Prove it," *The New York Times*, April 3, 2005, p.6, Business section.
16. Terry Gross, "Grover Norquist" *Fresh Air*, http://www.npr.org/templates/story/story.php?storyId=1452983
17. Dick Armey, *The Freedom Revolution*, Washington, D.C.: Regnery Publishing, 1995, p. 292.
18. Terry Gross, "Grover Norquist" *Fresh Air*, http://www.npr.org/templates/story/story.php?storyId=1452983
19. NY Times, Aug 31, 2000.
20. Benjamin Barber, "A Civics Lesson," *The Nation*, November 4, 1996, p. 21.
21. Bostrum, p. 17.
22. "Americans' View on Taxes," National Public Radio, April, 2003. www.npr.org/news/specials/polls/taxes2003/index.html
23. Bostrum, p. 27.

CHAPTER 6

More Government Does Not Mean Less Freedom

"FREEDOM!" has always been a rallying cry of anti-government activists. Many conservatives embrace and extol the libertarian principle that "Individual freedom and government power are polar opposites. More government means less freedom."[1] For them, the trade-off between government size and individual liberty is inevitable, and this is the main reason they work to minimize government.

As Ronald Reagan once put it: "Runaway government threatens ... the very preservation of freedom itself."[2] Charlton Heston, speaking to a college audience in the 1990s, argued that the government had become more than just a threat, that it had already reached oppressive proportions in the United States:

> There is now no aspect of American life, public or private, that the federal government does not invade, instruct and finally coerce to its will. Farm and factory, home and school, university and research center, club and playground – all are overlaid with a spidery network of laws, guidelines, restrictions and Draconian penalties that stifle the spirit, the energy, the creative capacity of what was once the freest nation on earth. In this hemisphere, now that Ortega and Noriega have fallen, the collectivists' sentiments discredited around the world fly best, I fear, in Cuba and Washington, D.C.[3]

In more recent years, the Tea Party has taken up the mission of alerting Americans about how much of a threat government has become to their freedom. In the election of 2010, more than one Tea Party candidate for Congress warned that the federal government had become so intolerably oppressive that an armed rebellion against it was not out of the question.

These views may seem extreme, but it is important to realize that many Americans have become convinced by these contentions that government is putting their liberty in danger. Almost a third of us now believe that the federal government "poses an immediate threat to the rights and freedoms of ordinary citizens." And many people resent it fiercely whenever the government prevents them from doing what they want to do – whether it is riding a motorcycle without a helmet, filling in a wetland on their property, or carrying a gun for their own protection.

Bashing the government in the name of freedom can be a very effective political tactic. After all, freedom is quintessentially American. It is our most basic political value and a fundamental part of our national political identity. We are "the land of the free" as we sing in our national anthem. And so, to the extent that government can be portrayed as interfering with our individual rights and freedoms, it will be seen as bad – as anti-American.

The political right's ability to convince many Americans that there is an inevitable trade-off between government and freedom has been one of its greatest ideological victories. In one stroke, it renders illegitimate virtually all liberal policy initiatives. Any effort to expand social programs or increase regulation becomes seen as an attack on freedom. If you value freedom, it is argued, you should strongly oppose any increase in public sector activity. If you love freedom, you should hate government.

Or so it seems. But things are not always as they seem. In reality, this view of the relationship between freedom and government is incomplete, distorted, and often wrong. It relies almost entirely on a misleading stereotype: government as "Big Brother." But if we can step back and look at the performance of our democratic government in a more objective and less dogmatic way, we begin to see that many of the basic conservative and libertarian assumptions about government and freedom are mistaken.

No Necessary Trade-off Between Government and Freedom

Let's start by seeing what is wrong with the assumption that there is an inevitable trade-off between government and our individual rights and liberties. Former U.S. House Majority Leader Dick Armey put this assumption succinctly: "The sheer mass of our federal government is simply inconsistent with a free society."[5] But it is a mistake to believe that the size or extent of government has anything to do with how oppressive it is. For example, you could have a country with a minimal public sector that was very repressive to its citizens. It would have low taxes, few social service programs, and hardly any regulations on business. But it could also be incredibly oppressive – allowing only one-party elections, banning free speech, muzzling the press, preventing freedom of assembly, jailing people arbitrarily, etc. On the other hand, we could have a society with a public sector much larger than we have now that has all the freedoms of a modern democracy. Belgium, for example, has a public sector almost twice the size of the United States as a proportion of GDP, and has much more extensive health care, unemployment, and pension programs. Yet Belgian citizens enjoy essentially the same rights and liberties as Americans. We see very few Belgian political refugees applying for asylum in the U.S. because they feel oppressed in their homeland.

So the size and extent of government activity, by itself, tells us nothing about how free or oppressive a society is. The necessary trade-off between government size and citizen's freedom simply does not exist. And the reason it does not exist is because many of the most common activities of the modern state – building roads and highways, putting out fires, fighting disease, treating our sewage, providing college loans, funding basic scientific research, providing medical care for the elderly, supplying clean water, feeding the poor, providing parks and recreational facilities, subsidizing farmers, educating our children, forecasting the weather, sending out Social Security checks, and so on – are not inherently coercive or oppressive at all. So it is simply mistaken to automatically equate more government with less freedom.

The minimal-government crowd uses this "more government = less freedom" formula to make all sorts of alarmist claims. For example, some suggest that every increase in government power is a step down the road to totalitarianism and repression. This is a favorite argument of many conservatives and they use it to oppose even small and seemingly reasonable increases in government programs or regulations. For example, they argue that if we allow the government to insist on background checks to buy guns, this will lead to mandatory gun registration, which will eventually lead to confiscation of guns, and this will put the government in a position to repress a disarmed and helpless citizenry. Or they suggest that legalizing assisted-suicide for terminally ill patients will only set the stage for government euthanasia programs aimed at the handicapped and others. Or they fear that mandating non-smoking areas is merely a step toward outlawing cigarettes altogether. Or they contend that if we allow environmental regulations to restrict how an owner deals with wetlands on their property, we are going down a road in which property rights will eventually be meaningless because the state will control all property. This seems to be the view of the conservative judge Janice Rogers – one of George W. Bush's appointees to the federal judiciary. In one of her opinions, she railed against local restrictions on the rights of real estate developers in California and concluded that "Private property, already an endangered species in California, is now entirely extinct in San Francisco."[6]

In his book, *Defending Government*, Max Nieman has labeled this argument the "Big Brother Road to Dictatorship." It suggests that the expansion of government powers in the U.S. during the last 75 years has been inevitably leading us down the path toward totalitarianism. But as he has noted, there is really no valid evidence for this theory. If we look at how modern dictatorships have come about, they have *not* been the product of gradually increasing social programs and regulations over property and business. As Neiman explains:

> It is common among conservative critics of public sector activism to characterize government growth in the arena of social welfare, environment, consumer and worker protection, and income security as steps toward the loss of liberty and even totalitarianism. Many critics of the emergence of the modern social welfare state ... have tried to convey the sense that the road to totalitarian hell is paved with the good intentions of the social democratic program. ...There is no record, however, of any oppressive regime having taken power by advancing on the social welfare front. Lenin and Stalin, Mussolini, Mao Tse-tung, Fidel Castro, and Chile's Pinochet did not consolidate power by gradually increasing social welfare programs, taxes, and regulation of the environment or workplace. Rather, these assaults on personal freedom and democratic governance involved limitation on civil rights and political rights, the legitimization of oppression and discrimination against disfavored or unpopular groups, and the centralization and expansion of military and policy forces. Hitler did not become the supreme ruler of the Nazi state by first taking over the health department.[7]

Government Coercion Can Be Good

So there is not an inherent trade-off between government and freedom. Much of what government does is not coercive at all, and expansion of government programs is not going to lead us down a slippery slope to totalitarian rule. But all of this is not to deny that some government activities do curtail our freedom. Conservatives are correct to say that many laws and regulations are inherently coercive – they prevent people and organizations from doing what they want to do. But anti-government conservatives seem to think this coercion is a bad thing. It is not.

What anti-government zealots fail to appreciate is that when our democratic government restricts people's behavior, this is usually a *very good thing*. We *want* the government to restrict the freedom of many people – people who would otherwise do a great deal of damage to us, our families, and our society. We don't want burglars free to rob, or rapists free to attack women, or murders free to kill people. Nor do we want shady businessmen free to defraud investors and customers, or factories free to dump poisons in our air and water, or drug companies free to sell dangerous or worthless medicines. To create an ordered, prosperous, and just society – something we all want – we inevitably have to have a government that will not let everyone do what they want. In short, restricting some people's freedom is in the public interest. Naturally, we don't always agree on when these coercive measures are justified. Sometimes the harm to individuals may not be worth the gains to the public interest. But while we can disagree on such matters, what is not disputable is that oftentimes it is entirely legitimate to restrict people's freedom in pursuit of the public interest – and that we are all much safer and better off for it.

While most conservatives will readily admit that the government is legitimate in restricting criminal behavior, they do not think it is legitimate for it to restrict the freedom of normal, law-abiding citizens. For example, they believe it's wrong for the government to use zoning laws to restrict how people use their private property, and for it to force people to wear motorcycle helmets or to prevent them from smoking in public facilities. They invoke the specter of "Big Brother" intruding into the private lives of citizens – telling us what to do in our everyday lives. But in virtually every case in which government tries to regulate the behavior of ordinary citizens, it does so for the same reason it restricts the freedom of criminals – to prevent harm and to promote the good of society as a whole. When people's actions only affect themselves, we usually could care less what they do. But when individuals' actions begin to harm others, then we do care and we want to stop it. No one cares if you smoke in your own home; but if you do it in a public place your secondhand smoke can harm others – as has been shown by numerous studies.

Perhaps the best example of this kind of issue has been motorcycle helmet laws – which have become a lightning rod for pro-freedom/anti-government activists. For them, this is the archetypal example of government bureaucrats interfering with our right to make our own decisions about our lives. If riders want to increase their chances of dying in a crash, that's their own business – the government should mind its own business. But the problem here is not so much the preventable deaths of these riders. The problem is that often they don't die. Motorcycle riders without helmets typically experience more frequent and more severe head injuries in accidents, which can often mean prolonged and expensive stays in hospitals and nursing homes. And this doesn't just affect them; it affects all us in terms of higher insurance costs, and increased government health care expenditures. For example, before enacting its universal helmet law in 1991, California's state medical program paid out $40 million for treatment of motorcycle-related head injuries. After passage of the law, that figure dropped to $24 million. Also, a National Highway Traffic Administration study has shown that if all states had mandated 100% helmet usage between 1984 and 1996, the total cost savings over those 13 years would have been $4,638,173,956.[8] This is money that came out of all our pockets and could have been put to better use. As Judith Lee Stone, president of Advocates for Highway and Auto Safety, has observed: "Citizens must fight for every penny at the state government level and recognize the trade-offs where they exist. In the case of motorcycle helmet laws, clearly the money spent on head injuries means that less money will be available to pay police officers or teachers."[9] And as one state senator, John Cullerton of Illinois, has concluded: "On behalf of the taxpayers I represent, I must ask: Is it worth spending these millions of dollars to pay for the wind in the hair of motorcyclists? My answer is No."[10] And yet in spite of the large public costs being imposed on taxpayers by the absence of these laws, the Republican Congress repealed federal incentives to the states to adopt these laws in 1995. As a result of this action and the growing power of conservatives in state legislatures, more states have been repealing and weakening their helmet laws, and now only 20 states have laws that cover all riders. We are all worse off for this.

Ironically, coercive government policies can sometimes actually have *liberating* effects on us and society as a whole. For many people this may seem counter-intuitive: How can having more rules increase our freedom? But it is true. This point has been made very effectively by the political commentator Garry Wills. He has argued that government restrictions on our behavior can often work to increase our freedoms. He uses a very common example to make his point – traffic laws. These laws, he points out, are often incredibly intrusive and restrictive:

> One must stop on the command of an inanimate red light or stop sign, yield to other drivers in a number of circumstances, drive at prescribed speeds (a maximum speed imposed everywhere, though at different levels place by place, and a minimum speed set on some highways). We are told where we *cannot* drive (the wrong way on one-way streets, the sidewalk, certain bus lanes, certain downtown areas at certain times). ...The very vehicle must be licensed, and the license periodically renewed. A car must have a mandated quantity and kind of lights, mirrors, windshield wipers, and unobstructed windows. Its width and turning capacity are determined by the state. It must have functioning brakes, mufflers, horn, and other parts. It must pass pollution tests. The car itself and its action upon others must be insured to prescribed levels. The accumulation of minor impositions is really quite staggering when one stops to add them up. ... How can we really be free when we are continually triggered to obey on so many fronts?[11]

But then Wills concludes, "Actually, these rules are immensely liberating." He explains that without these elaborate controls on our behavior, the traffic system would break down and we would not be free to drive anywhere. "If we all woke every morning, took out cars of uncertain performance, and tried to drive every which way, not heeding (nonexistent) signs or a right-side requirement, any speed laws or rules of precedence at crossings, we would either be crashing constantly, or would be immobilized by a fear of crashing or being crashed into."[12] In other words, without all those coercive traffic laws, we really wouldn't be free to drive. And such rules are not an example of "Big Brother" telling us what to do, but of "us" telling us what to do. They are not a form of dictatorial coercion; but a form of mutual coercion, decided on in a democratic manner. Without these kinds of democratically generated rules, we would lack the social order necessary for us to be free to go about our business.

We can see a similar liberating function of government rules at work in many other areas. For example, we are free to breathe clean air and drink untainted water only because environmental laws prevent the numerous private activities that could pollute those vital common resources. And our venerated "free" market would not work at all without elaborate government rules governing economic behavior, including complex laws about contracts, property rights, fraud, debt collection, and so forth. (See the chapter "Capitalism Requires Government.") Without these legal rules, markets would descend into chaos and cease to function effectively. We are free to participate in market activities precisely because acceptable economic actions are so highly circumscribed by government.

Conclusion

It is clear, then, that two of the central conservative assumptions about the relationships between government and freedom are wrong. There is no logical reason to assume that a growing government inevitably threatens the freedom of its citizens. Also, when the government does restrict the behavior of individuals, this is not necessarily a bad thing. These forms of "mutual coercion" are usually in the public interest and work to our common benefit.

---

1. Jo Jorgensen, "Why Republican politicians keep selling out Freedom," Libertarian Party News Archive, May 1997. http://www.lp.org/lpn/9705-Jorgensen.html
2. Joseph S. Nye, Jr., et al., *Why People Don't Trust Government* (Cambridge: Harvard University Press, 1997). p. 21.
3. Charlton Heston, Speech, September 9, 1990, Hillsdale College. http://www.libertyhaven.com/politicsandcurrentevents/governmentreformitsrealrole/reaganright.shtml
4. Meg Bostrum, *By, or for, the People: A Meta-Analysis of Public Opinion of Government* (New York: Demos, March 1, 2005) p. 38.
5. Dick Armey, *The Freedom Revolution* (Washington D.C.: Regnery Publishing, 1995), p. 291.
6. Dissenting opinion in San Remo Hotel L.P. v. City and County of San Francisco, 41 P.3d 87, 120, 128-9 (Cal. 2002).
7. Max Neiman, *Defending Government: Why Big Government Works* (Upper Saddle River, NJ: Prentice-Hall, 2000) pp. 160-161.
8. National Highway Traffic Safety Administration, "Universal Motorcycle Helmet Laws Reduce Costs to Society," http:// www.nhtsa.dot.gov/people/injury/pedbimot/motorcycle/safebike/costs.html
9. National Highway Traffic Safety Administration, "A Helmet Law is Not a Stand Alone Issue." http://www.nhtsa.dot.gov/people/injury/pedbimot/motorcycle/safebike/stand.html
10. NHTSA, "Universal Motorcycle Helmet Laws."
11. Garry Wills, *A Necessary Evil* (New York: Simon and Schuster, 1999) pp.305-06.
12. Ibid.

CHAPTER 7

Government as the Primary Protector of our Rights and Liberties

As seen in the previous chapter, the vast majority of public programs do little to threaten the liberty of Americans. But it would be naive to ignore the fact that democratic governments can sometimes step over the line and pass laws that do violate people's basic rights and civil liberties. Consider the political witch-hunts of the McCarthy era in the 1950s, the FBI's harassment of civil rights leaders and the Army's spying on the anti-war movement in the 1960s, and Nixon's "enemies list" and the Watergate scandal in the 1970s. More recently, in the wake of the 9/11 terrorist attacks, President Bush and the Republican Congress took a number of actions, including passing the Patriot Act, that undermined our basic rights and freedoms. The government greatly increased wiretapping and other forms of surveillance of citizens, often without any evidence of any wrongdoing on their part. Thousands of people were secretly detained for months without any charges against them. Suspected terrorists were denied lawyers and the right to a trial. Some suspects were even sent abroad to other countries so they could be tortured. And 2005 and 2006 revealed the existence of extensive domestic spying programs by the National Security Agency and other institutions that are legally forbidden from doing so – a very disturbing development.

But consider this: Who comes to the rescue when our government violates our rights in these ways? To whom do Americans turn to revoke or remedy those actions and to make sure that they don't happen again? *The government.* Sometimes the government acts independently in this protective role, as when federal authorities intervened in the 1960s when some states were violating the civil rights and voting rights of African Americans. But often it is citizens themselves who use one part of the government – usually the courts – to stop another part of the government from infringing on their freedoms and rights. Citizen organizations like the American Civil Liberties Union have been particularly active in using the courts to protect our freedom of speech, freedom of religion, the right to vote, etc.

In the end, then, we depend heavily on the tools of democratic government to protect people's rights. When we want to limit the abusive activities of government – such as unreasonable searches or unfair appropriations of our property – we need to rely on the positive actions of another part of the government to do so. This is a point that anti-government conservatives consistently ignore. Yes, government can violate our rights, but democratic government also functions as the main protector of our rights and freedoms as well – and it has often done so very effectively. Certainly totalitarian and dictatorial governments are the enemies of freedom, but democratic governments have constitutions and institutions that enable us to effectively protect our rights and freedoms.

We often make the mistake of seeing our rights and civil liberties as merely the *absence* of some kind of governmental action. We believe that we have free speech or freedom of religion when the government does nothing to impede those freedoms. But in reality, our rights depend heavily on *active* government – on *positive* government actions. In fact, the very existence of rights depends on government. In a very real way, rights and civil liberties are actually political constructs – creations of government. Formal rights do not exist until they are created by law or established in a constitution. We only have the right of free speech because it is guaranteed in our constitution. If we didn't have our constitution, or if we didn't have government, our civil liberties would literally not exist. In the preamble of the Constitution, the founding fathers did not say that in order to "secure liberty for ourselves and our posterity" they were going to *abolish* government; they said that they were going to "ordain and establish" a democratic constitutional government to do so.[1] They knew, as Benjamin Barber has explained, that "in democracies, representative institutions do not steal our liberties from us, they are the precious medium through which we secure our liberties."[2]

Our rights and liberties are not only created by people working through government, we also rely on government to enforce them and create remedies for their violation. This is a point made by Stephen Holmes and Cass Sunstein in their insightful book, *The Costs of Rights: Why Liberty Depends on Taxes.*[3] They argue that the traditional distinction that conservatives make between "negative rights" and "positive rights" is mistaken. Supposedly, negative rights, such as freedom of speech, simply require that the government not interfere with some activity. In this view, it is only positive rights, such as the right to health care, that require a government action to realize them. But Holmes and Sunstein argue that in fact *all* rights require government action. They all require an active and well-funded government to enforce them – to make them real. Without a well-functioning legal and court system, for instance, our rights would be unenforceable and meaningless. Rights and freedoms, if they are to mean anything, require a vigorous response by government whenever they are violated. Every effort to prevent the government or private organizations from violating our rights must be supported by court rulings, injunctions, damage awards, etc. As Holmes and Sunstein explain:

> Personal liberty cannot be secured merely by limiting government interference with freedom of action and association. No right is simply a right to be left alone by public officials. All rights are claims to an affirmative governmental response. All rights, descriptively speaking, amount to entitlements defined and safeguarded by law. A cease-and-desist order handed down by a judge whose injunctions are regularly obeyed is a good example of government "intrusion" for the sake of individual liberty. … If rights were merely immunities from public interference, the highest virtue of government would be paralysis or disability. But a disabled state cannot protect personal liberties, even those that seem wholly "negative," such as the right against being tortured by police officers or prison guards.[4]

Protecting and enforcing our individual rights in this way is no small job. Think of all the various rights we now take for granted: the right to a fair trial, the right to own property, parental rights, voting rights, the right to not be denied a job because of race or gender, landlord and tenant rights, the right to run for office, the right to practice our religion, mineral rights, consumer rights, the right to a minimum wage, the right to marry, copyright protections, the right to an attorney, the right to collect a debt, abortion rights, the right against self-incrimination, the right to free speech, the right to emigrate, intellectual property rights, the right to strike, the right to petition government, the right to privacy, child custody rights, the right to a safe workplace, the right to be free from illegal searches, and so on. Interpreting and enforcing all of these rights requires an extensive network of administrative and judicial organizations on the federal and state levels – courts, attorney generals' offices, civil rights agencies, etc. These large governmental efforts cost billions of dollars a year –

money that must come from taxpayers. In other words, our rights depend heavily on an active and well-funded government. When governments find themselves in a position where they can't effectively tax and spend – as has sometimes been the case in countries in the former Soviet Union – citizen rights and liberties become unenforceable and largely non-existent.

In short, while we often think of our rights as freedom from government, in fact we rely on an active government to establish and maintain those rights. This fact has led Holmes and Sunstein to conclude that efforts by anti-government ideologues to slash taxes and reduce government contradict their claims to also value individual liberties. They argue that "it is implausible to be 'for rights' and 'against government.' ...All-out adversaries of state power cannot be consistent defenders of rights, for rights are an enforced uniformity, imposed by the government and funded by the public."[5] Since the existence and protection of our rights depend so directly on a healthy and vigorous state, if we want to be pro-rights we have to be pro-government to some extent as well. Without the power and authority of a well-financed state, rights are worthless.

Government as the Way We *Expand* our Rights and Freedoms

Government not only protects our long-established constitutional rights and liberties, it has also enabled us to expand our freedoms significantly, especially during the last 75 years. As the power of government has grown, it has not resulted in significant losses in freedom for the average American – it has produced significant gains. In fact, government power has often grown precisely because citizens have demanded more rights and freedoms. Faced with harmful and debilitating social conditions, the American people have turned to government again and again to free themselves from these oppressive situations. And the government has come through and repeatedly expanded the rights and freedoms available to the average person. Social Security has liberated millions of citizens from destitution in their old age. Thanks to federal legislation, all Americans now have the right to vote. Our state and federal governments' public health efforts have freed millions of Americans from devastating and deadly diseases like polio and smallpox. Because of laws banning housing discrimination, all families are now free to live in any neighborhood they want. Millions of elderly Americans are freed from agonizing and worrying about how they will get medical care – thanks to federal programs like Medicare. Government-sponsored right-to-strike laws and workplace safety rules have freed countless American workers from oppressive and dangerous working conditions. Millions of minorities and women are now free to get jobs and receive equal pay, as a result of government anti-discrimination laws. Millions of handicapped citizens are now literally freer to move around their world due to passage of the Americans with Disabilities Act. And we all now have the right not to be fired simply because we are getting old.

All of these are examples of how the programs and actions of the modern democratic state have made most Americans more free, not less free – how government programs have more often worked to increase our opportunities and rights, not restricted them. So the reality has often been exactly the reverse of the contention of anti-government activists: more government has actually produced more freedom. Consider one final example of this: Indiana now has a policy of guaranteeing a college education for every low and moderate income child in the state. One mother of three, who never went to college and who couldn't afford to send her kids there, remarked about how this program was expanding the freedom and the career horizons for her children. "Now they can choose what they want to do," she said.[6] At last count, seventeen thousand Indiana teenagers have taken advantage of this newfound freedom.

The Real Threat to Rights and Freedom

Imagine for a moment a dictatorship where your rights and liberties are being constantly violated. There is no free speech and you can be punished for espousing your political views. Associating with groups that oppose official policy can invite reprisals. If you complain about the behavior of officials or blow the whistle on their illegal activities, you will be punished harshly. Privacy is non-existent. The authorities constantly spy on you. They tap your phone and use hidden cameras to monitor and record your daily activities. They know what you do on your computer and where you go on the internet. They open and read your mail; they routinely test you for illegal substances. Officials know virtually everything about you – your employment history, your financial situation, your medical problems, and even your genetic information – and will not hesitate to use this information to their advantage when necessary.

This would be a totalitarian nightmare. It is just this kind of situation that many anti-government ideologues fear, and it is exactly why they so desperately want to limit the power of the state. But they are too late – we already have this situation in the United States. It's called a corporation. Today, many of the main threats to our rights and freedoms do not come from the government – but come from the businesses we work for. The American Civil Liberties Union has noted this trend with some alarm.

> The Constitution does not apply to the workplace. In the 18th century, when the Bill of Rights was adopted, only the government was seen as a major threat to individual rights. Today, many if not most Americans are more vulnerable to violations of their rights by employers than early Americans were by the government. Private sector employees that are not unionized can be fired for any reason, without due process. They can be compelled to submit to urine drug tests on pain of losing their jobs. They can be punished for their political views. They can be subjected to secret computer, video and telephone monitoring.[7]

Believe it or not, your employer can fire you for expressing your views about a candidate, political party or a particular political issue. So much for free speech. And you can also get sacked for keeping company with people whom your management dislikes – like union organizers. So much for freedom of association. And some companies have even installed cameras in their bathrooms. So much for your right to privacy. In a very real way, when you go to work, you lose the protections of the Constitution. As one worker explained: "Every time I passed through those plant gates to go to work, I left America, and my rights as a free man. I spent nine hours in there, in prison, and then came out into my country again."[8]

"Prison" is probably not the most accurate analogy – most workplaces are not that punishing. But "dictatorship" would be an apt description. Workplaces are not democracies with civil liberties or the ability of people to affect their working conditions through elected representatives. They are virtual dictatorships: strictly hierarchical organizations where rules come from the top down, and where workers have few real rights and no say over who is running the show. This may sound too harsh, but it is a description to which any candid business owner would readily admit. And when employees complain about management practices, a typical response is often "This is not a democracy." Ironically, then, even though we live in a "free and democratic society," we in fact spend most of our waking lives working in quasi-totalitarian private institutions that are largely devoid of traditional democratic rights and freedoms. And the kinds of problems just described are just the *legal* actions that business can take to deprive people of their rights in the workplace. They don't include the illegal practices that some companies use to frustrate workers' rights to unionize, to violate child-labor laws, to ignore worker compensation rules, or to discriminate against women and minorities.

But anti-government conservatives seem largely blind to these routine violations of our rights and liberties. Their ideology assumes that the private sector is the realm of freedom and the public sector the realm of oppression. So they continue to point at the public sector as the source of threats to our rights, while in many ways, the main threats exist in the private sector. The average citizen is much more likely to have their rights violated in the workplace with phone taps, video surveillance, or drug tests, than they are to be beaten by the police or to have their house illegally searched by federal agents.

Freedom Often Requires a Collective Use of Power

The larger point here is that when it comes to freedom, anti-government conservatives are wrong about how they portray *both* government and the private sector. Government is not nearly the threat they make it out to be and it is actually the mechanism that allows us to best protect and expand our freedoms. Moreover, the private sector is not the realm of natural freedom that conservatives depict it to be. Minimal-government advocates want us to believe that government is the only source of oppressive power in society, and that if we prevent it from exercising that power over us in our private lives, we are then free. But this ignores the large concentrations of power in the private sphere that can still coerce us – that can still greatly limit our freedom. The fact is that during those periods of our history when the government kept largely out of the private sector, this approach allowed such private abuses of power as slavery, corporate monopolies, child labor, deadly workplaces, and racial segregation. Democratic government is really the only source of countervailing power that is strong enough to rein in the abuses that can result from the concentration of power in the private sector. As Benjamin Barber has explained it: "Big government – or let's call it strong democracy – is for the little guy; it's how he and his neighbors can take on the big bullies in the private sector. Naturally the bullies resent competition and make war on 'big government,' ostensibly on behalf of the little guy."[9]

In his book, *The Freedom Revolution*, former House Majority Leader Dick Armey defines freedom as "the ability and responsibility to control one's own destiny."[10] There is much truth to this, but he is mistaken when he also maintains that we can best assert that control when government leaves us alone and stays out of the private sector. He forgets that even when the government leaves us alone, there are still many forces in the private sphere that make it difficult for us to control our own destiny. Powerful institutions and individuals, along with large economic and social forces, make it hard for most people to "do what they want." As noted earlier, most of us work in strictly hierarchical institutions ruled by powerful superiors, and so we often have little control over our work life. More importantly, as private citizens, we are at the mercy of large, systemic economic realities: the ups and downs of the economy, the domestic impacts of globalization, the stagnation of wages, increasing income inequality, outsourcing of jobs, rising and falling stock markets, skyrocketing health costs, and so on. As Americans we no longer live in log cabins on the frontier, where it could be argued that our fate is in our own hands. We live in enormously large and complex economic and social systems – systems over which we can exert little control as individuals. In this context, the promise of Republicans to have government leave us alone sounds more like a threat – it amounts to abandoning us to larger societal forces over which we can have little influence. It's like someone dumping you in the middle of the ocean in a row boat and telling you that you are free to go wherever you want. You may be the "captain" of your boat, but in all likelihood if the storms and the sharks don't get you, the sunstroke and dehydration will.

In our world, being free to control our lives requires a great deal of power. If you happen to be rich, then you may have the economic resources to control your life as an individual. You have the luxury of choosing where you live, what job you have, whether you work at all, and what you do every day. But the rest of us do not have that kind of individual power. So we must rely on collective power – one major form of which is democratic government. If freedom really does mean exerting control over one's life, then it is government and the public sector that are the instruments of freedom for many people. In fact government has grown in the United States precisely because the American people have realized again and again that they must band together politically to gain some control over these forces buffeting their lives. They have sought out government power to neutralize the private powers and social and economic forces that are creating oppressive and harmful social conditions for them. Only the government is in the position to try to control the economy and prevent prolonged recessions and depressions. Only the government has the power to ensure that workplaces don't make people sick, or that you are not fired because of your race or religion. Only the government can provide a safety net that catches you after you have been laid off, allowing you to pay your mortgage until you get another job. Thus, to the extent that freedom has to do with controlling one's own life, people working through a democratic and representative government is in fact one of the best ways to realize that freedom. In other words, we can often be freer acting collectively than we can be acting alone – exactly the opposite of what anti-government zealots are preaching.

Rush Limbaugh is fond of saying that those who support government programs and oppose tax cuts do so "because tax cuts give people more power and take away from the role of government."[11] But what he and other anti-government pundits cannot see is that taxes and government can in fact be a way to empower people. They view government power as *power over us* – rather than as *our power*. Democratic government, when it is working correctly, gives us the power to have much more control over our lives. And as our democratic government has become more powerful, we ourselves have become more powerful and often more liberated as well.

When we see all the various ways that government actions can actually enhance our freedom, it also helps us to see how narrow and stunted the anti-government vision of freedom really is. They refuse to acknowledge that government power can enhance our freedoms. Also, they see freedom as merely being protected from the detrimental effects of government power, not from the equally detrimental effects of private power. And finally, while minimal-government advocates like to portray themselves as the champions of the general principle of freedom, the freedoms they are actually most concerned about are often very particular and only benefit certain limited groups in society, such as people who want the right to own assault rifles, or companies that want the freedom to pollute. They conveniently ignore broader freedoms and rights that would benefit many more Americans, such as the freedom to attend college or the right to adequate health care. Indeed they actively campaign against these kinds of rights and freedoms. Conservatives oppose them because they are only made possible by active government programs that require taxing and spending. In reality, then, while these conservative claim to be on the side of individual rights and liberties, they only truly support those that fit into their anti-government ideology.

Seizing Back the Idea of Freedom from Conservatives

Abraham Lincoln once said that freedom is our "political religion." Unfortunately, however, anti-government activists have been able to establish themselves as the high priests of this religion; and they have been spreading their simplistic and distorted dogma about how increased government activity will only reduce our freedom. We need to liberate this crucial political concept from the grip of these arch-conservative ideologues. The American people need to be reminded of how much government programs actually protect and enhance their essential rights and freedoms. Defenders of government need to seize back this basic American value and demonstrate how the programs and policies of the modern democratic state have on balance worked to promote freedom, not diminish it. We need to talk about how specific social programs and regulatory rules enacted by government have had a liberating effect on all of our lives.

Consider, for example, the issue of universal health care. Conservatives were able to block this policy for decades in part by convincing many Americans that it would bring a loss of freedom – that we wouldn't be able to choose our medical treatments or drugs, and that government bureaucrats would be telling us what to do. Of course they ignored the fact that private sector health insurance bureaucrats already restrict our freedom to choose various treatments and drugs. More importantly, the passage of the universal health care bill will have an enormously liberating effect on the 45 million Americans who until recently had no health insurance. It will free them to choose to go to the doctor when they need to, and it will free them from the risk of a serious illness bringing on financial ruin.

Freedom is a public value – along with others like justice, fairness, and equality – that can be enhanced through modern democratic government. So if we cherish freedom, then we must also value the institutions and policies of democratic government that create, protect, and expand our freedoms. We Americans enjoy an unprecedented bounty of rights and freedoms in our lives, not *in spite of* government but in large part *because of* government. Democratic government is the main instrument through which we preserve and enlarge our freedoms. That is the real story about freedom and government that Americans should be hearing.

---

1. Benjamin Barber, "A Civics Lesson," *The Nation*, Nov. 4, 1996, p. 21.
2. Ibid.
3. Stephen Holmes and Cass R. Sunstein, *The Costs of Rights: Why Liberty Depends on Taxes* (New York: W. W. Norton, 1999).
4. Ibid. p. 44.
5. Ibid. pp. 47, 58.

6. “College Track,” WGBY, September 19, 2004.
7. American Civil Liberties Union, “Workplace Rights,” http://archive.aclu.org/issues/worker/iswr.html.
8. Ibid.
9. Barber, p. 21.
10. Dick Armey, *The Freedom Revolution*, p.11.
11. The Rush Limbaugh statement can be found at “Quotes from Famous People,” http://home.att.net/~quotations/rush.html

CHAPTER 8

The Case FOR Bureaucracy

We all know the case *against* bureaucracy. Just say the word to yourself and consider the images it evokes. Massive waste. Inefficiency. Poor service. Ever-growing organizations. Mindless rules. Reams of useless forms. The term "bureaucrat" also comes loaded with a whole host of negative connotations: lazy, hostile, overpaid, imperious, and inflexible. In short, bureaucracy and bureaucrats are unmitigated bad things – with absolutely no redeeming qualities.

Conservatives like to play on this popular prejudice by constantly equating government with bureaucracy. The comments of Charlton Heston are typical: "Of course, government is the problem. The armies of bureaucrats proliferating like gerbils, scurrying like lemmings in pursuit of the ever-expanding federal agenda testify to that amply."[1] Once government is thought of as "bureaucracy," the case for reducing it becomes obvious. Who could complain if Republicans want to reduce these "armies of bureaucrats"? Everyone knows that we would all be better off with less bureaucracy and fewer bureaucrats in our lives. So when conservatives want to make shrinking government sound attractive, they say they are cutting "bureaucracy" – not "programs." Most people value government programs – especially in the areas of education, health and the environment – and do not want to see them reduced; but everyone hates bureaucracy. Using the term "bureaucracy" in this way is a rhetorical sleight-of-hand that obscures the real costs of cutting back on government programs.

But while disparaging and attacking government bureaucracy has become a very effective tactic for anti-government activists, it is based more on mythology than reality. Much of what we think is wrong with bureaucracy – and what conservatives keep telling us – is highly exaggerated and often simply mistaken. This chapter takes a careful look at bureaucracy and finds that there is little evidence to support most of the common criticisms of these administrative agencies. Studies show that bureaucracy and bureaucrats are not nearly as bad as we usually think they are. We will also consider the case *for* bureaucracy – that these much-maligned organizations and the public servants that work in them are actually playing many valuable and indispensable roles in our society. Many of the significant achievements of modern democratic government would in fact not be possible without the large bureaucracies that oversee and implement them. It turns out that government bureaucracies are actually good.

Myth No. 1: Bureaucracies Are Immensely Wasteful

A few years ago, local officials in my town were holding a public meeting to promote a referendum that would raise taxes to pay for vital city services. A man in the audience rose to object to the tax increase, arguing that instead the city should first get rid of all the waste in the city bureaucracy. The mayor explained that after years of cutbacks in city government, there really was no "fat" left to cut from the budget, and then asked the man what specific cuts he was suggesting. The man said that he didn't know much about the city budget, but that he "knew" that there "had to be" some waste that could be cut out instead of raising taxes.

Such is the strength of the notion that government bureaucracies are inherently wasteful. Even if we don't know much about government, we are absolutely certain that government agencies are wasteful. In fact, waste is the number one citizen complaint about government – and bureaucracy usually takes most of the blame for this. Seventy percent of Americans agree that when something is run by government, it is usually wasteful and inefficient.[2] And conservatives never tire of taking advantage of this view to lambaste the government. As two conservative economists have explained: "As every taxpayer knows, government is wasteful and inefficient; it always has been and always will be." Cutting bureaucratic waste has become a constant theme of conservatives, and it has become a major rationale for cutting taxes. They argue that we can have the best of both worlds: we can reduce taxes and also not cut back on needed government programs. How? By simply cutting out all the "fat" in government.

In the public's view, government agencies are not only wasteful, they are *enormously* wasteful. Surveys reveal that Americans believe that 48 cents of every tax dollar going to bureaucracies like the Social Security Administration are wasted.[3] Yet investigations by the Government Accounting Office and various blue-ribbon commissions have found that waste amounts to only a small fraction of that figure. Al Gore's

National Performance Review, conducted when he was vice-president, examined the federal bureaucracy in great detail and discovered that waste consisted of less than two cents of every tax dollar.[4] Of course we should be ever vigilant about waste and try to eliminate it wherever we can find it, but it seems clear that the extent of this problem is being highly exaggerated by conservative critics of government. As one set of scholars who examined a wide variety of the studies on government waste concluded: "There is ... little evidence to support the widespread impression that government inefficiency squanders huge amounts of money."[5]

People tend to think there is a large amount of waste in government in part because of the loose way this term is used. For instance, some conservative critics of government count as waste those programs they simply don't like – such as the Legal Services Corporation, the National Endowment for the Arts, Americorp, and subsidies for public television. But to use the term "waste" in this way makes it entirely a political judgment and renders it essentially meaningless. Normally the term "government waste" refers to the inefficient use of funds because of overstaffing, poor productivity, etc. But conservatives are not opposed to the National Endowment for the Arts because that agency is inefficient; they oppose it on ideological grounds. They wouldn't support the NEA no matter how "lean and mean" it was. It is misleading, then, to use the term "waste" in this way.

Another problem is that critics of bureaucracy often lump together "fraud" and "abuse" with "waste" to come up with high figures for government losses. But does it really make sense to blame government when doctors defraud the Medicare program, criminals scam the food stamp system, or private contractors cheat the Pentagon? We usually don't consider it the fault of business that they lose over $15 billion a year to employee theft and $10 billion to shoplifting. Most people blame the thieves for these losses and few consider these thefts to be an indication of something inherently wrong with capitalism. Similarly, it is unfair to consider the problems of fraud and abuse of government programs to be a product of inherently "wasteful" bureaucracies. Naturally, government should do everything it can to reduce these losses, but we should not be blaming the victim.

Myth No. 2: Business is Always Better than Bureaucracy

Another of the more persistent myths about bureaucracy is that "business is better" – that businesses are always more efficient than government efforts. Since government bureaucracies don't have to produce a profit and they are not subject to market competition, it is argued, they have much less incentive to be cost-efficient in their management and delivery of services. The assumed superiority of business has become so commonsensical that it is hardly ever questioned at all. This notion has also become an important argument for conservatives in their effort to reduce government and to privatize many of its functions. But are public agencies always less efficient than businesses? A careful look at this issue casts doubt on this common belief.

There have been many empirical studies examining the efficiency of government bureaucracies versus business in a variety of areas, including refuse collection, electrical utilities, public transportation, water supply systems, and hospital administration. The findings have been mixed. Some studies of electric utilities have found that publicly owned ones were more efficient and charged lower prices than privately owned utilities. Several other studies found the opposite, and yet others found no significant differences.[6] Studies of other services produced similar kinds of mixed results. Charles Goodsell is a professor of Public Administration and Public Affairs at Virginia Polytechnic Institute and State University who has spent much of his life studying bureaucracy. After examining these efficiency studies, he concluded: "In short, there is much evidence that is ambivalent. The assumption that business always does better than government is not upheld. ... When you add up all these study results, the basis for the mantra that business is always better evaporates."[7]

Further evidence that business is not always superior to government bureaucracy can be found in the area of health care. This is a critical issue today and it is well worth examining in some detail the question of whether market-based health care is superior to government run programs. Conservatives constantly warn us that adopting "socialized" medicine would put health care in the hands of government bureaucracies, which would be a recipe for incredible waste and inferior care. But is this really the case? We can answer this question by comparing the performance of public versus private health care systems. Every other developed country has some form of universal health care with a substantial amount of public funding and administration. In contrast, while the U.S. has a few programs like Medicare and Medicaid, most of our health care system is privately funded and administered. According to conservative mythology, this market-based system should produce better health care and do so more cheaply. But neither of these claims hold up when we look at studies of the actual performance of public and private approaches to providing health care.

First, studies have found that the U.S. health care system is by far the most expensive in the world. We spend 13.6% of our gross domestic product on health care – the highest in the world. The average for the other 13 industrialized countries in the OECD is 8.2%.[8] We also rank number one in terms of health care expenditures per capita, with U.S. spending $4,090 a year for every citizen. The highest figures for other industrialized nations are $2,547 per year for Switzerland, $2,339 for Germany, $2,340 for Luxembourg, and $2,095 for Canada.[9] But while we clearly have the most expensive health care system in the world, it does not always deliver the best health care nor does it provide health care in the most efficient way.

Research has shown that the U.S. ranks poorly compared to many other countries in terms of some common measures of health. For example, we rank 26th among industrialized countries for infant mortality rates.[10] We also do much less well in terms of life expectancy. In one typical study, the World Health Organizations (WHO) looked at "disability adjusted life expectancy"– the number of years that one can expect to lead a healthy life. The U.S. came in a disappointing 24th on this measure. As one WHO official concluded: "The position of the United States is one of the major surprises of the new rating system. ... Basically, you die earlier and spend more time disabled if you're an American rather than a member of most other advanced countries."[11] Moreover, an article in the *Journal of the American Medical Association* in 2000 noted with concern the results of a comprehensive study that compared how 13 industrialized nations were ranked on 16 different measures of health. The U.S. ranked an average of 12th – second to last.[12]

Why do Americans spend so much on health care but not get superior care? There are several reasons. One is that doctors tend to make more in the U.S. than in other countries, and another is that governments in other countries negotiate better deals with pharmaceutical companies on drug prices. But the other major reason is that our private, multi-payer system is much less efficient than the public single-payer systems in other countries. Consider this: the *New England Journal of Medicine* estimates that administrative costs take 31 cents out of every health care dollar in the U.S., compared to only 17 cents in Canada.[13] Why is this the case? Private insurance companies spend much more on paperwork and administrative overhead. The sheer number of people that are working in these private insurance bureaucracies far outstrips those required in government-funded programs. In Massachusetts alone, Blue Cross/Blue Shield employs 6,682 workers to cover 2.7 million subscribers. This is more people than work in *all* of

Canada's provincial health care plans, which cover over 25 million people.[14] Why do insurance companies need so many workers? One reason, as Paul Krugman explains, is that millions of health insurance personnel in the U.S. are employed not to help deliver health care at all, but to try to get someone else to pay the bills instead of their company.

Another source of administrative inefficiency in our private multi-payer health care system is the enormous amount of overlap between companies. Each insurance company must maintain its own records and develop its own billing processes. This is much more expensive than using a single government administrative structure. Moreover, our multi-payer system drives up the administrative costs for doctors and hospitals. They must deal with dozens of different insurance plans, each with their own coverage, payment rules, etc. We then need to add to all of this excessive overhead the need for private insurers to make a profit – something that government needn't do. This makes our private system become more expensive. It has been estimated that higher overhead and the need for profit together add from 15% to 25% to the costs of private insurance plans, while the overhead for the government-run Medicare program is a mere 3%. Given all this, it should not come as a shock to find that a 2004 study by researchers at Harvard Medical School and Public Citizen concluded that the U.S. could save up to $286 billion a year on paperwork if we switched to a single-payer, national health insurance program.[15] This money saved from eliminating the private health care bureaucracy would be more than enough to offset the costs of extending coverage to the millions of Americans who now have no health insurance at all. (Unfortunately, this single-payer plan was blocked by Republicans and conservative Democrats in the 2010 health care reform bill.)

To sum up, government-funded universal health care plans provide better care to more people at a lower cost. This one example by itself should be enough to explode the myth that business and privatization are always better than government bureaucracy in providing vital services to the public.

Myth No. 3: We Want the Government to Act Like a Business

The astronaut John Glenn tells a story about his first trip into space. As he sat in the capsule, waiting nervously on the launching pad, he couldn't stop thinking about the fact that NASA had given the contract for the rocket to the lowest bidder. This raises another important point about government bureaucracies: we don't always want them to act like businesses. Conservatives are constantly saying that we would all be better off if government were run like a business. But would we? Businesses are obsessed with their bottom lines and are always looking for the cheapest way to make a product or deliver a service. But in many cases, we don't want government services to be as cheap as possible. Often, with government, the main concern is the quality of the service, not its costs. For example, do we really want to spend the least amount of money possible on our air traffic control system? Obviously not – the main goal should be maximizing the safety of the aviation system. Also, do we want the cheapest possible workforce in charge of security at our airports? Again, of course not – and this point was even acknowledged by Republicans when they agreed to abandon private security companies in favor of a federalized system in the wake of the 9/11 tragedy. Private security had certainly cost less, but it is clearly better to have a federal program that spends more money on training personnel and pays higher salaries to attract employees who are more capable.

Similarly, we don't really want the cheapest system for dispensing justice in our society. We could certainly save a lot on court costs if we didn't pay for lawyers for those who can't afford them and if we got rid of jury trials and lengthy appeal processes. But this would undermine the main goal of providing justice. The point here is clear: unlike businesses, public agencies are not just concerned with the bottom line. We expect our government organizations to pursue a wide variety of important goals, and often cost is not the most important consideration. In this sense, it is unfair to expect many government bureaucracies to be as cheap to run as businesses.

Myth No. 4: Bureaucracy is a Major Cause of Government Growth

Conservatives also like to charge that bureaucracy is one of the main causes of government growth. They argue that government bureaucracies have an inherent tendency to expand. The reason is this: agency officials bent on their own career advancement are always pushing to increase their power and their budgets. Thus, bureaucracies – like cancer – inevitably become ever-growing entities with ever-increasing destructive effects. Bureaucracies are constantly eating up more tax-payer dollars and imposing more and more rules on American citizens.

This criticism of bureaucracy seems plausible, but is it really true? The evidence suggests that it is not. Consider, for example, the assumption that we are plagued by an ever-growing federal bureaucracy. Figures show that federal agencies have not been growing at an alarming rate. If we go back to 1970, we find that 2,997,000 civilians worked for the federal government at that time. By 2009, that figure had actually gone down – to 2,804,000.[16] So much for the constantly expanding federal bureaucracy.

Second, it is not clear at all that bureaucrats are always seeking to expand their agencies and their budgets. This budget-maximizing thesis was directly contradicted by a study conducted by Julie Dolan.[17] She compared the views of members of the federal senior civil service to those of the general public when it came to whether we should be spending more or less in a wide variety of policy areas, including education, healthcare, defense, welfare, environment, college financial aid, AIDS research, homelessness, etc. She found that in most areas the public was willing to support increased spending much more than the agency administrators. And in most cases, a majority of these administrators did not support increased budgets. This was due, she believed, to administrators having a more realistic and sophisticated knowledge of these issues and programs. Her conclusion: "In sum, the budget-*minimizing* tendencies of federal administrators reported here suggest that self-interest is not as powerful a motivator as previously believed, and they suggest we should revise our theories about self-interested bureaucrats inflating government budgets for their own gain."[18]

Another theory of bureaucratic expansion suggests that the government grows because once an administrative agency is established, it will stick around even when its program is no longer needed. In short, the bureaucracy never shrinks, it only grows. However, studies have shown that the conservatives are just plain wrong when they claim that outmoded programs are rarely purged from government. Robert Stein and Kenneth Bikers completed a study in which they examined the number of federal programs that were eliminated between 1971 and 1990. During that twenty-year span, an average of thirty-six federal programs were terminated each year.[19] A pretty amazing figure. The commonly held notion that bureaucracies never die is clearly false.

The Real Causes of Government Growth

Ironically, during the last several decades, as right-wing complaints about ever-increasing government have escalated, little growth has actually occurred in the federal government. However, if we look back over a longer historical period, say to the early 1900s, there is no denying that the size and scope of the federal and state governments have grown considerably. Our governments have much greater responsibilities in regulating corporations and the economic system, and we have many more programs in areas like health care, education, and the environment. But the question is whether this kind of historical growth in government has been caused by the inherent tendency of bureaucracies to expand. The answer is no. As one political scientist, Max Neiman, who studied this question extensively, has concluded, "Bureaucratic imperialism, by which public agencies generate an autonomous force for government growth, seems fairly insignificant as a cause of growing government size."[20] But if this is true, what has driven the historical expansion of government in the United States?

One important clue can be found by identifying those periods in which government has expanded the most. For example, 70% of the growth in federal regulatory agencies occurred during three decades, the 1930s, the 1960s, and the 1970s.[21] What these decades have in common is that they were times of enormous economic and social upheaval and increased political activism. In other words, *government responsibilities increased because the public demand for social programs and economic regulation increased.* During those eras, mass-based social movements – including the labor movement, the civil rights movement, and the environmental movement – insisted that the government address a wide variety of pressing social and economic problems.

We have big government today primarily because citizens have realized that large-scale public programs are necessary to solve big problems – economic depressions, an elderly population mired in poverty, widespread racism, growing environmental degradation, a health care crisis, etc. As Nieman has concluded, "A substantial source of growth in government activity in democratic societies is driven ... by citizens and other groups using government to improve their life-chances."[22] So it makes little sense to argue that growth in government has been something forced onto the American people by power-hungry bureaucrats. Government has grown mainly because we have wanted it to grow – something conservatives seem unable to admit. Growth in government is primarily a product of democracy at work, and so it should be something that is celebrated, not condemned.

Myth No. 5: Bureaucracies Usually Provide Poor Service

Yet another common criticism of government bureaucracies is that they routinely provide very poor service to the public. Unlike businesses, where the rule is "the customer is always right," public agencies seemed to adhere to the rule that "it's my way or the highway." Many people have stories of at least one frustrating encounter with a government worker where they received rude or inadequate service.

But how frequent are these bad experiences? How widespread is dissatisfaction with government workers and the services they provide? Studies show that negative experiences are not nearly as common as many think and that most people's encounters with government workers actually turn out well. For example, when a survey was done in Virginia about the quality of the services provided by local government workers, the results were surprisingly positive. Over 80 percent of citizens said that the services they receive from the fire department, EMS service, police department, public library, and parks and recreation were either "excellent" or "good." An average of a mere 2.7 percent of citizens rated these public services as "poor."[23] Pretty impressive figures for any organization.

Perhaps more surprisingly, surveys show high citizen evaluations for most large *federal* agencies as well. The Pew Research Center conducted a survey in 2000 of citizens and businesspeople who used the services of the Social Security Administration, the Environmental Protection Agency, the Food and Drug Administration, the Internal Revenue Service, and the Federal Aviation Administration. Predictably, only 47.6 percent had a favorable view of the IRS. But 84.5 percent had favorable views of the FDA. For the Social Security Administration that figure was 72.0; for the FAA, 69.3; and for the EPA, 68.0. What makes these strong favorable ratings all the more impressive is that they include the views of people from businesses being regulated by these agencies – respondents who are going to naturally feel some hostility toward these bureaucracies.

Of course, to really evaluate the quality of services being provided by public sector bureaucracies, we need to compare them to services provided by the private sector. Such a study was done by Theodore Poister and Gary Henry, who conducted a survey of citizen satisfaction with both public and private services in Georgia.[24] They compared satisfaction with public services like the police, public health clinics and trash collection, to that of private doctor's offices, fast-good restaurants, banks, etc. As they explained their findings: "Given the conventional wisdom about the poor quality of services provided by government and the general superiority of the private sector in delivering services, the private services included in this survey might have been expected to receive consistently higher ratings than the public services. But this was clearly not the case." [25] We can see this in their findings summarized in Table 4. Both public and private service providers received consistently high scores from people who had recently used their services. On a scale of 0-100, the public agencies averaged a score of 73.5 for customer satisfaction, while the private businesses averaged 73.9 – a negligible difference. Clearly, people's actual experiences and evaluations of public agencies runs directly contrary to the negative stereotype that government organizations consistently provide inferior service to that available in the private sector.

Table 4: Citizen Ratings of the Quality of Public and Private Services

	Ratings by Recent Customers
Public	
Fire department	82.8
U.S. Postal Service	76.1
Public health clinics	74.4
Municipal trash collection	75.5
Police	71.3
Parks and Recreation	77.1
Public transportation	76.6
Public schools	68.2
Street maintenance	59.2
All Public	**73.5**
Private	
Private mail carriers	84.5
Grocery stores	77.1
Banks and savings and loans	81.7
Private doctors' offices	80.6
Fast-food restaurants	68.5
Movie theatres	75.5
Auto garages	71.7
Cable TV providers	66.2
Taxicabs	59.6
All Private	**73.9**

Source: Theodore H. Poister and Gary T Henry, "Citizen Ratings of Public and Private Service Quality: A Comparative Perspective," *Public Administration Review* 54, no.2 (March/April 1994), p. 158.

This is not to suggest that people don't sometimes have bad encounters with government bureaucracies – we all have. The point here is that these encounters are not the rule, and we usually get pretty good service from our public agencies. It is also worth keeping in mind that bad encounters with bureaucrats are not limited to the public sector. Who hasn't had a horrible time trying to get approval for a drug or a medical procedure from the rigid bureaucrats in private health insurance companies? And who hasn't wandered through seemingly endless phone trees and spent hours on hold just trying to get some technical help from large computer and software companies? Instances of poor service are hardly confined to government bureaucracies.

Myth No. 6: Agencies Should Treat Us as Individuals

People are sometimes frustrated because government administrators do not treat them as individuals. Instead, they are treated like a "number" – simply one case among many others – without any seeming sensitivity to the distinctiveness of their particular situation. Why must bureaucrats slavishly follow the rules, and not treat each person uniquely depending on his or her circumstances? Why can't that police officer see that we were speeding because we were late in picking up our child at school, not because we were being irresponsible? Why can't that city official simply wave the zoning rules so that we can run our new business out of our home?

It is true that bureaucrats' treatment of us *is* often based on general rules and policies, rather than who we are as individuals. But what we fail to see is that this is actually a good thing. We should *want* bureaucrats to not treat people as individuals. Treating everyone the same is in the public interest – and often in our own interest as well. It is what ensures that government agencies treat everyone fairly and impartially. Dealing with us impersonally is what guarantees that our treatment is not arbitrary, discriminatory, or abusive. It is what discourages police officers from handing out tickets based on your race or the political bumper stickers on your car. It is what helps to ensure that government contracts are given to the lowest bidders, not those companies that give the most in campaign contributions.

If government workers had the ability to ignore procedures and treat us as individuals, this would also give them enormous power over us – which is exactly what we don't want to happen. Imagine that you had been waiting in a long line at the Department of Motor Vehicles. A clerk recognizes a friend at the end of the line and decides to serve them next. It is unlikely that you would praise this "bending" of the rules for this individual – you would undoubtedly be mad about the unfairness of this action. You would be upset about the lack of impersonal, rule-based treatment by officials.

When things go terribly wrong in bureaucracies, it is often because they are not acting bureaucratic enough. We often hear horror stories about someone being caught in a government bureaucracy in some developing country, where nothing can get done unless you have the right connections or unless you offer a bribe to an official. But the problem in these situations is not that officials are being "bureaucratic," but that they are not being bureaucratic enough. These abuses occur because officials are engaging in personal favoritism and not treating people the same according to a set of administrative procedures. The cure in these situations involves creating a civil service that is strongly committed to more impersonal, rule-based form of bureaucratic behavior.

So we should not be so quick to condemn government officials for not dealing with us as unique individuals. While we might not always enjoy being treated like everyone else by government workers, we should try to remember that this practice is an important political safeguard of the modern democratic state.

Bureaucracy is Good

So far, we've seen that government bureaucracies are not nearly as bad as conservative critics and popular mythology make them out to be. However, there is a much more *positive* case that can be made here – the case for bureaucracies actually being a good thing. It is not a difficult case to make. It begins with a simple fact: the modern state as we know it cannot exist without large bureaucratic agencies to implement its programs. Modern democratic governments are necessarily bureaucratic entities. And if this is true, then the successes of modern government have to also be considered the successes of government bureaucracies as well. The fact that Social Security has dramatically reduced poverty among the elderly should be counted as an achievement of this agency's bureaucracy. The Environmental Protection Agency should also get much of the credit for our being able to breathe cleaner air and drink safer water.

In short, if government is good, then government bureaucracies are good. If government programs have had many enormously positive impacts on the lives of every Americans, some of the credit for this has to go to the agencies that make these programs work. Without bureaucracy, modern democratic governments could not possibly fulfill all the crucial roles it plays in society – including creating more economic security, curing diseases, caring for the environment, dispensing justice, educating our children, and protecting us from a variety of harms.

Most of us also know, on some level, that public agencies are primarily there to help us, and that they often do so reasonably well. That is why we keep asking for more of them. Kevin Smith and Michael Licari are two political scientists who have written a textbook about public administration. They have noticed a curious fact: that even those of us who say we don't like government are usually more than willing to demand and accept a new bureaucracy if it will make our lives better off. Even people who live in that notoriously anti-government state of Texas. As Smith and Licari explain.

> Rural Texans tend to be an independent bunch. The stereotypical image is a politically conservative business owner, farmer, or rancher, raised on the myth of rugged individualism and a strong supporter of property rights. Not the sort of people, in other words, who favor big government programs. Or even small ones. Surely such citizens are the least likely group to start agitating for more government bureaucracy. So what does a conservative, small-government group like this do to help spur economic development and advocate for their issues? Well, it asks for a bureaucracy. And it gets one: the Office of Rural Community Affairs (ORCA). Created in 2001 by the Texas legislature, ORCA annually spends tens of millions of dollars on a wide variety of programs ranging from health care initiatives to business development to disaster relief. Rural Texas communities and their legislators are by all accounts pleased with ORCA. Now there is an agency full of bureaucrats whose job, as Texas State Representative Warren Chisum put it, is to get to work in the morning and ask themselves, "What are the people out in rural Texas doing, and how can we help them?" [26]

However, it is important to see that the case for bureaucracy is about more than what those agencies can do for us as *individuals*, it is about the crucial role they play in creating a better society for *all of us*. As Charles Goodsell has noted, government bureaucracies form the public infrastructure that is essential to maintaining a free and prosperous society:

> A good bureaucracy is indispensable to a free society, a democratic polity, and a capitalist economy. The freedom to wander the streets at night, for example depends on competent law enforcement. The ability to vote governments out of office

> without disruption requires a reliable administrative apparatus. A prosperous business community demands good schools, highways, health departments, post offices, and water and sewer systems.[27]

So if you feel that America is a good place to live, at least part of the credit for that must be given to government bureaucracies. Literally, the good life as we know it in the United States could not exist without the numerous and various essential tasks being performed by these public agencies on all levels of government.

Bureaucrats or Public Heroes?

If we should be thankful for government bureaucracies, we should also be thankful for the people – the "bureaucrats" – who work in them. Yet they are one of the most maligned groups in our society. They are constantly the butt of jokes and are stereotyped as being lazy, rude, rigid, arrogant, and controlling. Of course, some are like that. But you find these kind of people in every organization, including business bureaucracies. Moreover, studies have found that government bureaucrats are much like all other Americans and that there is no credible evidence supporting the charge that a pathological "bureaucratic mentality" is prevalent among government workers.[28]

On the whole, our civil servants are hard workers dedicated to serving the public and improving our lives. There are times when this point is made in such dramatic way that no one can deny it. In the wake of the 9/11 tragedy in New York, there was an outpouring of public praise and appreciation for the incredibly brave and self-sacrificing actions taken by numerous police officers and firefighters. What we tend to forget is that for these public employees this was not unusual – they are putting their lives and health on the line every day, not just during terrorists attacks.

And we also tend to forget that police officers and firefighters are not the only heroes working for the government. Our government bureaucracies are full of "everyday heroes" – public servants who labor away in anonymity to protect us from harm and to make our lives better. As Robert Kuttner has observed:

> [We] should not let a week go by without celebrating a public hero, and not just the firefighters and the veterans. The civil servant at the Food and Drug Administration who fights drug-industry pressure and keeps a harmful drug off the market is a

> public hero. So is the SEC auditor who busts a corporate thief so a million people don't lose their pensions, and the Environmental Protection Agency scientist who safeguards our water from some scofflaw mogul.[29]

Or consider the government workers of the National Highway Traffic Safety Administration. These are the people who do automobile crash tests, evaluate child safety seats, initiate recalls of defective cars, and so on. The motto of the agency is, appropriately enough, "People Saving People." They will never meet you or know your name, but they are working week in and week out to protect your health and safety. Unfortunately, we rarely celebrate these kinds of public servants – instead they must put up with the public disdain leveled at everyone who works for the government. This is the reward they get for choosing to work for the government and to promote the public interest. It is no wonder that many of our best young people are discouraged from taking on these kinds of public service jobs.

The Role of Reform

Let me be clear: I am not suggesting that we look at bureaucracy and bureaucrats through rose-colored glasses – or ignore their shortcomings. There are some inherent problems that can afflict government bureaucracies – most notably corruption and waste. And a hundred years ago, these were rampant problems. The enormously corrupt political machines that existed in many large cities during the early part of the twentieth century are examples of how badly bureaucracies can go wrong. But decades of reform efforts have greatly reduced these problems. We have rooted out large-scale corruption and are increasingly minimizing the amount of bureaucratic inefficiency, excessive paperwork, etc. These problems have not completely disappeared, and we must continue to try to improve the performance of our administrative institutions. A good example of this on-going effort was Vice-President Al Gore's project, called the National Performance Review, which sought to reduce excess federal workers. Between 1993 and 2000, the number of civilian employees in the executive branch was reduced by 193,000. But while we must be vigilant about pursuing these kinds of reform efforts, we must not exaggerate the extent of the problems in our administrative agencies. And we should not allow the occasional failures of government bureaucracies to overshadow their achievements. A more realistic and accurate view of these institutions recognizes that on the whole they are working well and they continue to play a crucial role in administering vital programs that are improving the lives of all Americans.

The Real Lessons from Katrina

And yet, what are we to make of the kind of massive bureaucratic failure that occurred when hurricane Katrina when it hit New Orleans in the fall of 2005? The Federal Emergency Management Agency's response was too little too late, and the agency was harshly criticized for its inadequate and bungling efforts. This fiasco seemed merely to confirm many peoples' worst assumptions about the problems of bureaucracy.

However, it would be a mistake to use the failures of FEMA to paint a negative picture of government bureaucracies. FEMA failed in New Orleans not because of something inherently wrong with government bureaucracies, but because of a policy of neglect by the Bush administration. First, the administration appointed Michael Brown to head the agency, a political crony with no experience in emergency response management and who was fired from his previous job for mismanagement. The agency was then downgraded and folded into the Department of Homeland Security, where its mission was re-oriented toward fighting acts of terrorism. Finally, FEMA's budget was slashed, with Bush officials arguing that "Many are concerned that federal disaster assistance may have evolved into an oversized entitlement program..."[30] As the *Washington Monthly* concluded, "FEMA was deliberately downsized as part of the Bush administration's conservative agenda to reduce the role of government."[31] In the end, then, FEMA's failure in New Orleans was in large part a result of a conservative administration that had only contempt for the role of government in society and had little interest in ensuring the wellbeing of vital government agencies.

Ironically, the real problem with many public bureaucracies today is not that they are bloated institutions who are over-staffed and spend too much money, but that they are understaffed and don't have the funds to do their jobs. The continuing right-wing attack on government has left many agencies in a weakened state, unable to vigorously pursue their missions. There are not enough mine inspectors to protect mineworkers. The IRS lacks the personnel to detect and retrieve the billions of dollars lost every year from individuals and corporations that cheat on their taxes. Many school districts lack the teachers to keep their class size down to a reasonable level. In many cases, we have gone way past cutting "fat" out of these bureaucracies and we have begun to cut into flesh and bone. The main threat to the public interest posed by government bureaucracies these days is not that they are wasting huge amounts of our money, but that many are not healthy enough to do their job of promoting and protecting our collective wellbeing. To make matters worse, the very right-wing forces who are starving these vital agencies then turn around and cite any poor performance by these debilitated organizations as evidence of the ineptness of government.

When President Obama was elected in 2008, he was committed to revitalizing important federal agencies. For example, he worked to enable the FDA to have enough inspectors to ensure that our foods are safe to eat; and the Democratic Congress acted to increase the funding for the Consumer Product and Safety Commission. These were important steps in the right direction, but much more needs to be done to strengthen the numerous bureaucracies that serve our vital public interests. Unfortunately, the Republican takeover of the House of Representatives in 2010 threatens to undermine any systematic efforts to reinvigorate many federal agencies.

Beyond Bureaucratic Stereotypes

The negative stereotypes of bureaucracy that we have looked at in this chapter contribute to a political atmosphere that legitimizes the right-wing attack on government. The problem with these stereotypes is not simply that they are exaggerated and mistaken, but that conservatives and libertarians are able to exploit these misperceptions to justify their attempts to defund and hamstring the public sector. The more Americans believe that bureaucracies are bad, the more likely they are to agree with efforts to slash taxes and gut government programs. That is why it is increasingly important that we begin to see that most of the criticisms of government bureaucracy are based more on myth than reality, and that these administrative agencies play a central role in promoting the important missions of a modern democratic government.

---

1. Charlton Heston, in a speech given at Hillsdale College.
http://www.libertyhaven.com/politicsandcurrentevents/governmentreformitsrealrole/reaganright.shtml
2. Jacob Weisberg, *In Defense of Government* (New York: Scribner, 1996), p. 32.
3. Joseph Nye, et al, *Why People Don't Trust Government* (Cambridge MA: Harvard University Press, 1997) p. 62

4. Ibid.
5. Ibid.
6. Charles Goodsell, *The Case for Bureaucracy: A Public Administration Polemic*, 4th ed. (Washington, D.C.: CQ Press, 2004), p. 52. This excellent and much underappreciated book is the basis for most of the arguments made in this chapter – and for its title.
7. Goodsell, p. 54.
8. Bureau of Labor Education, "The U.S. Health Care System: Best in the World, or Just the Most Expensive? (Orono, Maine: University of Maine, 2001), p. 4.
9. Robert Evans and Noralou Roos, "What Is Right about the Canadian Health Care System," *Physicians for National Health Care Newsletter*, March 2000.
10. Bureau of Labor Education, p. 5.
11. World Health Organization, "WHO Issues New Healthy Life Expectancy Rankings," June, 4, 2000. http://www.who.int/inf-pr-2000/en/pr2000-life.html
12. Barbara Starfield, "Is U.S. Health Really the Best in the World?" *Journal of the American Medical Association* 284(4), July 26, 2000, pp.483-485.
13. Paul Krugman, "The Medical Money Pit," *The New York Times*, April 15, 2005, p. A19.
14. "The Deteriorating Administrative Efficiency of the U.S. Health Care System, *New England Journal of Medicine* 324, May 2, 1991, pp. 1253-1258.
15. Physicians for National Health Care, "National Health Insurance Could Save $286 Billion on Health Care Paperwork," January 14, 2004. http://www.pnhp.org/news/2004/janaury/national_heath_insu.php.
16. U.S. Government, *Statistical Abstract of the United States* (Washington D.C.: U.S. Government Printing Office, 2011) Table 494.
17. Julie Dolan, "The Budget-Minimizing Bureaucrat? Empirical Evidence from the Senior Executive Service," *Public Administration* 62, no. 1 (January/February 2002).
18. Dolan, p. 47.
19. Cited in Goodsell, p. 123.
20 Max Neiman, *Defending Government: Why Big Government Works* (Upper Saddle River, NJ: Prentice Hall, 2000), p. 212.
21. Neiman, p. 38.
22. Neiman, p. 139.
23. Goodsell, p. 25.

24. Theodore H. Poister and Gary Henry, "Standards of Excellence: U.S. Residents Evaluations of Local Government Services," *Public Administration Review* 54, no. 2 (March 1994)..
25. Poister and Henry, p. 158.
26. Kevin Smith and Michael Licari, *Public Administration: Power and Politics in the Fourth Branch of Government* (Los Angeles: Roxbury Publishing, 2006), p. 1.
27. Goodsell, p. 157.
28. See Goodsell, chapter 5.
29. Robert Kuttner, "Teachable Moments: Every Week, Celebrate a Public Hero," *The American Prospect*, August 1, 2004.
30. Kevin Drum, "Political Animal," *The Washington Monthly*, September 1, 2005, http://www.washingtonmonthly.com/archives/individual/2005_09/007023.php
31. Ibid.

CHAPTER 9

How Government is Good for Business

The Doge's Palace is a popular tourist destination in Venice. It was the seat of government when Venice was one of the most powerful and wealthy city-states in the world. In the 16th century, the rooms where the various councils of the "Serene Republic" met were decorated with paintings by the leading Italian Renaissance artists – works now considered masterpieces. In one room, the paintings on the ceiling are by Paolo Veronese and they are intended to represent the virtues of the Republic's government. On one panel are figures of women representing "Peace" (with an olive branch) and "Justice" (carrying a sword and scales). Another contains the figure of "La Prosperita" – prosperity. She is dressed elegantly and is surrounded by mounds of fruit. She is clearly meant to celebrate the idea that the various activities of the city's government – managing trade, conducting foreign policy, and defending against the armies of rival city states – played a large role in creating the incredible financial success of Venice.

What a difference five hundred years makes. These days, in the United States, many people see the government as the *enemy* of business and economic prosperity – a notion that is relentlessly promoted by anti-government conservatives. Their complaints and those of the business community are familiar ones: environmental and workplace regulations raise the cost of doing business and hamper corporate expansion; minimum wage laws raise costs for employers; and consumer protection laws raise the prices of goods and discourage innovation.

Crying Wolf: Exaggerating the Costs of Regulation

There is no denying that some government policies – particularly regulations – do raise the cost of doing business for some firms. This is true. But advocates of active government argue that companies and conservatives often "cry wolf" about regulations and that they are often not as economically damaging as claimed. For example, a report by Public Citizen called "Not Too Costly After All," found that businesses routinely exaggerate tremendously the potential costs of regulations and usually end up adapting to them with much less cost than they predicted. Public Citizen also found that government critics typically ignore the fact that environmental regulations that impose costs on the companies that must comply with them often also generate large economic gains for companies that make pollution control technologies, like catalytic converters.[1]

A current example of crying wolf is the corporate complaints about the Sarbanes–Oxley Act. Though not perfect, these regulations go a long ways toward preventing the kinds of massive corporate frauds perpetuated by Enron and WorldCom. But many in the business community have been warning that these rules are stifling business. In particular, Wall Street firms have been arguing that these regulations are discouraging foreign investment in the U.S. and are threatening to dethrone New York and its stock markets as the financial capital of the world. But *New Yorker* writer James Surowiecki looked into these concerns and found no evidence of the economic harms alleged by critics. It is, he concluded, just one more example of how Wall Street has consistently claimed impending dire effects from any attempts at regulation:

> Wall Street … has greeted practically every important market regulation introduced in this century with howls of dismay and predictions of disasters. In 1934, the head of the New York Stock Exchange told Congress that if the Securities Exchange Act, which became the foundation of market regulation in the U.S., was made law there was a chance that stock trading in the U.S. would be "entirely destroyed." Needless to say, it wasn't. In 1975, when the S.E.C. abolished fixed commissions, the Street claimed that its business would be demolished. Instead, after transaction costs fell, trading volume shot up. And in 2000, when the S.E.C. required companies to disclose material information to all investors, rather than just to insiders, we were told that this would strangle the flow of information to the market and make stock prices swing wildly. But, as numerous academic studies have found, it has actually done the opposite.[2]

Examples like these make it clear that we cannot trust the business community to tell us whether it is being harmed by regulations. In many cases, the reality is that the costs to business of complying with regulations are often not that onerous.

Regulations Make Us All Better Off

Defenders of the public sector also point out that the benefits we enjoy as a society from these government regulations far exceed the costs to most businesses. These policies may have a negative impact on some businesses' profits and growth, but they also produce a better society. Environmental regulations ensure drinkable water and breathable air for all of us. Consumer and workplace regulations protect millions of people from harm. Minimum wage laws help raise families out of poverty. And so on. In general, government regulation of business and markets has made Americans safer and healthier, and has created greater economic security and economic equality.

Apparently even a conservative administration cannot deny this. In 2003, George W. Bush's Office of Management and Budget issued a report that summarized the cost and benefits from 1992 to 2002 of the most significant 107 regulatory rules implemented by eight main federal agencies. As Table 5 clearly shows, the benefits that Americans enjoy from these regulatory programs far outstrip the economic costs. The benefits of these regulations are from $147 to $231 billion versus $37 to $43 billion in costs – so the net benefits to society are huge. And what makes this study's result even more impressive is the fact that it comes from an administration generally hostile to regulation and uses traditional cost-benefit techniques that are notorious for underestimating social and environmental benefits. In any case, the record clearly shows that Americans are much better off for having these rules and regulations.

Table 5: Estimates of the Total Annual Benefits and Costs of Major Federal Rules, October 1, 1992 to September 30, 2002 (Millions of 2001 dollars)

Agency	**Benefits**	**Costs**
Agriculture	3,094 to 6,176	1,643 to 1,672
Education	655 to 813	361 to 610
Energy	4,700 to 4,768	2,472
Health & Human Services	9,129 to 11,710	3,165 to 3,334
Housing & Urban Development	551 to 625	348
Labor	1,804 to 4,185	1,056
Transportation	6,144 to 9,456	4,220 to 6,718
Environ. Protection Agency	120,753 to 193,163	23,359 to 26,604
Total	**146,812 to 230,896**	**36,625 to 42,813**

Source: Office of Management and Budget, *Informing Regulatory Decisions*, 2003.

Government Can Also be Good for Business

Not only are the economic impacts of active government not as bad as business claims, many of the programs and policies of the modern democratic state are often actually *good* for business and the economy. But you will rarely hear about this from the advocates of reduced government. They deliberately turn a blind eye to the many significant ways that government aids the business community. The rest of this chapter will detail some of the main ways that government actively supports a growing economy – ways that most Americans often don't think about. This more accurate and complete view of the relationships between government and the business community reveals that the democratic state often functions as a friend of business, not its enemy. We will see, for instance, that numerous government policies provide crucial direct and indirect subsidies to the business community. In the next chapter, "Capitalism Requires Government," I will continue this analysis and document how government establishes the elaborate legal and regulatory infrastructure that enables a market economy to function efficiently and grow. Understanding all of this will get us much closer to understanding the true relationship between government and business in the United States.

Companies Can Benefit Economically from Regulations

It may seem counter-intuitive, but government regulations can often work to increase the profitability of business. That's because the success of a business requires a certain crucial amount of consumer confidence. For example, consumers want to be sure that the products they buy are not going to hurt them. When this confidence is lost, this can be a disaster for a company as customers become less likely to buy their product. Consider the case of salmonella-tainted peanut butter in 2008. Even though only one large peanut company was implicated, many consumers stayed away from all peanut products. This lead to a loss of revenue for the peanut industry that was estimated to be a billion dollars – a huge economic impact.

Government rules that ensure the safety and efficacy of products function to maintain consumer confidence in those regulated industries. The peanut company involved in the salmonella scandal chose to use private inspectors – who were poorly trained and who rarely pushed companies to correct unsanitary conditions. Undoubtedly this saved the company some money in the short run. But the resulting scandal and loss of public confidence drove that company into bankruptcy and severely damaged the entire industry. In the long run, then, many industries can actually benefit from strict enforcement of regulations designed to ensure that their products do not harm the public. This is clearly one way that more government can be good business.

Government Subsidies to Business: Obvious and Hidden

A more obvious way that government helps business is through direct government subsidies of various corporate activities – what is sometimes called "corporate welfare." Reasonable estimates of corporate welfare from the federal government range from $100 billion to $200 billion dollars a year – depending on what is counted as "welfare." The main forms are direct grants to business, aid for corporate research and development, subsidized loans and insurance, tax loopholes and tax breaks, and discounted fees for use of public resources. A typical example is the Import-Export Bank, which spends about $1 billion a year to help private companies like Boeing and General Electric sell their goods abroad. Typical tax breaks include accelerated depreciation and elimination of taxes on profits earned abroad. One study estimated that in 1996, government subsidies and tax breaks to corporations outpaced all the federal money spent on programs for the poor, including welfare, food stamps, housing subsides, and student aid.[3] State and local governments also have their own extensive corporate welfare programs – often designed to attract businesses to their area or to keep them there. They include such things as tax deferrals, abatements and credits of property and income taxes, low-interest loans, tax-free enterprise zones, tax-exempt industrial development bonds, and employee training subsidies.

These kinds of business subsidies are controversial. Many anti-government and libertarian types do not like them because they believe businesses should go it alone without government handouts. Many on the left criticize them because they resent government help going to big corporations when it is being cut back for the poor. But all of this controversy is misleading. It gives the false impression that these policies are the only government subsidies for business and that it they were discontinued, business would be on their own without any government aid. This is far from the truth. Besides these direct subsidies, there are many indirect and hidden government subsidies designed to promote businesses and economic growth in the United States.

One of the largest and most significant indirect subsidies for business is the hundreds of billions of dollars local, state, and federal governments spend on creating and maintaining crucial infrastructure facilities – things like roads, bridges, harbors, navigable rivers, clear water facilities, waste disposal facilities, airports, and so on. Businesses cannot grow and prosper without these things. Imagine trying to run a profitable large business without a well-functioning interstate highway system or adequate airport facilities. Another enormous public investment necessary for a well-functioning business system is education. Companies need skilled and well-educated employees. The public education system – from grade schools to public universities – plays a key role in providing that kind of workforce. Also, community amenities – such as well-planned and vibrant urban centers, well-funded and successful schools, a clean environment, public funded parks and cultural activities – also help to attract skilled workers to an area. The crucial importance of such hidden subsidies are shown by studies that found that good schools, a skilled workforce, clean water, and community amenities often do more to attract a business to a particular area than the obvious subsidies like tax breaks.[4]

Another immense source of hidden subsidies for business is government-sponsored research and development. Actually, the business community is highly aware of these benefits, even if most Americans know little about them. They are more than willing to accept this kind of government aid – even if it contradicts their stated position of opposing government "intrusions" into the private sector. Direct government R& D spending amounts to over $80 billion a year. The federal government alone runs over 700 research laboratories and funds 49,000 fellowships and research assistantships in graduate level science and engineering programs. Virtually all of the research done in "basic science" – whose payoffs are often in the future – is sponsored by government. The government has also heavily subsidized R&D work in many ostensibly "private" research institutions such as Bell Labs. It is not an exaggeration to say that this spending is part of the reason that Americans industries remain on the technological forefront in areas such as medicine, communications, and engineering.

The direct economic payoffs to businesses of this kind of research have been immense. If we only consider the commercial spin-offs from military research done during the Cold War, we find such things as supercomputers, advanced microprocessors, computer-controlled machine tools, advances in metallurgy and materials science, and optical fiber cables.[5] Spin-offs from research for the space program are also numerous. In medicine: cool laser surgery technology, body imaging systems, infrared thermometers, cardiac monitors, and digital mammography. For the airline industry: lightening protection, wind shear predictors, and collision avoidance systems. The pay-offs of NASA research also find their way into many products like scratch-resistant eyeglass lenses, sports protectors, golf balls, infant formula, ski boots, firefighters' breathing systems, smoke detectors, home insulation, cordless power tools, and many others.

One business sector that benefits tremendously from government R&D is the drug industry. Our government conducts fully half of the research and development of new drugs – the economic benefits of which are then largely captured by pharmaceutical companies. The National Institutes of Health alone spend about $20 billion a year on research, a good portion of which is devoted to developing new drugs. One study found that publicly funded research played a part in the discovery and development of 67% of the 21 most important drugs introduced between 1965 and 1992.[6] Another found that all five of best-selling products of the drug industry for a recent period – Zantac, Zovirax, Vasotec, Capoten, and Prozac – were initially aided in their development by tax-payer funded government research.[7]

Subsidies are Only Part of the Story

But here is the most interesting thing about all this: even if we add these various hidden government subsidies to the more obvious kinds of corporate welfare, all of this together is only the tip of the iceberg of how government aids the business community. To see the rest of the iceberg, we need to go to a different and deeper level of analysis. We need to appreciate not only how government subsidizes particular businesses, but how government activities are necessary to make business and free market capitalism possible at all. This is the topic of the next chapter, "Capitalism Requires Government."

---

1. Public Citizen, "Not Too Costly, After All: An Examination of the Inflated Cost Estimates of Health, Safety and Environmental Protections," February 2004. http://www.citizen.org/documents/ACF187.pdf
2. James Surowiecki, "Over There," *The New Yorker*, February 5, 2007, p. 29.
3. Charles Noble, *The Collapse of Liberalism* (New York: Rowman and Littlefield, 2004) p. 5.
4. See Mimi Abramovitz, "Everyone is on Welfare: The Role of Redistribution in Social Policy," *Social Work*, Vol. 46, No. 4, October 2001, p. 305.

5. Robert Kuttner, *Everything for* Sale (New York: Alfred A. Knopf, 1997) p. 215-216. I rely heavily on Kuttner's analysis throughout this section.
6. Public Citizen, *Rx R&D Myths*, July 2001, p. 8. http://www.citizen.org/documents/ACFDC.PDF
7. Public Citizen, *Rx R&D Myths*.

CHAPTER 10

Capitalism Requires Government

One of the most common and misleading economic myths in the United States is the idea that the free market is "natural" – that it exists in some natural world, separate from government. In this view, government rules and regulations only "interfere" with the natural beneficial workings of the market. Even the term "free market" implies that it can exist free from government and that it prospers best when government leaves it alone. Nothing could be further from the truth. In reality, a market economy does not exist separate from government – it is very much a product of government rules and regulations. The dirty little secret of our "free" market system is that it would simply not exist as we know it without the presence of an active government that creates and maintains the rules and conditions that allow it to operate efficiently.

Government Rules Make Markets and Capitalism Possible

Markets, like governments, are very much social constructs. The market is a set of behaviors that is structured by rules, and many of the most important rules have been developed and enforced by government. Without these rules, our prized free-market economy would be a stunted and feeble version of what we see today. To see how this is the case, lets looks at these essential "rules" – the vast infrastructure of laws and policies that make a modern capitalist economy possible.

- **Limited Liability Laws.** Capitalism requires capital – lots of it. But without limited liability laws, investors are unlikely to risk investing their money in businesses. In the 19th century, before the passing of laws that limited the liability of investors, anyone who put money into a business that then went under could be held liable for the debts of the company. They could have their personal assets seized and could be financially ruined. Needless to say, this discouraged investment. Without limited liability laws, the economy would not have access to the capital it needs to grow and prosper.[1]

- **Property Rights.** Without the right to own property and dispose of it as you wish, capitalism as we know it could not exist. These legal rights are created and protected by the government. Moreover, in the U.S., the federal courts have extended to corporations the same property rights given to citizens. Corporate property rights – one of the main legal instruments that insulate business from government power – can be created and maintained only by government.
- **Law and Order.** A market system cannot work well without a functioning criminal justice system. Otherwise, organized crime would easily take over large sectors of the business community. Extortion, bribery, kidnapping, and murder would become the reigning corporate model. Without the rule of law, our economy would resemble the "mafia capitalism" that Russia has suffered from in its transition to capitalism.
- **Bankruptcy Protection.** Business is inherently risky and one of the largest risks is business failure, particularly during recessions and depressions. In the 19th century, before the creation of bankruptcy laws, business failures would usually saddle entrepreneurs with large and ongoing debts, making it impossible for them to make a fresh start and often putting them in debtors' prison. Investors and creditors also often failed to get any of the money due to them. Bankruptcy laws protected otherwise healthy businesses that were temporarily short of funds. And these laws allowed entrepreneurs to be eventually freed from crushing debts. Along with limited liability, bankruptcy rules formed a crucial financial safety net for entrepreneurs. It is important to note, however, that bankruptcy laws were passed not simply out of concern or sympathy for failed entrepreneurs, but also as a way to lessen economic risk and therefore encourage more investment and economic growth.[2]
- **A Stable Money Supply**. Without reliable money, markets would be based primarily on barter and thus be extremely limited. In the U.S., before the Civil War, almost all paper money was issued by private banks – not the government. This was an unreliable and incredibly chaotic system. Sometimes merchants would not even accept certain currencies. It also meant there was no real control over the money supply – which has a crucial

impact on inflation and economic growth. Widespread commerce and a stable economy both require a stable and dependable money system – one in which consumers and merchants have faith. This can only be provided and maintained by the federal government.

- **Patents and Copyrights.** Large portions of our economy would grind to a halt if the government did not grant patents and copyrights. Without this massive intervention into the free market, the drug, music, publishing, and software industries could not exist. Bill Gates likes to think of himself as a self-made man, but he would not be one of the richest men in the world if the government did not make it illegal for anyone but Microsoft to copy and sell Windows.
- **Banking Regulation and Insurance**. As we have seen recently, a capitalist economy depends heavily on stable banks to finance growing businesses. But banks are inherently vulnerable to "runs" – where worried depositors all seek to take out their money at the same time. Banks cannot survive runs because they have loaned out most of the money deposited with them and therefore cannot pay it out to a large number of depositors at once. Before the passage of banking regulations and federal deposit insurance, banks regularly had runs and failed. The main reason that we had no disastrous runs on banks (and money market funds) during the financial panic of 2008 was that government was there to guarantee those deposits.
- **Corporate Charters.** Capitalism today is corporate capitalism. But the corporation itself is a creation of government. Corporations can come into being only through charters: the legal instruments by which state governments allow businesses to incorporate. These charters and state business laws define what a corporation is, how it is organized, how it is governed, how long it may exist, who has a say in decision making, the rights of stockholders, the extent of its liability, and so on. Most states also retain the right to revoke the charters of corporations that break the law or harm the public interest, though this power is seldom used these days.
- **Commercial Transaction Laws**. Businesses could not operate effectively without laws governing commercial transactions. Few would risk doing business on a wide scale unless there was some way of making and enforcing contracts. Who would sell goods if they couldn't be sure they would be paid, and who would buy goods if they couldn't be sure they would receive them? The

Uniform Commercial Code is a set of legal rules that determines, among other things, what a valid contract is, how contracts can be enforced, and various remedies for fraud, default, etc. It is over 800 pages long and covers every aspect of commerce in great detail, including laws governing the sales of goods, payment methods, receipts, warrantees, titles, shipping of goods, storage of goods, how sales are financed, and the leasing of goods. It is the legal infrastructure that allows business to be conducted smoothly and reliably.

- **International Trade Law.** Global capitalism would be impossible without trade. Governments create the legal frameworks – the treaties and international trade laws – that facilitate and make this trade possible. "Free trade" is a misnomer because it implies that it is international trade that exists free of any political framework. But this is hardly the case. The North American Free Trade Agreement, for instance, takes up two volumes and is over 900 pages long – covering such things as tariffs, customs, dumping, corporate and investor rights, intellectual property rights, financial services, government procurement, and dispute resolution procedures. It also establishes a secretariat, a commission, dispute panels, scientific review boards, eight industrial sector committees, and six working groups to oversee implementation of this agreement. It turns out that free trade requires a great deal of regulation.
- **Enforcement of Laws.** All of these rules and laws that facilitate business and markets have to be enforced, otherwise they are worthless. Just as international trade treaties require elaborate enforcement mechanisms, so do all our national laws that facilitate the business process. And this is no small effort. We and our governments spend billions of dollars every year to provide police to protect private property, courts to interpret and enforce contracts, and agencies to protect patents, oversee banks, and act as watch dogs in the stock and bond markets. It is revealing that most civil suits are not brought by individuals harassing corporations – as conservatives would have it – but by businesses suing other business. The courts are indispensable for resolving business disputes and thus ensuring the smooth operation of the economic system.

To see just how essential these government contributions are to the workings of a free market system, you merely have to imagine what it would be like if these measures didn't exist. Or if we didn't enforce these laws. Imagine that investors were liable for all debts of a company, that there were no patents, copyrights, or property rights, that contracts couldn't be enforced legally, that there was no official and stable money supply, and so on. In such a world, markets would be very limited, and economic growth severely stunted. It would hardly resemble the economic world we now live in.

Conservatives would like us to think that there can be a strict boundary between public and private in modern economies. But this is impossible. As the points above make clear, markets and capitalism are quasi-public entities – made possible by a myriad of government rules and laws that establish many of their basic inner workings. We may think of the "private market" as existing separately from the public sphere, but it does not.

Football and Capitalism: The Rules Make the Game

Consider this analogy: free-market capitalism is constituted by government laws in the same way that sports are constituted by their rules. When we watch football, for instance, we usually see it as a free-wheeling game with exciting runs and daring passes. But in reality, football is a highly circumscribed and regulated activity. It is only made possible by a large numbers of rules and regulations that cover everything ranging from the size of the field and the ball, to the number of downs, how scoring occurs, how tackling and blocking must take place, what constitutes a legal play, and so on. And without referees to interpret and enforce these rules, football as we know it would descend into chaos. The defining nature of these rules is shown by the fact that there are different kinds of football, depending on the rules. In Canada, for instance, the field is much larger, teams have one more player, and there are only three downs. In Arena League football, the clock rarely stops, the fields and goal posts are much smaller, and substitutions are very limited. The rules make the game.

Just as rules can create different kinds of football, government laws can create different kinds of capitalism and market relations. This clearly shows how market economies are actually political constructions – with their basic institutional arrangements being developed and managed by government rules. In some European countries, for instance, the government has not granted to firms the broad property rights that corporations have in the United States. This means, among other things, that large businesses are not free to simply move facilities from one region of the country to another. Because these relocations can dramatically alter the economic fortunes of entire communities, businesses must apply to the government for permission to move. In addition, in many other Western countries, government laws give much more power to unions in their relationships with businesses – thus altering the basic nature of the labor market. In some places, for instance, unions are actually mandated by law. These kinds of market relations are no more or less "natural" than those we have in the United States. There is no one natural form of market relations – just as there is no one "natural" form of football. This is simply an illusion that business interests and conservatives like to foster. Capitalism itself can take on different forms depending on the government rules that form it.

The Fantasy of our Laissez-Faire History

There is nothing new in the way that government aids business and a market economy. Conservatives would have us believe that our nation began and prospered under a laissez-faire arrangement, until the twentieth century and the advent of the New Deal and big government as we know it. But in fact, there has never been a complete wall between the public and private sectors. Government has always been involved in the economy. Active government support for business and the encouragement of economic growth can be traced back to the very beginnings of our Republic. Consider, for example, section eight in our Constitution – the one that describes the powers given to the newly created Congress. What is striking about most of the powers listed in this section is how mundane they seem. Here are the first eight of those powers:

> Clause 1: The Congress shall have Power To lay and collect Taxes, Duties, Imposts and Excises, to pay the Debts and provide for the common Defense and general Welfare of the United States; but all Duties, Imposts and Excises shall be uniform throughout the United States;
> Clause 2: To borrow Money on the credit of the United States;
> Clause 3: To regulate Commerce with foreign Nations, and among the several States, and with the Indian Tribes;
> Clause 4: To establish a uniform Rule of Naturalization, and uniform Laws on the subject of Bankruptcies throughout the United States;
> Clause 5: To coin Money, regulate the Value thereof, and of foreign Coin, and fix the Standard of Weights and Measures;
> Clause 6: To provide for the Punishment of counterfeiting the Securities and current Coin of the United States;

> Clause 7: To establish Post Offices and post Roads;
> Clause 8: To promote the Progress of Science and useful Arts, by securing for limited Times to Authors and Inventors the exclusive Right to their respective Writings and Discoveries;

What is remarkable about most of these topics is that they have little to do with promoting freedom, justice, equality, or the other lofty political values for which the American Revolution was fought. What they are promoting is economic prosperity. This was the first attempt to create a legal and policy infrastructure that would promote and encourage business growth – establishing protective patents, providing a stable money supply, preventing counterfeiting, creating uniform duties on goods, establishing uniform bankruptcy rules, regulating foreign trade, and so on. Even the creation of post roads was not simply for the mail – these roads were the main avenues of commercial transportation in the states. Later, in clause ten, the Constitution also forbids states from imposing duties on goods from other states and prevents them from impeding the enforcement of states across state lines – all absolutely necessary if businesses are to grow into nationwide enterprises.

So as far back as the 18th century, American government has been working hand in glove with business interests to promote economic growth. In the 19th century, this government effort to aid the economy intensified and took on new forms. As seen earlier, numerous laws were passed on the federal and state level to protect investors and entrepreneurs from excessive risk and to give an artificial boost to economic growth. In addition, the key infrastructure development of that century – and one that fueled rapid economic development in the entire country – was the railroads. These were extremely risky ventures that had to be heavily subsidized by state and federal governments through loans, credits, and land grants. Government also greatly strengthened and increased farm production through its establishment of agricultural colleges and agricultural extensions services. Further, research and development in public universities and land grant colleges were largely responsible for giving U.S. industries technological leads in areas such as metallurgy, and mechanical, electrical, and chemical engineering during the latter 19th century.[3] Extensive and ongoing government tariffs also continued to protect and promote many vital domestic businesses throughout that whole period.

So the conservative idea that until recently we had a laissez-faire economy that prospered without any help from government is really a myth. Robert Kuttner, one of our most insightful commentators on the relationship between government and business makes this point very strongly. Looking at this long tradition of government aid for business in this country, he concludes that it "gives lie to the idea that the United States has historically been a laissez-faire nation. Despite the constitutional restraints on state power and the generally libertarian national creed, government action for economic and industrial development is deeply ingrained in our heritage."[4]

Government and the Deification of the Market

Up until this point, I have been talking about how government policies and programs actually help businesses and stimulate economic growth. These have clearly positive effects on business, and even most conservatives would not deny the beneficial economic results of the government enforcing contracts, keeping the money supply stable, limiting liability of corporations, and so on. But the fact is that modern democratic governments also do a lot of things that are not necessarily good for particular businesses – at least in the short run. And these are what really bother anti-government conservatives – things like environmental and workplace regulations that add to the cost of doing business, taxes that lower the profitability of corporations, and social programs that insulate people from the discipline of the labor market. There is no getting around the fact that some governmental actions do indeed reduce profits for some businesses.

For free-market, anti-government conservatives, most of this damaging government interference in the economy is simply unnecessary. In their view, if we simply leave the market alone, it can be trusted to produce virtually all of what we need for the good life in America. This unbridled enthusiasm about the wondrous abilities of markets is expressed well in a variation of the old light bulb joke:

> Q: "How many conservatives does it take to screw in a light bulb?"
> A: "None. If the government would just leave it alone, it would screw itself in."

A silly joke – but it does capture well the sense of delusional optimism that many conservatives have about markets. The market is seen as a marvelous self-regulating mechanism that if left unfettered will provide all our basic needs – and a great many luxuries as well. This view rests in large part, as mentioned earlier, on the notion that markets are "natural" and can achieve a kind of perfection that manmade, artificial government cannot. It assumes that market-based decision-making will always produce the public interest – and that attempts by government to regulate markets only distort them and cause problems. As Rep. Dick Armey liked to quip: "The market is rational and the government is dumb." [5]

In many ways, then, the conservative movement's demonizing of government is merely the flip side of its deifying the market. And the term "deifying," with all its religious connotations, may not be that far off. After all, it was Rep. Armey who suggested that our inspiration to participate in the market may come from above. "We have all been called to Freedom by God," he said. "I think the free market arose from the calling."[6] Of course, most anti-government conservatives would not take it so far as to claim some kind of divine endorsement of the market; but many do adhere to a kind of "market fundamentalism." This fundamentalism consists of an unquestioning faith that unrestricted markets are the best way to organize human activity and that they can largely do no wrong. We all need only follow our own selfish economic interests, and the "invisible hand" of the market will inevitably weave this all together to produce the public interest. Moreover, free market mechanisms, if allowed to, would eventually solve virtually every pressing problem we have, including spiraling health costs, poor quality education, environmental pollution, unsafe products, retirement insecurity, and so on. So if we simply place our faith in laissez-faire capitalism, then we will all reap the rewards.

The Inherent Problems of a Market Economy

The problem with market fundamentalism is the problem with all forms of fundamentalism – the faith of the adherents blinds them to significant portions of reality. In the case of market fundamentalism, it blinds them to most of the serious problems inherent in a capitalist economic system – the problems that necessitate government action. If pressed, most conservatives will admit that unregulated markets do suffer from a few "market failures," such as a tendency to ignore pollution. But they see such failures as episodic and limited. For them, these problems only occasionally interfere with the smooth operation of markets to produce the public interest and thus only necessitate a modicum of government interference to set them straight. But they are wrong. The failures of markets are many, serious, widespread, and ongoing. This is not to suggest that capitalism is "bad" or to deny the many economic advantages and achievements of markets. It is simply to acknowledge that when left on their own, market economies will inevitably produce a whole host of economic and social problems. Let's consider a list of some of the basic built-in problems, limitations, and failures of capitalist market economies.

- **Economic Bubbles.** Market economies are susceptible to "bubbles" — where the price of an asset rises high above its real value. These bubbles then burst, leading to the destruction of large amounts of wealth. Recent examples include the Dot-Com bubble crash that wiped out $5 trillion in the market value of technology companies, and the $2 trillion lost when the housing market bubble burst in 2008.
- **Environmental Pollution**. Pollution is a classic example of one common form of market failure: externalities. Externalities are created when decisions by businesses cause costs to groups outside of the business. Since businesses don't have to bear these costs, they typically ignore these side effects – but the public is harmed by them. So a company has no incentive to clean up air or water pollution caused by its production facilities, even though it will do great harm to the environment and to humans. This kind of problem cannot be solved within a market framework. Voluntarily assuming the costs of cleaning up its own pollution would be irrational for a business – it would lower profits and put it at a competitive disadvantage with rival companies. Only government can effectively address this problem by devising policies to ban or discourage pollution. Without government, a laissez-faire capitalist economy is inherently and inevitably bad for the environment.
- **Exploitation of Workers**. Corporations and their employees have conflicting interests. Businesses want to pay their employees as little as possible and not give benefits like health insurance and pensions. Also, businesses do not have an incentive to invest in safety measures in the workplace, which would lower profits. Owners of sweatshops, mines, and other businesses found out long ago that it is cheaper to replace injured workers than to improve working conditions. Given that corporations are often in a position of power over their employees, only a countervailing power on the side of these workers – in the form of unions or the government – can protect them from exploitation.

- **Unsafe and Ineffective Products.** Without government help, consumers are vulnerable to products that are unsafe or ineffective – such as tainted foods and worthless medicines. Some shady businesses engage in outright deception about their products, but even legitimate businesses have an incentive to pad their bottom line by not being overly concerned about how safe or effective their products are. For example, the auto industry fought for decades against such things as mandatory seat-belts, air-bags, and other important safety features because these safety devices lowered their profits. Without government, the reality of the market is "Let the Buyer Beware!"
- **Marketing Bads.** Left alone, markets and businesses will sell anything for which there is a demand. But there are many things that shouldn't be sold. We don't want women sold into slavery in the sex industry, or the peddling of child pornography, or the sale of dangerous and addictive drugs. Only government can control what should or should not be marketed. Where appropriate, it can try to eliminate markets entirely (such as underground markets that provide Stinger ground-to-air missiles to terrorists), or act to limit markets (as in not allowing cigarettes to be sold to minors).
- **Resource Depletion.** Like individual businesses, capitalist economic systems must grow or die. But as the worldwide economy grows, depletion of non-renewable resources necessarily increases dramatically. For example, the United States, with five percent of the world's population, currently consumes twenty-six percent of the world's energy – most of it in non-renewable forms. If the rest of the developing world were to rise to our levels of energy use, non-renewable energy resources would quickly be used up. A worldwide capitalist economy engaged in unlimited growth is fundamentally incompatible with a world where many vital resources are limited.
- **Corporate Fraud and Theft.** Without the government playing watchdog, there is a constant and strong temptation for companies to cheat their investors and their customers. The Bernie Madoff ponzi scheme that defrauded investors of $50 billion is simply the latest example of this problem. This happens so often, it cannot be considered an aberration. In just the last decade, many large businesses, including Enron and World-Com, have used deceptive accounting procedures to give the illusion of profitability, defrauding investors out of billions of dollars. Insurance brokers have rigged prices to steal hundreds

of millions from their customers. Investment companies have routinely told customers to buy stock in companies they have underwritten, knowing full well that these are poor investments. Several prominent mutual fund companies have been convicted of allowing illegal "late trading" by a few favored customers that lowered the profits of other customers. Drug companies have paid hundreds of millions in government fines for bribing doctors to prescribe their medicines. Corporations also routinely cheat the public by using questionable, unethical, and sometimes illegal strategies to avoid paying taxes, thus forcing citizens to pay more to fund public services.

- **Neglect of Public Goods**. Another classic example of market failure. A public good is something that is hard or impossible to produce for private profit – primarily because once it is produced, you can't limit who enjoys or consumes that good. The classic example is a light-house, because you can't prevent any ships from using it. More important examples are national defense, law enforcement, and clean air. Such goods are inevitably under-produced or neglected in a market economy and we must produce them collectively through government.
- **Neglect of Social and Public Investments.** Typically, businesses will not invest in large public projects that are necessary for the long-term health of our economy or society. A typical example is infrastructure facilities like roads, bridges, harbors, airports, etc. Such projects are usually too risky and provide too little profit for most businesses or investors to want to take them on. Education, sanitation, and public transportation are other examples of important social investments that would be neglected if left to the market.
- **Hidden Information.** For markets to work effectively in the public interest, consumers must have the information they need about products to make an intelligent choice about what meets their needs. But businesses often have an interest in not fully disclosing all relevant information. So government must step in and force companies to reveal that crucial information, such as what is in their food products, how safe their cars are, how efficient their air conditioners are, or what side effects their drugs have.
- **Inability to Plan.** Markets cannot plan. Capitalism is basically an anarchical economic process. Economic development is a function of the activities of separate and uncoordinated businesses and customers – all largely oriented toward the short-term. While this

arrangement produces great economic efficiencies, it has the disadvantage of disallowing any coordinated planning to make our lives better. Planning is essential if we want to have cities with livable neighborhoods, to create an efficient interstate highway system, to have an energy system not so dependent on foreign oil, to save rare ecosystems for future generations, and so on. Only government can provide rational, long-term plans for the development of society.

- **Boom and Bust Cycles**. As history has shown, *laissez-faire* capitalism is subject to regular cycles of boom and bust, where economies heat up too rapidly and then cool down into a period of deep stagnation. This process produces run-away inflation, recessions, depressions, rampant unemployment, etc. – and the widespread and profound human suffering that accompanies these serious economic problems. Government policies are often the only way to dampen these swings. For example, in an economic downturn, when businesses are shrinking, consumers are not buying, and banks are not lending, only government is in a position to revive the economy through the use of monetary and fiscal policies.
- **Lack of Markets.** Not everything we need for a good society can be provided by markets and business – especially things such as justice, fairness, equality, or basic rights and freedoms. Even if markets were possible for these things, we would not want them. For example, when the well-off are able to buy more justice in our court system, we consider that illegitimate and unfair. Only government can properly supply things like justice and freedom to all Americans.
- **Monopoly.** Competition in capitalism does not foster more competition – it eventually creates monopoly. Unrelenting competition eventually drives many companies out of business or forces them to merge, thus allowing fewer companies to take over increasingly larger shares of a market. Unchecked, this process leads to monopolies and oligopolies. This inevitably produces price-fixing, low-quality products, and other abuses of overly concentrated economic power. The only cure? Government anti-trust laws and other "regulation for competition" policies.
- **Ignoring Needs**. Markets and business do not respond to our *needs*, they respond to *demand*, as expressed in money. Thus social needs are sometimes neglected. What concerns producers is not what social needs or functions are fulfilled by their products, but how much people will pay for them. Henry Ford put it

best when he said that he was in the business of making money, not making cars or providing transportation. So while there is a pressing need for low-cost, affordable housing in America, what are being produced are huge McMansions and luxury condominiums – because these are more profitable. And while we may desperately need universal health care in this country, it will not be provided by the market alone. It can only be mandated by government policy.

- **Devaluing the Future.** As a rule, businesses are only oriented to the short-term. The accounting practices of firms utilize "discount rates" that require them to consider money, goods, and resources in the future to be worth less than those in the present. So it is better to develop resources like oil and old-growth forest now, rather than leaving them for later. The result: values like long-term environmental sustainability and the welfare of future generations tend to be neglected in corporate calculations.
- **Poverty and Economic Inequality**. On their own, market economies tend to produce high levels of poverty and economic inequality. In the last twenty years, the distribution of income and wealth has become more unequal in the United States, and we far surpass other Western democracies in our poverty rate. Also, the top 10% of wealthy Americans now own 70% of the wealth of the country. Economic inequality inevitably produces unequal distribution of other vital goods. The poor, for instance, have less access to health care, adequate housing, and retirement security. Only government action can address the low wages and lack of jobs that fuels poverty and can provide an economic safety for citizens. Studies have shown that Western countries that spend more on social programs and do the most to promote worker interests are the ones who have the fewest poor and the lowest economic inequality.[7]
- **Lack of Opportunity and Economic Mobility**. The economic inequality characteristic of market economies also undermines equal opportunity. The poor face many obstacles to financial success, while the well-off enjoy the advantages of superior education, social connections, and family wealth.[8] Unsurprisingly, studies show that citizens in countries like the U.S. with relatively high levels of poverty and lower government spending to equalize educational opportunities have less intergenerational economic mobility.[9] Even the *Wall Street Journal* has admitted that "Despite the widespread belief that the U.S. remains a more

mobile society than Europe, economists and sociologists say that in recent decades the typical child starting out in poverty in continental Europe or in Canada has had a better chance at prosperity."[10] Only government programs – like Head Start, high quality public schools, federal student aid, and low cost public colleges – can begin to level the economic playing field and help to equalize life chances for all Americans.

Taken together, all of these failures and problems totally undermine any notion of the "perfection" and "self-regulating" nature of the market. Virtually all of these problems are *built-in* to a capitalist, free-market system. They are *systemic* problems – products of the normal operation and the inherent attributes of this kind of economic system. This means that they occur irrespective of who is running our businesses. They are not the product of greedy owners or evil corporate CEOs; they are a product of the systemic priorities that all companies must adhere to if they are to stay in business and prosper. It is the internal logic of capitalism that forces firms to pay low wages, ignore the environment, devalue the future, and hide information from consumers.

Being systemic also means that these problems cannot be cured from within the economic system itself. These problems can only be addressed from the outside by coordinated collective efforts – the efforts of people acting through their governments. This doesn't mean that the government cannot at times utilize the forces of the market to help solve these problems – such as when it creates a market in pollution rights, or when it auctions off a limited number of licenses to harvest lobsters. But these are not "market solutions" as conservatives like to trumpet; these are "government solutions" that utilize markets to achieve their goals.

Once the extent and severity of the shortcomings of a market economy become obvious, it becomes much clearer why we have big government in the United States. The public has repeatedly turned to government to provide important things the market cannot – such as clean air, retirement security, equal access to a good education, city planning, and health care for those who cannot afford it. Nor can we rely on markets to provide a more just, free, and secure society. Government is also necessary to make sure that market economies don't hurt people in a variety of ways, including cars that blow-up or roll-over, or mines that collapse. That is exactly why most Americans say they do not want to see consumer or workplace regulatory protections dismantled. [11] Even David Stockman, ardent free-marketeer and lead man in the effort to reduce government in the Reagan administration, eventually had to reluctantly admit that the American public would simply not put up with capitalism in its raw form. Upon leaving office as budget director, he observed rather sadly that "The American electorate wants a moderate social democracy to shield it from capitalism's rougher edges."[12]

Why Taxes, Regulations and Social Programs are Good for Capitalism

That, then, is the traditional justification for government regulation of business and market: only government can address the many serious problems caused by laissez-faire capitalism. Even if government rules decrease somewhat corporate growth and profits, they promote important things that Americans care about – like better health care, safer workplaces, a cleaner environment, and more economic security. But this rationale leaves out an important – and more intriguing – reason why government "interference" in the economy is desirable. The fact is that many government actions that hurt businesses in the short run are actually *good* for business in the long run. Most regulations, for instance, are not only good for the American people, they are also ultimately good for business as well. This point may not seem obvious at first. But I will argue that the central pillars of the modern democratic state – the regulations and social programs that conservatives and business interests often oppose so vehemently – actually work in important ways to the benefit of the business community and capitalism itself. What business thinks is bad for it economically can be very beneficial, and even essential, for it politically.

How can this possibly be true? To see, we need only asks ourselves a simple question: What would happen to market capitalism without all of these regulations and social programs? Fortunately, we don't have to try to speculate about the answer to this question; we merely need to go back to the first several decades of the twentieth century. This was the time before big government – before extensive regulations and expensive social programs – an era that anti-government conservatives consider a golden age. But what they forget is that at that time, around the world and even in this country, growing numbers of people were becoming very discontent with capitalism. They were also becoming increasingly interested in alternatives such as socialism, communism, and anarchism. The communist revolution in Russia prompted a wave of attempted socialist uprisings or threats of uprisings throughout much of Europe after World War I. Rosa Luxemburg led one uprising in Germany, and the communists actually overthrew the government in Bavaria and briefly established a soviet state. Another short-lived communist government was established by revolutionaries in Hungary in 1919. The success in Russia also inspired a host of anti-capitalist movements and incidents in other countries: there was a wave of factory occupations in Italy, a wide-spread series of strikes in Britain, and a general strike in Winnipeg, Canada. Later, in the 1930s, in the Spanish Civil War, anarchists and communists fought side by side for control of the country.

Many people today wonder how anyone could have become such a radical, anti-capitalist revolutionary. But they are forgetting the horrendous conditions that many people were living under in unregulated capitalist economies – the grinding poverty, the enormous economic inequality, the lack of adequate health care for most people, the absence of old-age pensions, the widespread unemployment, the unchecked and abusive power of monopolies, the environmental squalor of the cities, the dangerous and often lethal working conditions, the inevitable and hugely destructive economic depressions. It was these unaddressed problems of capitalism that led to the creation of communism and communist revolutions. Some people were so upset and disgusted with the widespread injustices and suffering caused by of laissez-faire capitalism that they were willing to take up arms and risk their lives to throw out the entire system and to start over with new and untried economic systems. The extreme problems of capitalism drove them to those political extremes.

The United States was not immune to these problems or this kind of political and social unrest. In 1912, Eugene Debs, the Socialist Party presidential candidate, offered a radical critique of capitalism and won the support of nearly a million voters. Some unions, like the Industrial Workers of the World, wanted to replace capitalism with worker-controlled production. The IWW was instrumental in organizing the Seattle General Strike of 1919 where 60,000 workers went out on strike and paralyzed the city for a week. The influence of the Socialist Party and the IWW only abated when federal and state authorities jailed their leaders, deported many of them, harassed their members, shut down their newspapers, and denied them use of the mail.

The 1930s and the Great Depression, however, saw a resurgence of interest in anti-capitalist ideas and movements. Political unrest was growing. There were food riots, widespread labor violence, street protests, and increasing political instability. In this atmosphere, communist and socialist parties experienced growing support and began to exert more influence in unions as well. In addition, socialist and communist groups became very popular on college campuses. To students, they seemed to be the only organizations that could explain the causes of the Depression and who offered alternatives to a malfunctioning capitalist system. Into this highly volatile and precarious political situation stepped Franklin Delano Roosevelt and his New Deal programs. Anti-market conservatives have reviled Roosevelt ever since as a "socialist" who betrayed capitalism; but in reality, his government programs actually saved capitalism by stabilizing the economy and developing programs to alleviate the suffering it was causing – all of which had the effect of undermining political unrest.

Examining the deeper political implications of New Deal, the political scientist Edward Greenberg concluded in his book *Capitalism and the American Political Ideal* that Roosevelt's efforts can best be seen as ultimately aiding the cause of business and conservatives:

> [T]he New Deal is best understood as a series of attempts to save a faltering and depressed capitalist system by further regulating and rationalizing the economy, by bringing important elements of the labor movement into the established political life, and by staving off social disruption and revolution through expansion of the welfare role of government. … the New Deal represents, paradoxically, a conservative expansion of government activities. While it is traditional to define any expansion of government activities as "liberal," I would argue that since this expansion was directed toward preserving and cementing the position of capital and maintaining the social class system, it must, in the end, be judged "conservative."[13]

Ironically, then, free-market conservatives and business leaders who worked so hard against Roosevelt and his policies were actually working against their own long-term interests. They failed to see that capitalism actually needs some "socialism" to make it less destructive and more palatable to most people.

Today, the corporate community and anti-government conservatives fail to see this point as well. They fail to understand that government policies that protect consumers, make workplaces safe, provide economic security, eliminate poverty in old age, provide health care to the poor, and prevent and repair environmental damage are what "humanize" capitalism and make it tolerable to people. In this way, businesses are a lot like sulky teenagers. They resent their parents' rules – such as no drinking and driving, no unsafe sex, no experimentation with hard drugs – which they simply see as constraints on their freedom and their fun. They refuse to see that these rules are for their own good, their own long-term health and welfare.

Similarly, businesses and free-market conservatives have been unable to appreciate how government efforts to humanize capitalism have been for their own good. Instead, they have resented and opposed virtually every effort to make capitalism less harsh – from the 40-hour week and the abolition of child labor to Social Security and Medicare. They should see the costs they pay for these policies as a premium on a vital form of political insurance. Government regulatory policies and social programs are crucial in undermining popular discontent about the problems of a free-market economy and serve to co-opt potential anti-capitalist and anti-business political movements. These "liberal" reforms provide and sustain the social and political peace on which profitable business activity ultimately depends.

Even Ben Bernanke, chairman of the Federal Reserve, understands how essential government safety net programs are to maintaining public support for our market system. He has warned of the "painful dislocations" associated with capitalism and has stated that if "we did not place some limits on the downside risks to individuals affected by economic change, the public at large might become less willing to accept the dynamism that is so essential to economic progress."

There is one final ironic twist to all of this. Modern government's achievements in reining in abuses of corporate power and humanizing capitalism have actually backfired on those who champion an active role for government in society. These successes have fostered an illusion that a market economy is relatively harmless. Few people remain alive who actually experienced the severe problems of the "bad old days" of capitalism before the New Deal. Today, many think we are living in a natural "free market" system, but in reality it has been extensively tamed by myriad government policies. It is as if we lived in a world where all we knew about wild animals is what we learned by going to the circus, and thus came to believe that bears and elephants were naturally gentle creatures. Frustratingly, then, it has been the government's triumphs in addressing the many problems inherently caused by a free-market economy that has allowed conservatives to argue that markets are naturally benign and largely problem free – and so we do not really need much government.[14]

Beyond the Myths of Government and Markets

In the end, anti-government conservatives get it wrong about both markets and government. In their zeal to justify shrinking the state, they intentionally misrepresent both of these institutions and how they interact. The market is not God and the government is not the Devil.

Despite their enormous advantages, markets are not benign and self-regulating. They create numerous social, economic, and political problems that only government can correct. Government is also not the sworn enemy of business and capitalism. Conservatives can only promote this misleading caricature of government by deliberately ignoring the myriad ways that government aids business and makes a market economy possible.

Anti-government conservatives are constantly warning that government is primarily a threat to business and the economy – that unless we reduce it, it will "kill the goose that lays the golden eggs." But as we've seen, this is far from the truth. The modern state is more like the farmer who feeds and waters the goose, builds the facility that houses it, inoculates it from disease, clips its wings so it can't fly away, protects it from predators, cleans up its excrement, and tames it so it won't bite people. If we appreciate those golden eggs, we should also appreciate the efforts of the farmer who helps make the egg production process possible. Similarly, those who celebrate the achievements of business and a market economy should also acknowledge and celebrate the role government has had in those accomplishments. This would be the fair thing to do; but of course it would not fit into anti-government conservative orthodoxy.

The basic lesson is this: we Americans need to realize that our economy has thrived not *in spite* of government, but in many ways *because* of government. The American economy that so many people admire is not the mythical free market that operates without government interference. Our version of a market economy is highly constructed, regulated, subsidized, and humanized by government laws and policies. And we are all better off for it. Even if it were possible to create a world of free markets that were left entirely alone by government, none of us would want to live there.

---

1. For more on this issue, see David Moss' excellent book, *When All Else Fails: Government as the Ultimate Risk Manager* (Cambridge, MA: Harvard University Press, 2002) chapter three.
2. Moss, chapter five.
3. Robert Kuttner, *Everything for* Sale (. New York: Alfred A. Knopf, 1997) p. 212.
4. Kuttner, p. 218.
5. Dick Armey, *The Freedom Revolution* (Washington D.C.: Regnery Publishing, 1995), p. 316.
6. Armey, p. 68.

7. See for example, Timothy M. Smeeding, et al., "United States Poverty in a Cross-National Context." In Sheldon H. Danziger and Robert H. Haveman, editors, *Understanding Poverty* (New York and Cambridge, MA: Russell Sage Foundation and Harvard University Press, 2002) pp. 162-189.
8. Benard Wasaw, "Rags to Riches: The Americans Dream is Less Common in the United States than Elsewhere," Century Foundation, March 19, 2004. http://www.tcf.org/4L/4LMain.asp?SubjectID=1&TopicID=0&ArticleID=456
9. Jo Blanden, et al., "Intergenerational Mobility in Europe and North America," April, 2005. www.suttontrust.com/reports/ IntergenerationalMobility.pdf
10. "As Rich-Poor Gap Widens in the U.S., Class Mobility Stalls," *The Wall Street Journal*, May 13, 2005.
11. Charles Noble, *The Collapse of Liberalism* (New York: Rowman and Littlefield, 2004), p. xvi.
12. David Stockman, *The Triumph of Politics: Why the Reagan Administration Failed* (New York: Harper and Row, 1986) p. 394.
13. Edward S. Greenberg, *Capitalism and the American Political Ideal* (Armonk, NY: M.E. Sharpe, 1985) p. 93.
14. Thanks to Sam Rosen-Amy for making this point to me.

CHAPTER 11

Why We Need More, Not Less, Government

For decades, conservatives have been pushing for smaller government, and have consistently called for reduced social spending, less regulation, and more tax cuts. But not everyone agrees. When the financial crisis hit in the fall of 2008 and the economy began to melt down, suddenly there were calls for bigger and more active government. Many people wanted a massive federal stimulus plan to ward off an economic depression, and others demanded the widespread re-regulation of financial markets to prevent a recurrence of these problems. On top of this, many Democrats have argued for increased government involvement in a wide variety of areas, ranging from education and energy development to infrastructure repair and health care reform. But is this broad expansion of the public sector really justified?

Whether we need more government in this country really depends on the answer to three other questions. First, is there room for improvement in government programs? Have we reached the limits of what government can do in most policy areas, or could expanding these current programs produce significant added benefits for the public? Second, are any of our current social and economic problems worsening? Are we facing new and serious threats to our wellbeing? If so, this would logically indicate the need for more government. And finally, can we rely on markets and individual effort to solve these current and emerging problems? If so, then we don't need more government. But if markets and individual initiative are not up to the task, this bolsters the case for a more collective, governmental approach. All three of these questions are complex ones, but as this chapter will show, we can begin to get some definitive answers to all of them. These answers strongly indicate that we do need more government – not less – in the United States.

Room for Improvement

As impressive as the accomplishments of government are in the U.S., there is clearly room for it to play a much more constructive role in people's lives. In fact, many Americans sense this already. One of the most common complaints about government is that it is not doing enough to address a whole raft of problems. Sure the air is cleaner than it was, but we still have major smog problems in many cities. Of course we have done much to reduce poverty among the elderly, but a high level of poverty among the general population still exists. And while energy efficiency has improved, we still have an economy that is dangerously dependent on oil and other fossil fuels. Some may be tempted to conclude from these situations that government simply can't do anything more to help – that we have reached the limits of what government can do in these areas. But this is not the case. We know that government could actually do much more. How do we know this? Because governments in many other advanced democracies have already done much more to effectively address these problems.

In an earlier chapter, "Government's Forgotten Achievements," I cited a study done by Derek Bok which showed that a myriad of government programs have in fact been successful in addressing many of our social, environmental, and economic problems. But this study also found that there is considerable room for improvement. Bok discovered this by comparing the accomplishments of the U.S. in important policy areas to the accomplishments of the government of other major democracies – primarily those in Western Europe. What Bok found in this comparative study was not comforting: "Over the past several decades, America has moved ahead more slowly than most other leading countries in most areas of activity that matter to a majority of the people."[1] Of the more than sixty areas examined, the efforts of the U.S. government were below average in two-thirds of the cases, and at or near the bottom of the list in more than half.

Among the areas where we have under-performed other democracies:

Growth of per-capita income.
Reducing pollution.
Cost of health care system.
Life expectancy.
Infant mortality.
Effective job training.
Gender earnings gap.
Income inequality.
Health care system coverage.
Affordable long-term care.
Job-related illness or injury.
Safeguards for laid-off workers.

Ability to establish unions.
Severity of poverty.
Affordable rental housing.
Segregation in cities.
Availability of child care.
Children in pre-school.
Crime rates.
Number of families in poverty.
Affordability home ownership.
Child nutrition.
Student performance in math.
Availability of parental leave.

The fact that we lag behind our democratic neighbors in so many policy areas demonstrates unequivocally that our government could accomplish even more than it has done already. There is a real possibility that increased government efforts could do much more to improve our lives in significant ways. The greater success of other democratic governments in addressing serious economic and social problems shows that it can be done and that we could be following their lead.

We Can Do Better at Fighting Poverty

Let's consider just one particular policy area, poverty, where we lag far behind other democracies. We have an abysmal record in reducing the level of poverty in this country. It went down in the 1960s, but for the last 40 years it has hovered stubbornly at around 11-13%. Today, over 43 million Americans continue to suffer severe economic hardship. Conservatives consider our failure to reduce poverty as evidence of the inherent limitations of government. They conclude (wrongly) that since our current anti-poverty policies have failed, that there is nothing the government can do and that it should get out of the business of trying to eliminate poverty. It is this attitude that has animated Republican attempts to cut back on programs for the poor, such as welfare and job training. For them, our failures in poverty policy only contribute to the case they are making for a more limited government.

But the record of fighting poverty in Europe clearly demonstrates that governments are quite capable of addressing poverty much more effectively. Anti-poverty policies in the U.S. only lift 36% of people out of poverty, while government policies reduce poverty in Germany by 76%, by 83% in the Netherlands, and by 89% in Sweden.[2] Not surprisingly, all of these other countries end up with much lower rates of poverty. While our poverty rate continues to hover around 12%, Germany, the Netherlands, and Sweden have reduced their poverty rates to 4%, 4% and 2% respectively.

These are very impressive differences. And it is not a mystery how these other countries have been more successful in addressing poverty. First, these countries simply spend more on helping people out of poverty – welfare payments are higher, unemployment benefits are more generous and last longer, and so on. Spending more money helps lift more people out of poverty. In addition, social welfare policies in these other countries are much more universal – they include everyone, not just limited groups. Everyone has national health insurance; everyone qualifies for day care subsidies, and so on. Because of this, the social safety net is much more complete and effective than in the U.S., and this means that fewer people are likely to slip into poverty because of personal disasters such as a serious illness, a divorce, or the loss of a job. Most other democracies also pursue policies that help to raise wages. They encourage rather than discourage the formation of unions and they set a much higher minimum wage – both of which help to lower the number of the working poor in these countries.

As Bok found, poverty is just one of dozens of areas in which the U.S. lags behind other Western democracies. Clearly our government could be doing much more to address a wide variety of problems and could make even greater strides in improving the lives of Americans. This fact by itself is a powerful argument in favor of more government in the U.S.

Things are Getting Worse

The case for more government is strengthened even more if it can be shown that some of our current problems are worsening and/or that we face significant new threats to our quality of life. In the wake of the 9/11 attacks, few Americans disagreed with the idea that we needed major new government initiatives to deal with the growing menace of terrorism. Likewise, it also makes sense that we would need more government if we are facing other worsening problems. And in fact we are. Let's just consider a few of them.

- **Growing Economic Insecurity.** The effects of the deep recession continue to linger for many families. Long-term unemployment has become chronic and is at its highest rate since the Great Depression in the 1930s. Add to this the millions who can only find part-time work, and we have more than 40% of Americans who want a full-time job but cannot find one. A Rockefeller Foundation report found that over 20% of Americans have experienced a drop of more than 25% in income. The bottom line is that more and more families are facing economic disaster: out of a job, their savings gone, and nowhere to turn for help.

- **Unsafe Food.** The last decade saw increasing threats to our food system. Problems have ranged from e. coli infected beef and peanut butter to tainted spinach and botulism-laced chili sauce. Every year seems to bring new instances of Americans getting sick and dying from the food they eat.
- **Financial System Breakdown.** Deregulation and lax enforcement allowed the financial industry to operate with little public oversight. One disastrous result was the mortgage loan crisis that eventually wiped out billions of dollars of investors' assets and brought on a severe recession. The 2010 financial reform bill addressed some of these issues, but many crucial proposed regulations were blocked by the fierce lobbying of the financial industry. The bill left in place two of the main causes of the financial crisis: the ability of banks to engage in high-risk speculation, and the use of dangerous derivatives like the credit-default swaps that led to the collapse of AIG. The financial system is still at risk.
- **Health Care Crisis.** There is almost universal agreement that the U.S. health care system is increasingly in crisis. Tens of millions have been uninsured and costs have been spiraling out of control. Amazingly, the elderly must spend a larger proportion of their income on their medical expenses today than they did in the early 1960s before the passage of Medicare.[3] The 2010 health care reform bill did address the issue of lack of access for many Americans. But whether this bill will rein in the growth of health care costs is very doubtful. Many experts believe that new significant policy changes are necessary to address this cost issue.
- **Growing Environmental Problems.** A number of environmental problems are getting worse. The most obvious one is global warming, which will bring with it extensive coastal flooding, agriculture crop declines, rising danger from tropical diseases, increasingly severe weather, and so on. But there are also other environmental issues that are getting worse rather than better. Consider the plight of U.S. fisheries. Over-fishing has resulted in disastrous declines in fish stocks off New England, the Gulf of Mexico, and other areas. Increasing toxic waste from discarded computers and other electronics is another emerging problem.

- **Increasing Economic Inequality.** The rich are getting richer and the poor are getting poorer and the middle class is shrinking – all threatening to further divide American society along class lines. Income inequality is getting worse. Between 1979 and 2009, the incomes for the richest 5% of families grew by a whopping 73%; and incomes for the richest 20% by an impressive 49%. But the increases for the bottom 60% of families have been pitiful in comparison – their gains were a meager 7%. Today over half of all income in this country (50.3%) goes to the top fifth income class of families. The income going to the top 5% of richest families is actually more than the combined income of the bottom 40% – the 110 million Americans living on low and moderate incomes. The inequalities in wealth are even larger – with the top fifth richest families owning a staggering 84.7% of all the wealth of the country, the next 40% owning only 15.1%, and the poorest 40% owning less than 1%. Most other Western democracies have a much fairer distribution of income and wealth. In Sweden, for example, the poorest 40% own 32% of the wealth.
- **Crumbling Infrastructure.** Around the country, crucial infrastructure facilities – roads, bridges, sewers, etc. – are rapidly deteriorating. For example, 27.5% of the nation's bridges (162,000) are structurally deficient or functionally obsolete. In addition, the nation's 16,000 wastewater systems face enormous needs. Some sewer systems are 100 years old and many treatment facilities are past their recommended life expectancy. Currently, there is a $12 billion annual shortfall in funding for these infrastructure needs. Also, airport capacity increased only 1% from 1991 to 2001, yet air traffic increased 35% during that same period. The American Society of Civil Engineers argues that we must dramatically increase funding to solve these and other infrastructure problems – and it estimates that it will take at least $1.6 trillion to bring these facilities into an acceptable state.[4]
- **New Disease Threats.** A whole host of new and evolving diseases now threaten public health in the United States. They range from the Hantavirus to new drug-resistant strains of microorganisms. Globalization and tourism mean that new diseases are more easily finding their way into this country. The West Nile virus and eastern equine encephalitis have already arrived. The main concern now is that a more virulent and deadly form of swine-flu or bird-flu is going to eventually come to the United States, with potentially devastating results.

- **Cyber Security Threats.** Threats in cyberspace have risen dramatically in the last 15 years. Individuals are vulnerable to viruses, worms, financial scams, and identity theft. Embezzlement, fraud and other cyber crimes cost businesses billions of dollars a year. More importantly, key parts of the economic infrastructure are vulnerable to cyber attack, including the banking system, the telecommunications system, and the electricity grid. Cyber-attack tools are spreading rapidly worldwide and are being employed by foreign nationals and foreign intelligence services. Cyber warfare and cyber terrorism are very real threats to our national security.
- **Looming Retirement Crisis.** Social Security is in good shape at least for the foreseeable future. But the other two forms of support that retirees hope to rely on – private pensions and private savings – are in terrible shape for most people. Fewer and fewer companies are offering fixed benefit pension plans, and it is estimated that U.S. companies are underfunding current pension plans to the tune of $350 billion – a disaster waiting to happen. Stagnant wages have made it difficult for many workers to save any money for retirement: 36% of workers contribute nothing to their retirement and 43% have less than $10,000 saved for their "golden years." As a result, many Americans will be facing poverty – or at least a much lower standard of living – when they retire.
- **Deteriorating Public Education System.** Many local public school budgets are in crisis, with teachers being laid off and textbooks in short supply. There is a growing divide between the quality of public education offered in rich communities and that in poor communities. Due to either aging, outdated facilities, severe overcrowding, or new mandated class sizes, 75% of our nation's school buildings remain inadequate to meet the needs of school children. State colleges and universities — which produce three quarters of all degrees in the United States – are also in trouble. Class sizes are spiraling, and needed maintenance is being neglected. In addition, states have been raising their tuitions and cutting financial aid. A study by the National Center for Public Policy and Higher Education gave the public college and university systems in 43 states a grade of "F" for affordability.[5] This means that many low- and middle-income students simply cannot afford college anymore – a half million were turned away for lack of money in 2004 alone.

The existence of these and other growing problems clearly justifies the expansion of public sector efforts to deal with them. And increasingly, many Americans have realized that more government action is necessary in many of these areas. A 2010 poll found that when people look ahead 10 to 20 years, they say by 42% to 18% that the federal government will become more rather than less important in terms of improving the lives of the American people.

Can Markets Substitute for Government?

Of course, even if we have serious social, economic, and environmental issues facing us, this may not necessarily require more government. There might be better, non-governmental ways to solve these problems. Conservatives have long maintained that we would be better off relying on the market or on individual efforts, rather than government. Let's consider both of those claims.

First, can the market really solve most of these problems? There are several reasons to be skeptical of this claim. First, as was discussed in some detail in the chapter "Capitalism Requires Government," many of our country's current problems are in fact *caused* by our market-based economy. Free-market economies are incredibly productive, but they inevitably bring with them a whole host of social and economic troubles. Clearly issues like poverty and increasing economic inequality are directly traceable to how the market distributes income and wealth. Our looming retirement crisis is due in large part to the effort of businesses to increase profits by abandoning their traditional pension programs. And there is a good deal of evidence to indicate that our health care system is overly expensive in large part because we rely so much on the private sector for insurance. As these examples illustrate, the market is often the source of our problems, not the solution.

It is also clear that we cannot depend on markets to solve their own problems. Conservatives and libertarians are fond of arguing that markets are "self-correcting." If we would just leave them alone and not burden them with onerous regulations, they would correct their own problems. This is one of the core assumptions underlying the push for the deregulation of markets that has been a hallmark of the Republican Party. But in recent years, we have seen that this idea of self-correcting markets is often more myth than reality.

A good example of how markets do not fix their own problems is the food supply system. In the last decade, we have seen one food safety problem after another, including contaminated spinach, E. coli infected beef, and salmonella tainted peanut butter. These problems have sickened tens of thousands of Americans and in some cases have led to death. Many food businesses have little incentive to adopt costly safety standards, in part because they know that in many cases it is difficult to trace the sources of food-borne illnesses. The food industry has claimed that it can rely on private food inspectors, but these auditors are hired by the very companies they inspect and have often failed to point out problems in facilities. In the case of peanut butter, the offending plant had gaping holes in the roof and walls, was infested with rats and roaches, and had employees washing mops in the same sinks as peanut butter production equipment. And yet the private inspector reported that "The overall food safety level of this facility was considered to be: SUPERIOR." After the salmonella outbreak was made public, that inspector told a food safety expert: "I never thought that this bacteria would survive in the peanut butter type environment. What the heck is going on?"

Another classic example of markets failing to correct themselves is the mortgage loan fiasco and the resulting economic crisis. For years conservative had been working hard to de-regulate the financial industry. They asserted that regulations did more harm than good. In 2006, Bush Treasury Secretary Henry Paulson argued that "the solutions to our nation's problems are not always found in Washington." And he maintained that one of the two main threats to financial markets was "excessive regulation."

Other conservatives argued that any regulation of financial markets should be "voluntary." As traditional financial regulations were being stripped away, right-wing analysts insisted that Wall Street could be relied on to police itself and thus protect the public interest. We now know that this was wishful thinking. Even Bush's head of the Securities and Exchange Commission, Christopher Cox, had to admit in the fall of 2008 that "The last six months have made it abundantly clear that voluntary regulation does not work."[6]

These are just two examples of why we can't rely on markets and business to solve society's problems. There are plenty more. Past experience has shown that corporations will not always provide safe working conditions or livable wages, that private schools cannot ensure that all our children get a decent education, that companies will not clean up their pollution on their own, and that "let the buyer beware" is not going to protect us from dangerous products. No – if we want to address these kinds of problems, there is really no alternative to public sector programs.

Can Individual Efforts Substitute for Government?

The other alternative that conservatives offer to more government is more effort on the part of individuals. They argue that we need to empower individuals to take responsibility for their own problems, and thus reduce their dependency on government. This was the principle behind a major set of Republican initiatives that they called the "ownership society." Policies like 401(k) retirement plans, individual health savings accounts, privatized Social Security, and private education were seen as ways to allow people to take control of their own fates and solve their own problems. As a leading libertarian intellectual, David Boaz, has explained it:

> An ownership society values responsibility, liberty, and property. Individuals are empowered by freeing them from dependence on government handouts and making them owners instead, in control of their own lives and destinies. In the ownership society, patients control their own health care, parents control their own children's education, and workers control their retirement savings.[7]

This may sound good to some people, but the record of these kinds of programs does not inspire much confidence. Consider, for example, how 401(k) plans have helped to solve the retirement crisis. The 401(k) option has been around for decades and so it is a good test for this approach to retirement security. Unfortunately, it is flunking that test. On the one hand, these plans *have* been a boon for businesses. They have been able to greatly reduce the money they spend on retirement for their employees. They no longer have to invest in fixed benefit pension plans. Moreover, most donations to these 401(k) accounts come from the workers themselves. Mutual funds firms have also benefited from these accounts as well. But most workers don't seem to be getting much security from them. First, only half of the American workforce even has access to these accounts, and only 40% of those feel that they can afford to contribute to one. Also, the vast bulk of the money contributed to these plans comes from already well-off employees – not your average worker. The myth is that the average worker now has tens of thousands of dollars in these funds ready to provide for a comfortable retirement. But in reality, the median amount of funds for these account holders – what's most typical – is a mere $13,000.[8]

As Jacob Hacker has explained, despite the growth in the total funds in these accounts – especially during the 1990s stock market boom – most workers are actually worse off in terms of their retirement prospects than they were before.

> To be sure, defined-contribution accounts [401(k)s] grew handsomely during this period, especially in the 1990s. Yet, at the same time, median defined-benefit holdings [pensions] declined as employers stopped offering defined-benefit programs. So too did expected Social Security benefits, thanks to the cutbacks in Social Security passed in 1983. When all the gains and losses are added up, the median family approaching retirement – that is the family exactly in the middle of the retirement wealth distribution – ended the 1990s with 11 percent *less* in retirement wealth than the median family had in 1983.[9]

Today, of course, the situation for 401(k) accounts is even worse. In the stock market collapse that followed the mortgage loan crisis, workers lost billions of dollars in these accounts. Many people had to put off retirement. Those already retired were threatened with poverty and many were forced to try to find work again. And imagine how much more dire this situation would be if the Republicans had had their way and we had privatized Social Security and allowed people to invest this money in the stock market.

Clearly, as companies rapidly retreat from providing people with reliable retirement plans, individual efforts, like 401(k) accounts, are not going to be able to provide the kind of economic security that most people need as they grow old.

Health Savings Accounts (HSAs), another much vaunted approach being push by the Right, are also doing little to help with the ever growing problems of health care in the United States. In this approach, individuals buy health insurance plans with very high deductibles – such as $2,000 and then make up the difference in money they save in their own HSAs. But despite a big push by Republican lawmakers and corporations, polls show that most people don't like this approach and would rather have regular, low-deductible health insurance. These plans mostly appeal to the wealthy (who can afford high out of pocket expenses) or the young and healthy (who don't need much care). However, draining these people out of the traditional health insurance programs means that premiums will have to go up for the less well-off and the less healthy people in this insurance pool. In addition, when average Americans are forced into these plans, they can often run into trouble. Studies have shown that HSA users are much more likely than those with traditional medical coverage to have trouble paying their medical bills. They are also much more likely to avoid or postpone treatment for serious medical problems because of the cost.[10]

Shifting Risks from Society to Individuals

But there is a deeper problem with the individualistic approach – one that goes beyond the inadequacies of these particular programs. The whole "ownership society" approach is actually a way of shifting economic risks from businesses and government on to the backs of individuals. It makes us responsible for dealing with all the significant financial risks that we face in an advanced capitalist society – getting sick, retiring, becoming disabled, losing our job, and so on. But in fact, individuals are usually the least able to deal with these risks – and that is why we have used government to create all sorts of "social insurance" programs (like Social Security and Medicare) to spread these risks among society as a whole and create more economic security for all of us.

Jacob Hacker has written an entire book about this topic, called *The Great Risk Shift.* In it, he gives an eloquent description of why we originally embraced the government-based, "social insurance" approach back in the 20th century. He explains the basic political and economic insights that led to the creation of Social Security and other collective efforts to deal with common risks:

> Social insurance transformed individual misfortunes into common problems. It made the inevitable dislocations of capitalist society into risks that could be managed and distributed, rather than blows of fate that could only be feared and suffered. The 'insurance" in social insurance came from the power of aggregation: Risks that could devastate an individual or community could be managed if they were spread across many individuals and many communities. The "social" in social insurance came from the principle of shared fate, the reassurance that "we are all in this together." All insurance pools risks. Only social insurance pools risks on terms that enable the poor as well as the rich, the aged as well as the young, the ill as well as the healthy to afford protection. The crafters of the Social Security Act believed that insurance had to be available and within the means of those who needed insurance most. At the heart of this belief was a simple conviction: broadly distributed threats to economic well-being – sickness, injury, disability, unemployment, penurious old age – were not the

> responsibility of individuals alone. They were a widespread and often unavoidable feature of an interdependent industrial society. And because they were, the cost of these risks should be distributed widely across the citizenry, not concentrated on those unlucky enough to experience them – a goal made possible by the unique power of government to compel participation and require contributions. Government could pool the risks of millions of citizens. It could guarantee that even workers of limited means are able to afford basic protections.[11]

As Hacker makes clear, social insurance programs are one of the greatest inventions of modern democratic government and they have gone a long ways toward making all of our lives much more secure. We could be doing even more with social insurance programs, as they have done in Europe, but it is this proven approach that has been directly under attack by conservatives. They want us to move from a "we are all in this together" society to a "you are on your own" society. But this individualistic, anti-government approach cannot provide the kind of economic security that most Americans need and want.

Public Support for More Government

Many Americans are aware of the serious problems we face as a country and say they want more government involvement to help solve them. For example, over 60% of Americans say that they want the government to spend more on education and health, 69% favor more generous government aid to the poor, 77% say the government should do all it takes to protect the environment, and 83% favor raising the federal minimum wage. And with numbers like these, this is clearly not just liberals talking. There have to be a lot of moderates and even conservatives that recognize the need for more government in these areas. In fact, a 2010 poll by the Center for American Progress found that 40% of conservatives and libertarians support a *larger* federal government role in areas like improving public schools, reducing poverty, and developing new energy sources.[12]

Only More Government Will Do

To sum up, there is a great deal of evidence that strongly suggests that Americans would be better off with more – not less – government. We know from the experience of other advanced democracies that our government could be doing more to address many of the problems we face as a society. We also know that some of these problems are getting worse, and other additional serious problems are emerging. Finally, it is clear that non-governmental approaches – markets and individuals efforts – are in many cases not sufficient to deal with all of these problems.

Of course all of this does not tell us exactly what new kinds of public efforts are needed. We still need to carefully analyze proposed policies and programs to figure out which ones will be most effective in addressing these social, economic, and environmental problems. And there is also the difficult question of deciding how much we can afford to spend to alleviate these problems. As the chapter on the deficits will make clear, we can afford to spend a lot more on these problems than conservatives say we can. But this still leaves the question of how much we *want* to spend. In any case, one thing that we do know for sure at this point is that if the government does nothing more, or actually does less, our quality of life is going to suffer. In today's world, we need a well-funded public sector that will do more to reduce the risks we face and to improve the lives of all Americans.

---

1. Derek Bok, *The State of the Nation* (Cambridge, MA: Harvard University Press, 1996) p. 387.
2. Timothy M. Smeeding, Lee Rainwater, and Gary Burtless, "Luxembourg Income Study working Paper No. 244: United States Poverty in a Cross-National Context," (Differdange, Luxembourg, Luxembourg Income Study, 2000).
3. Jacob S. Hacker, "Privatizing Risk without Privatizing the Welfare State: The Hidden Politics of Social Policy Retrenchment in the United States," *American Political Science Review*, Vol. 98, No.2, May 2004, p. 253.
4. American Society of Civil Engineers, "Report Card for America's Infrastructure: 2003 Progress Report," http://www.asce.org/reportcard/index.cfm
5. National Center for Public Policy and Higher Education, "Measuring Up 2006: The National Report Card on Higher Education. http://measuringup.highereducation.org.
6. The Paulson and the Cox quotes are from OBM Watch, *The Bush Legacy: An Assault on Public Protections*, http://www.ombwatch.org/node/3877
7. David Boaz, "Ownership Society Defined." http://www.cato.org/special/ownership_society/boaz.html

8. Jacob Hacker, *The Great Risk Shift* (Oxford: Oxford University Press, 2006) p. 122.
9. Ibid.
10. Think Progress, "Health Savings Accounts Fail to Provide Savings or Address Costs." http://thinkprogress.org/2006/01/31/sotu-health-savings-accounts-fail-to-provide-savings-or-address-costs/
11. Hacker, *The Great Risk Shift*, pp. 41-42.
12. Guy Molyneux and Ruy Teixeira, with John Whaley, "Better, Not Smaller: What Americans Want from their Federal Government," July 2010. http://www.americanprogress.org/issues/2010/07/what_americans_want.html

PART II

THE WAR ON GOVERNMENT

CHAPTER 12

The Anti-Government Campaign

The first part of this book described how the American people have been using government to effectively promote the public interest. It showed how government social and regulatory programs are by and large working well and have vastly improved the lives of everyone in our society. This part of the book will chronicle the political effort to tear much of this down. Make no mistake – there is a well organized and well funded political campaign to demonize government and shrink it dramatically. And if it succeeds, all Americans will have to pay the price. This chapter describes how this anti-government movement has grown and why it has become so powerful.

The Goal: To Drown Government in the Bathtub

If there is one person who for many years has exemplified this anti-government campaign it has been Grover Norquist who heads up Americans for Tax Reform. He is one of the most powerful conservative figures in Washington D.C. and he is a leading advocate of slashing taxes and dismantling government programs. Every week he hosts a breakfast meeting at his organization's headquarters on L Street in Washington. This meeting serves as one of the informal nerve centers for the anti-government campaign in the United States. The attendees of the invitation-only affair normally include members of Congress, corporate lobbyists, Republican National Committee representatives, the House and Senate leadership staff of the GOP, conservative media editors and reporters, right-wing think-tank intellectuals, and prominent grassroots activists. The topics of discussion vary from week to week, but the general theme is the same: how to wage war on the government. When the Republicans are in power, they discuss what tax cuts to promote and which regulations to get rid of. When the Democrats are in power, they strategize about what new programs must be blocked and how best to portray liberals and their policies as dangerous and anti-American. And Norquist has always made it clear what the ultimate aim of all of this activity is: "My goal is to cut government in half in twenty-five years, to get it down to the size where we can drown it in the bathtub."[1]

This goal of a radically reduced government is not simply the dream of small-state ideologues within the Beltway in Washington D.C. Consider the 2008 platform of the Republican Party in Texas. It called for the elimination of every federal agency not mentioned in the original constitution – including the Environmental Protection Agency, and the Departments of Energy, Housing and Urban Development, Health and Human Services, Education, Commerce and Labor. Programs like Social Security and policies like the minimum wage would also be abolished. And Texas Republicans believe that not only should taxes never be increased, but that most current taxes should be abolished, including income taxes, inheritance taxes, capital gains, corporate income taxes, payroll taxes, and property taxes.[2] In short, this GOP platform is a blueprint for how to cripple the federal government.

Some people had hoped that the election of President Obama would signal a reduction in the relentless government bashing that has come from the political right. But the President's attempt to create new public sector programs actually prompted conservatives to dramatically escalate their attacks on government. In fact, the anti-government rhetoric quickly reached near hysterical levels. Fox News commentators like Glenn Beck repeatedly accused the President of being a "closet communist" and warned of the coming of a "totalitarian state." For the conservative political activist Alan Keys, Obama's policy initiatives showed that he was clearly a "radical communist." And the right-wing media pundit, Michael Savage, described the Obama administration as a "fascist dictatorship."

The emergence of the Tea Party movement was another manifestation of this virulent backlash against government. This grassroots effort has sought to whip up public anger and resentment and channel it directly at "big government." In the 2010 elections, several Tea Party candidates for Congress maintained that the federal government had become so overwhelmingly repressive that armed resistance was not out of the question. The Republican candidate for the Senate in Alaska serious argued that many major government programs – ranging from Social Security to Medicare to unemployment compensation – were unconstitutional and should be abolished.

When the Republicans took over the House of Representatives after the 2010 elections, the anti-government movement went on the offensive again. Virtually all congressional Republicans signed Norquist's radical No New Taxes Pledge, promising never to raise taxes under any circumstances. In 2011, Republican Representative Paul Ryan introduced a GOP budget plan that proposed to savagely cut the federal budget by $4.5 trillion dollars and to effectively end Medicare and Medicaid as we know it. Dramatically shrinking the size of the federal government is once again on the national agenda.

How did we reach the point where this kind of extreme hatred for government has became part of mainstream politics in this country? Where did this anti-government movement come from?

The Evolution of the Modern Anti-Government Movement in America

To understand this intense hostility toward government we need to understand its history. The roots of the modern anti-government movement can be traced to the 1940s and 50s. It was largely a reaction to Franklin Delano Roosevelt's New Deal, which introduced many of the policies and programs that now define the modern state: federal mechanisms to manage the economy, large social programs like Social Security, the increased regulation of business, and progressive taxation. These liberal policies created a conservative counter-reaction which condemned FDR's programs as "creeping socialism." Right-wing critics called for a return to the laissez-faire days of the 1920s, when businesses and financial institutions were largely unregulated, taxes were low, and people were free to deal with social and economic problems on their own.

However, the New Deal programs proved widely popular among most Americans and few had any real interest in returning to the "bad old days" of the 1920s and 30s. This meant that during the 1940s and 50s, the anti-government movement remained small and largely intellectual – kept alive by a handful of conservative writers. In 1953, for instance, Russell Kirk published *The Conservative Mind*, still considered a seminal work in right-wing anti-state ideology. In it he condemned federally sponsored school lunch programs as a "vehicle for totalitarianism," and labeled Social Security as a form of "remorseless collectivism." Another writer, Ayn Rand, was also promoting a radically pro-individual/anti-government vision of society in her novels *The Fountainhead* and *Atlas Shrugged.*

In 1955, William F. Buckley founded *The National Review*, widely considered to be the first serious intellectual journal of conservatism in the U.S. Buckley and his colleagues were heavily influenced by libertarianism – a radical anti-state ideology that had few adherents among the public, but was attractive to conservatives fighting an uphill battle against growing government. Libertarianism maintains that individual freedom is the highest political value and that virtually all government activity inevitably impinges on that freedom.[3] In this view, the only legitimate purposes of government are to maintain order and protect individual rights, particularly property rights. Governments should not run schools, regulate business, or establish any social welfare programs. Government funding of armies, police, and the courts are considered necessary evils – all other government activities are just evil.

In the 1950s, most mainstream Republican politicians, like President Eisenhower, wanted nothing to do with the libertarian-tinged anti-state ideology of Buckley and his cohort. They believed that they had little choice but to accept New Deal economics and social programs – these were simply a given of modern government. Other leading Republicans in the 1960s and 70s, like Nelson Rockefeller, Richard Nixon and Gerald Ford, also accepted many of the basic tenets of New Deal liberalism. They were political moderates who at times actively supported the expansion of government programs and responsibilities.

The one exception to this trend was Barry Goldwater, who ran for president on the Republican ticket in 1964. Among other controversial stands, Goldwater made his anti-government hostility perfectly clear. He often stated that his primary goal was not to improve government, but to shrink it. As he put it at the time:

> I have little interest in streamlining government or in making it more efficient, for I mean to reduce its size. I do not undertake to promote welfare, for I propose to extend freedom. My aim is not to pass laws, but to repeal them. It is not to inaugurate new programs, but to cancel old ones that do violence to the Constitution or that have failed their purpose, or that impose on the people an unwarranted financial burden.

Goldwater's views and policies proved wildly unpopular among voters and he lost in a landslide, garnering only 36% of the vote. But even though he lost this political battle, he was to eventually win his political campaign to put anti-government ideology at the center of the Republican Party. Young Goldwater supporters had infiltrated many parts of the party in their successful attempt to get him the nomination.

Many stayed on and continued to push his political agenda and to move the party toward more of an explicit minimal government stance.

Throughout the 1970s, anti-government activists in the Republican Party were able to take advantage of a number of developments that contributed to growing public disenchantment with government, such as the failure of the Vietnam War and the Watergate scandal. Conservatives also played on public resentments, such as the perception by some whites that government policies like civil rights and affirmative action unfairly favored minorities. Finally, Republicans also benefited from increasing public worries about economic insecurity. They offered the appealing argument that it was government that was causing the stagnant economy and rampant inflation of the late 1970s, and that all we needed to do to solve these problems was to reduce government, curtail business regulation, and unleash the free market.

Corporations also played crucial role in the growing power of the anti-government movement in this era. In the 1960s and early 1970s, they were caught off guard by citizen activism and suffered a series of embarrassing policy defeats. Congress passed major legislation to increase environmental protection, workplace safety regulations, and consumer protection – all of which business strongly opposed. Reeling from these political losses, business leaders began meeting in the mid-seventies to plot their political counter-offensive. Their main weapon was money and they started to funnel huge amounts of it into a variety of political efforts. They put significant funds into corporate political action committees, the number of which grew from under 300 in 1973 to over 1,200 by the 1980s. Business PAC spending increased 500% between the late 1970s and late 1980s. This money greatly boosted the prospects of pro-business and anti-government candidates. Corporations also increased their lobbying presence in Washington and began pushing hard for deregulation and smaller government. The number of firms with registered lobbyists skyrocketed from 175 in 1971 to almost 2,500 by 1982. Another tactic was for corporations to pour tens of millions of dollars into "advocacy advertising" in an effort to sell Americans on the virtues of business and the evils of big government. Firms also became adept at organizing their employees, shareholders, and suppliers to generate "grassroots" letter writing campaigns (what some have called "Astroturf campaigns") to pressure Congress.

In 1980, Ronald Reagan rode to victory thanks to public discontent and a Republican party awash in corporate funds. He was the first modern Republican president to run on an openly anti-government platform. And he made his "government is bad" perspective clear in a famous sentence he uttered during his first inaugural speech: "Government isn't the solution; it is the problem." In the end, Reagan had very little real success implementing his anti-government agenda. He did succeed in pushing through several large tax cuts, but his efforts to cut back on many federal programs were routinely defeated by a Democratic Congress.

What Reagan did achieve was to put minimal-government sentiments at the center of mainstream Republican ideology. Since the 1980s, virtually every Republican candidate (and even many Democratic ones) has made running against government a major part of his or her campaign. And once in office, conservatives have spent a lot of their energy demonizing and denigrating government. Being anti-government – sometimes radically so – has simply become part of what it means to be a Republican.

The 1980s also saw the growing dominance of right-wing, anti-government think tanks in Washington. Fueled by hundreds of millions of dollars from conservative philanthropists and the business community (more on this later), these libertarian and conservative think tanks grew to be much larger and influential than their liberal counterparts. Organizations like the Heritage Foundation, the American Enterprise Institute, and the Cato Institute began to provide much of the intellectual ammunition used in the war on government. These idea factories produced hundreds of books, reports, articles, news releases, op-ed pieces and editorials making the case for cutting taxes, curbing spending, and rolling back regulations. They also produced enormous policy handbooks that were used by conservative administrations as a detailed guide to anti-government initiatives. The *Washington Post* described Cato's *Handbook on Policy* as "a soups to nuts agenda to reduce spending, kill federal programs, terminate whole agencies and dramatically restrict the power of the federal government." This handbook became especially influential during the administration of George W. Bush.

The 1990s saw the emergence of a crucial new element in the political offensive against government: the increasing power and presence of conservative pundits in the media. First came the explosive growth of conservative talk radio. This was made possible when, in 1987, the Federal Communications Commission was ordered by President Reagan to abolish the Fairness Doctrine. This policy had required stations to cover public issues in a balanced way that included contrasting views. Once that was out of the way, right-wing radio hosts like Rush Limbaugh and Sean Hannity could spend hours a day broadcasting one-sided tirades against big government and liberal politicians. By the turn of the century, these anti-government programs became the most popular talk shows on the air, with millions of listeners. Even today, these shows occupy 11 of the top 11 spots in talk radio in the United States.

Then, in 1996, Rupert Murdoch and Roger Ailes, a former Republican Party strategist, started Fox News with the explicit intention of making it a vehicle for spreading conservative ideas. It quickly became the 24/7 anti-government channel. The right-wing commentators on Fox dispensed misinformation about government programs and spread rumors about government malfeasance. They regularly resorted to malicious slurs against government officials, calling them "idiots," "Nazis," "communists," "fascists," and "Satanists." Ever since then, they have played a crucial role in the anti-government movement with their continuous efforts to defame, denigrate, and delegitimize government. It is hard to underestimate how instrumental media outlets like Fox News and conservative talk radio have been in encouraging many Americans to distrust, fear, and even hate government.

The anti-government movement received another big boost when the Republicans took over Congress after the 1994 elections. A central part of the "Republican Revolution" was an immense hostility toward many established government programs – from welfare, to business regulation, to environmental protection. One Republican leader, House Majority Leader Dick Armey, said that one of his political ambitions was "reduce the federal government by half." He even had a hit list of dozens of agencies to be axed, and the "first to go must be the Department of Education, which produces nothing but puffed up rhetoric, while squandering billions of dollars annually."[4]

But again, the Republicans were not successful in pulling off this anti-government revolution. President Clinton was successful in blocking most of their efforts to cut back on government programs. And these conservatives also found that they were out of step with public opinion. While most Americans liked the ideas of tax cuts, they did not like the idea of cutting back on programs that they valued – like education, health care, etc. There was a particularly strong public backlash against the Republican effort to roll back environmental regulations. Any truly successful effort to implement an anti-government agenda on the federal level would have to wait until the Republicans controlled both Congress and the White House.

The Bush Attack on Government

When George W. Bush was elected in 2000, the conservatives were finally in a position to effectively promote their anti-state ideology. Of course, they were not hostile to all parts of government. They were happy to spend hundreds of billions of dollars a year on defense programs and foreign wars. And many were quick to endorse the unprecedented expansions of George W. Bush's presidential powers – all in the name of fighting terrorism.

When Bush and his fellow conservatives talked about reducing government, what they were targeting were the three main pillars of the modern democratic state: social programs, regulation of business, and the taxes needed to support these two efforts. For them, "too much government" really meant too many social programs, too much regulation, and too much taxation. And "reducing government" meant starving social programs, rolling back regulations, and cutting taxes. All three of these were important goals during the eight years of the Bush administration.

Cutting taxes was one of the most successful Bush administration attacks on government. Taxes were seen as the life blood of government; so if taxes could be reduced, then it would become more and more difficult to maintain funding for government programs. George W. Bush pushed through a number of enormous tax cuts during his administration. These tax cuts cost the federal government over two trillion dollars in lost revenue from 2001 to 2010 alone.[5] This helped to create huge deficits and a growing national debt – all of which are now used by conservatives to argue that we can't afford any new government programs. (For more on this issue, see the chapter "The Deficit Scare: Myth vs. Reality.")

President Bush also took aim at social programs during his tenure in office. He repeatedly targeted education, housing, job training, community development, Medicaid, food stamps, and children's services for budget cuts. Probably most emblematic of his hostility to social programs was his push to partially privatize Social Security. As *The New York Times* columnist Paul Krugman pointed out at the time, administration officials made it clear that they were not as interested in "saving" Social Security as they were in weakening it and striking a blow against government and social programs in general. One high placed Bush White House official argued that the ultimate goal of overhauling Social Security was to cut benefits and to "help the nation move away from dependency on government."[6] And as another conservative ideologue explained, the real agenda was to attack the whole notion of government social welfare spending: "Social Security is the soft underbelly of the welfare state. If you can jab your spear through that, you can undermine the whole welfare state."[7] (For more on Bush's tax cuts and attacks on social programs, see the chapter "Starving the Beast.")

During the Bush years, conservatives also made progress in their quest to "deregulate" American society. They were not only trying to roll back regulations on business, they were also busy handing over federal regulatory agencies to the special interests they were supposed to be regulating. Under Bush, the United States Department of Agriculture official in charge of regulating the meat packing industry previously worked for a group that lobbied for the National Cattleman's Beef Association. Bush also named a mining industry executive to head the Mine Safety and Health Administration, and a lawyer who specialized in representing corporations seeking to block environmental regulations to be a top administrator in the Environmental Protection Agency. Officials who were supposed to be protecting workers, consumers, investors and the environment spent much of their time quietly dismantling existing regulations, delaying the development of new ones, and downplaying enforcement efforts. (For more on Bush's anti-regulatory efforts, see the chapter "Stealth Deregulation: The Untold Story.")

The Political Appeal of Anti-government Ideas

To understand the growth and influence of the anti-government movement in the United States, you also need to understand the powerful political appeal of government bashing. The idea that "government is bad" serves two important political functions for conservatives: (1) it provides a convenient scapegoat for many people's problems, and (2) it serves as a common complaint to unite the disparate parts of the right-wing coalition. Let's look at each of these things in turn.

Blaming government for virtually all of society's problems can be very alluring. As the anxieties and insecurities of average Americans mount, the anti-government movement offers them a simple – and simplistic – explanation for who is at fault. Is the economy stagnant? It is because of government over-regulation of business. Are you having trouble paying your bills or sending your children to college on your current wages? It is because government takes so much of your salary in taxes. You didn't get that job or that promotion? It is probably the fault of government promoted affirmative action programs. Worried about the moral decay of society? Blame government for taking prayer and God out of schools. Don't have enough money for retirement? It's the fault of government for not letting you invest your Social Security money in the stock market. Blaming government is a convenient, one-size fits-all explanation that can be stretched to fit just about every problem in this country.

Scapegoating government also has the advantage of not requiring a great deal of analysis to formulate solutions to our complex societal problems. All we have to do is reduce government. If big government is the cause of our problems, then obviously small government is the solution.

Using the government as a scapegoat also appeals to many conservatives because it allows them to ignore the real – and more disturbing – causes of some of our problems. For example, die-hard government bashers have strained to blame the disastrous mortgage crisis and financial meltdown of 2008-2009 on bad government policies. This means they don't have to acknowledge the numerous questionable practices of the banking and financial sectors that actually precipitated this crisis, and they can thus maintain their cherished illusion that unregulated markets are always good for society. (For more on how and why conservatives scapegoat government, see the chapter "Why the Government Becomes the Scapegoat.")

Government-Hating as Political Glue

Disdain for government also serves as much of the ideological glue that holds the Republican electoral coalition together. The groups that make up this coalition are actually quite diverse – well-off suburbanites, gun owners, libertarians, fundamentalist Christians, the wealthy, small farmers, business interests, fiscal conservatives, and anti-tax activists – and they often have very different political priorities. Such a coalition is always in danger of falling apart. Much of what holds them together is their common dislike for government. So while they are all promoting somewhat different issues – the NRA wants the freedom to own guns, business wants less regulation, fundamentalists want prayer in school – what they do share is a common conviction that government often works against their interests and that they would be better off with less of it. As Grover Norquist has explained, this resentment is what binds these different groups into what he has called the "Leave Us Alone Coalition." "The issue that brings people to politics is what they want from government. All our people want to be left alone by government. To be in this coalition, you only need to have your foot in the circle on this one issue."[8]

Who Funds the Anti-Government Campaign?

Another key reason that the anti-government movement has become so powerful in the United States is that it has been able to massively outspend pro-government groups. Huge amounts of money –

amounting to billions of dollars – have fueled virtually every part of this political campaign. For example, conservative anti-government think tanks have a collective budget four times larger than their liberal counterparts.[8] Hardly surprising since it is estimated that conservative donors have funneled over $1 billion into the top-twenty right-wing think tanks during the last several decades.[9]

So where does all this money come from? Certainly not from the pockets of average Americans. Some minimal-government groups, like the NRA, receive most of their funding from members' donations. But much of the billions of dollars that have been donated to various parts of the anti-government movement have come from super-wealthy right-wing philanthropists and the foundations they have set up. For example, many of the major conservative and anti-government think tanks were created, virtually single-handedly, by grants from these philanthropists and their foundations. Joseph Coors initially bankrolled the Heritage Foundation in the 1970s. Then, between 1985 and 2003, right-wing foundations provided Heritage with over $57,000,000. The bulk of the Heritage's yearly income still comes from foundations and wealthy individuals – 72% – with the rest coming from corporate donations, return on investments, and sales of materials.[10]

These right-wing foundations donate money to many different parts of the anti-government coalition, funneling millions not only to think tanks, but also to academic institutions, lobbying groups, conservative media outlets, and grassroots organizations.[11] The major givers include the Sarah Scaife Foundation, the Lynde and Harry Bradley Foundation, the John M. Olin Foundation, the Shelby Cullom Davis Foundation, and the Richard and Helen DeVos Foundation. The spending pattern of the ultraconservative Koch family is typical. They own Koch Industries, the second largest privately owned company in the United States, with yearly revenues of $40 billion. Charles Koch founded the libertarian Cato Institute. His brother David ran as the Libertarian candidate for president in 1980 and founded Citizens for a Sound Economy, another conservative think tank. They also direct three family foundations, which have made substantial donations to both of these think tanks – more than $12 million to each one between 1985 and 2002. Other think tanks receiving substantial Koch family support include the Heritage Foundation, the Hudson Institute, and the Heartland Institute. David Koch also founded Americans for Prosperity, an advocacy group that organized over 300 rallies against health care reform and has funded over 80 events targeting global warming legislation. Considerable Koch family money also goes to the Reason

Foundation, publisher of the libertarian *Reason* magazine, and to various conservative and libertarian legal organizations, including the Federalist society and Institute for Justice. The Koch foundations have funneled huge sums into academia to support conservative scholars and programs. The primary beneficiary has been George Mason University, which has received over $23 million between 1985 and 2002, including a $10 million grant to help set up the James M. Buchanan Center for the Study of Political Economy.[12]

Finally, money from the Koch brothers has also been instrumental in funding the Tea Party movement and its electoral successes in 2010. Writing in her *New Yorker* profile of the Koch family, Jane Mayer described their influence this way:

> The anti-government fervor infusing the 2010 elections represents a political triumph for the Kochs. By giving money to "educate," fund, and organize Tea Party protesters, they have helped turn their private agenda into a mass movement. Bruce Bartlett, a conservative economist and a historian, who once worked at the National Center for Policy Analysis, a Dallas-based think tank that the Kochs fund, said, "The problem with the whole libertarian movement is that it's been all chiefs and no Indians. There haven't been any actual people, like voters, who give a crap about it. So the problem for the Kochs has been trying to create a movement." With the emergence of the Tea Party, he said, "everyone suddenly sees that for the first time there are Indians out there—people who can provide real ideological power." The Kochs, he said, are "trying to shape and control and channel the populist uprising into their own policies."[13]

The Role of Big Business

The other main funder of the anti-government campaign is big business. But its motivations differ substantially from that of many philanthropists. While the Koch family is clearly opposed to government as a matter of deep political principle, business is not. The opposition of corporations to government is based almost entirely on economic selfishness – they are concerned about their own bottom line. Their lack of principle is obvious in their inconsistency – if not to say hypocrisy – when it comes to opposing government programs. The business community is adamant about opposing taxes or regulations that cut into their profits, but it is more than willing to take government subsidies and other forms of "corporate welfare." And many businesses are not opposed to government interference in free markets as long as they themselves benefit. Their selective opposition to government is thus a matter of self-interest, not ideology.

As mentioned earlier, business began funneling large amounts of money into anti-government efforts as far back as the late 1970s and has long played a crucial role in the growth of this movement. For example, hundreds of millions have been invested in anti-government think tanks and corporations now play a major role in governing many of these organizations. Today, for instance, most of the board of directors of the American Enterprise Institute are CEOs of major companies, including American Express, ExxonMobil, Motorola, State Farm Insurance and Dow Chemicals.

Business has also ramped up its incredibly powerful lobbying machinery to support various anti-government efforts in Congress. Corporations and industry trade groups far outnumber all the other lobbies in Washington put together, and these well-heeled organizations are also able to employ more lobbyists and better-paid lobbyists than anyone else. Corporations lobby on a wider variety of anti-government measures than any other conservative interest group. They not only pressure lawmakers to lower corporate taxes, they also strongly oppose environmental and consumer protection regulations. They work against pro-labor policies like the minimum wage and workplace safety rules. They even push for cutbacks in social programs like welfare and unemployment insurance because these give workers a temporary alternative to working, and thus increase their bargaining power with employers. No other lobby matches the business community in either its resources or its wide-ranging policy agenda.

Corporations also funnel money to various other "advocacy" groups that promote their anti-state agenda of cutting taxes and reducing regulations. For example, Grover Norquist's Americans for Tax Reform tries to portray itself as a grassroots organization, but it really relies on business to survive. A mere forty corporate donors supply fully a third of the budget for Norquist's organization. Or consider another advocacy group, Citizens for Sensible Control of Acid Rain, one of the most active lobbies working against air pollution regulations in the 1980s and 1990s. In fact, this group had no citizen members at all and was entirely funded by the utility and coal industries.

Business also invests heavily in anti-government politicians, mostly in the form of campaign contributions that help these candidates win office. One conduit for this money is corporate political action committees, where their donations have far outpaced the spending of any other interest group. In the 2008 election cycle, for instance, environmental PACs donated $813,000 to Congressional candidates. But donations from just four industries likely to oppose environmental regulations (oil and gas, chemicals, forest products, and mining) exceeded $16 million – twenty times that of the environmental groups.[14] And none of this takes into account the Supreme Court's 2010 ruling in the *Citizen's United* that has now opened the floodgates to virtually unlimited corporate spending in elections.

And we need to also count the large individual donations given to campaigns by business owners, executives, and managers. We like to think of individual campaign donations as representing a broad cross-section of Americans, but this is not true. Close to eighty per cent of the billions given in individual donations for federal elections come from big donors – donors who make up only 0.2% of the population, and four out five of whom earn more than $100,000.[15] Needless to say, most of these well-off donors are likely to have strong corporate connections, to be conservative, and to support an anti-government agenda.

In short, the business establishment has not only been the chief pressure group in the anti-government movement, it has also served as its cash cow. For the past 30 years, it has been a generous and dependable source of financial support for the attack on government. It is not an exaggeration to say that the anti-government movement would not be as influential as it is today in American politics without the constant and massive infusions of money that it has received from corporations and business owners.

Government Bashing as a Political Smokescreen for Elite Interests

The role that business and wealthy philanthropists have played in providing the financial life blood of the anti-government campaign betrays its elitist underpinnings. Despite the presence of some grassroots elements like the Tea Party in this political movement, it has been largely created and supported by rich individuals and organizations, largely for their own interests. Irrespective of its populist rhetoric, this movement is clearly working to promote the agenda of some of the most powerful and moneyed interests in American society.

In fact, one of the main reasons the anti-government crusade is so popular among well-to-do interests is because it provides them with a smokescreen that they can use to obscure their real political goals. For example, drug companies and the health insurance industry have constantly exploited people's misgivings about big government as a way to promote their own economic self-interest in maintaining private control over the health system. In debates about health care reform, these businesses and their conservative allies have constantly raised the specter of "government bureaucrats controlling your health care decisions" as a way of scaring people away from reform plans that might cut into their corporate profits.

Similarly, when businesses want to reduce regulatory protections for workers, they argue that they are only trying to reduce the government red-tape and bureaucracy. They are not putting their workers at risk; they are simply "opposing unreasonable intrusions of big government into the private sector" and "getting government off the back of businesses." Who could complain about that? Similarly, conservative consultant Frank Luntz has told business lobbyists and Republican lawmakers that when they are trying to weaken environmental protections, they should describe their activities as "streamlining" and "modernizing" government. They can thus seem to be attacking "excess government," not the environment.

Anti-government rhetoric also allowed Republicans to sidestep the accusation that their policies are a form of "class warfare." Clearly, most of the benefits of the Republican tax cuts during the Bush administration fell to the rich and to corporations, and the costs of cuts in social programs fell disproportionately on working people, minorities, and the poor – the very definition of class warfare. But such criticisms were blunted by Republican claims that they were only waging war on government. President Bush claimed that his numerous tax cuts were simply an effort to reduce the onerous burden of government taxes – and everyone knows taxes are bad. And cuts in social programs were portrayed as simply "reining in out of control government spending" and "reducing big government."

This anti-government spin on conservative policies works to obscure the fact that an attack on government is often an attack on those Americans who are least well-off. In reality, reducing government takes away power away from those in society who most need the government to protect their interests – those who are most vulnerable to job layoffs, those who need to protect themselves from workplace discrimination and dangers on the job, or those who need government to ensure equal educational opportunity or a fair minimum wage. As Max Neiman explained in his book, *Defending Government*, shrinking government not only eliminates programs that aid the less well-off, it also reduces their political power as well.

> The attack on government has involved … a focused effort to make it more difficult for the less privileged of society to have access to governing authority. If the assault on public programs and the capacity to produce them is permanently and broadly successful, then making life fairer and better for the least advantaged and less politically connected members of society will be more difficult.[16]

The basic point is this: the deeply disturbing nature of many conservative policies is being hidden behind a political smokescreen – an effort to portray these policies as mere attempts to reduce government and the "bad effects" it is having on society. The whole anti-government campaign has become a very handy way for some powerful and well-off groups to disguise the true intentions of their policies and to deflect potential public opposition.

Even More Worrisome

This has been the story of where the anti-government movement came from and how it came to be such a powerful force in American politics. But even more disturbing is what it wants to do with that power – how it is committed to undermining many of the essential progressive government programs that have been created during the last 100 years. To see just how radical the anti-government agenda really is and how it conflicts with the political views of most Americans, turn to the next chapter.

---

1. Quoted in Robert Dreyfuss, "Grover Norquist: 'Field Marshal' of the Bush Plan," *The Nation*, April 26, 2001.
2. http://www.tfn.org/site/DocServer/GOP_-Final_2008_Platform.pdf?docID=582
3. For a summary of Libertarian philosophy and policy positions, see the Libertarian Party's website, http://www.lp.org/issues/issues.shtml.
4. Dick Armey, *The Freedom Revolution* (New York: Regnery Publishers, 1995) p. 304.
5. Urban Institute, "Bush Tax Cuts," January 16, 2008. http://www.urban.org/decisionpoints08/archive/01bushtaxcuts.cfm
6. Daniel Schoor, "Bush's Social Security Plan Carries Ideological Underpinnings," *All Things Considered*, March 7, 2005.

7. Paul Krugman, "Spearing the Beast," *The New York Times*, February 8, 2005, p. A25.

8. Karen M. Paget, "Lessons of Right Wing Philanthropy" *The American Prospect*, Number 40, September-October 1998, p. 92.

9. David Brock, *The Republican Noise Machine* (New York: Crown Publishing, 2004), p. 48.

10. This figure is for 1988. See Sourcewatch, "Heritage Foundation," http://www.sourcewatch.org/index.php?title=Heritage_Foundation, June 17, 2006.

11. People for the American Way, "Buying a Movement," http://www.pfaw.org/pfaw/general/default.aspx?oid=2052, June 17, 2006.

12. Media Transparency, "The Koch Family Foundations," http://www.mediatransparency.org/funderprofile.php?funderID=9, June 15, 2006.

13. Jane Mayer, "Covert Operations: The Billionaire Brothers Who Are Waging a War Against Obama," *The New Yorker*, August 30, 2010.

14. Open Secrets, "PACs by Industry," http://www.opensecrets.org/pacs/list.php

15. Public Campaign, "Hard Facts: Hard Money in the 2000 Election," http://www.publicampaign.org/publications/studies/hardfacts2000/fullreport.htm, June 17, 2006

16. Max Neiman, *Defending Government: Why Big Government Works* (Upper Saddle River, NJ: Prentice-Hall, 2000) p. 2.

CHAPTER 13

The Anti-Government Movement's Radical Agenda

Anti-government activists like to portray their ideas as mainstream and claim to speak for the political aspirations of common Americans. They would have us believe that their vision of the minimal state is as American as apple pie – merely an extension of Americans' traditional skepticism toward government. Americans have always disliked government, they say, and we are only following their lead. But once we get beyond this rhetoric and get a good look at the underlying ideas and goals of these anti-government zealots, it becomes clear that their views are far different from the political sentiments of most Americans. Their agenda is much more radical and their hatred of government goes way beyond the natural political cynicism that most citizens have about this institution. The anti-government movement is out of touch with mainstream America; and at its core, it is nothing less than a form of political extremism.

Out of Step with America

It is true that part of the American tradition is to distrust power and those who wield it – whether they are in government, corporations, churches, labor unions, or any large organization. This is all to the good, because power can be abused and needs to be kept in check. We need to constantly question our governmental leaders and we need to keep them accountable in order to ensure that they are responsive to our needs and that they spend our money wisely. But the views of the anti-government movement go far beyond this kind of healthy suspicion about governmental power – they actually hate government. They sometimes call it "the beast" or "the monster" – and actually consider it to be some kind of malevolent force in society. They demonize it, loathe it, and see it as the source of all of our problems.

Of course, all of us have probably said at times that we "hate" the government. But what we mean by that is usually very different from what these anti-government crusaders mean. We usually mean that we detest the particular politicians in power and/or that we hate the policies they are pursuing. So liberal Americans hate it when conservatives are in charge of government, and vice versa. In other words, we hate *a particular government*. But the anti-government right hates government *in general* – government *itself*. This is a very different and much more extreme view.

Similarly, these ideologues' criticisms of government are also much more sweeping than the typical complaints about government voiced by most Americans. Consider, for example, the issue of wasteful government bureaucracies. Most of us strongly support efforts to cut the "fat" out of government bureaucracies and to make them more efficient. But for proponents of minimal government, this kind of reform is really beside the point. As one early icon of the anti-government movement, Barry Goldwater, explained it: "I have little interest in streamlining government or making it more efficient, for I mean to reduce its size."[1] And by "reducing," they often mean lopping off entire agencies and programs. The conservative hit list of agencies that should be eliminated has at various times included the Department of Education, Department of Energy, the Environmental Protection Agency, Department of Commerce, the Occupational Safety and Health Administration, plus hundreds of other small agencies and programs. They don't want to cut fat; they want to cut meat.

Americans also sometimes have problems with government regulations. We can all probably identify at least a few regulations that seem particularly wrongheaded or burdensome, and we would certainly support changing or eliminating them. But many anti-government zealots condemn the legitimacy of government regulation itself. Some conservative legal scholars actually argue that the federal government has no constitutional right to regulate the workplace or the environment.[2] And most libertarian-leaning conservatives would reduce regulations drastically – even those protecting our health and safety. Dick Armey, former Majority Leader of the U.S. House, seriously proposed that we eliminate half of all federal regulations. He didn't specify which ones – he just seemed to know that half of them were unneeded. Another Republican House Leader, Tom DeLay, went Dick Armey one better and actually told a reporter that he could not think of a single federal regulation he would like to leave in place.[3] Such irresponsible and extreme hostility toward consumer protection, environmental, health, and workplace regulations is clearly out of touch with mainstream America. Only a very small minority of Americans – less than 18% – say they want *less* government regulation of most industries.[4]

Some Americans also have issues with our social safety net programs, but they are usually confined to complaints about welfare payments going to people who do not really need them. In general, most Americans strongly support programs like Social Security, unemployment insurance, Medicare, and the minimum wage. However, many in the anti-government crusade want to get government out of the business of providing this kind of economic security for Americans. For example, some leading conservative intellectuals like Charles Murray don't just want to cut back on welfare, they want to eliminate it entirely. In his famous book, *Losing Ground*, he proposed "scrapping" welfare, Medicaid, and food stamps and leaving the poor to be taken care of by friends, churches, and charities.[5] Minimum wage and workplace anti-discrimination policies have also come under attack as improper uses of government power. Even unemployment insurance is looked upon with great suspicion by some critics of government. As Ronald Reagan, an anti-government icon, once declared: "Unemployment insurance is a pre-paid vacation for freeloaders."[6] And he did not think much better of Medicaid, whose recipients he once described as "a faceless mass, waiting for handouts."[7]

George W. Bush's attempts to "reform" Social Security also revealed a deep underlying hostility toward social programs in general. A limited-circulation memo written in January 2005 by Peter Wehner, the director of the White House Office of Strategic Initiatives, was particularly instructive in this regard. He made it clear that an essential part of the privatization plan was to actually reduce benefits and weaken Social Security, and he said that any proposal that didn't include this was a "bad idea." More importantly, he revealed how radical the privatization effort really was. "The overhaul of Social Security will be one of the most conservative undertakings of modern times. And if successful, will rank as one of the most significant conservative governing achievements ever." The ultimate goal of this effort, he concluded, was to "help the nation move away from dependency on government."[8] There is a clear refusal here to realize what most Americans know to be true: that it is sometimes necessary for us to use collective institutions like government to deal with the many serious financial risks and insecurities that are part of living in a modern market economy – risks like unemployment, retirement, sudden illness, and so on.

Getting Rid of Public Schools

Remarkably, some anti-government activists are even against our public schools. For much of our history, public schools have been seen as a vital symbol of our nation's commitment to equal opportunity for all. But in their zeal to condemn anything and everything governmental, some conservatives have set their sights on greatly reducing or even eliminating public education. As Thomas Johnson of the Future of Freedom Foundation has explained:

> Famous supporters of public education include Hitler, Stalin, Castro, Mao Zedong, Mussolini .... The best possible reform that could ever be affected is eliminating completely politicized socialist government schools and replacing them with private, profit-making, and charitable education businesses that offer courses of instruction only to willing customers.[9]

And it's not only far-out libertarians like Johnson who express these kinds of hostile views of our public schools – these ideas extend into the mainstream of the conservative movement. Conservative luminaries including Milton Friedman, Dinesh D'Souza, Howard Phillips, and Marvin Olasky have publicly endorsed the goal of eliminating public education.[10] A story told by Reed Hundt, head of the Federal Communication Commission in the Clinton administration, illustrates just how deep the conservative contempt for public schools can go. He had a meeting with William Bennett, who had been Secretary of Education under Ronald Reagan, in order to ask him to support a bill in Congress that would have paid for internet access in all classrooms and libraries in the country.

> [Bennett] told me he would not help, because he did not want public schools to obtain new funding, new capability, new tools for success. He wanted them, he said, to fail so that they could be replaced with vouchers, charter schools, religious schools and other forms of private education.[11]

In contrast to these extremely antagonistic attitudes towards public education, most Americans support and even cherish their local public schools. In a poll, Americans ranked public schools as "the most important public institution in the community" by at least a five-to-one margin over hospitals, churches and other institutions.[12] And by 69% to 27%, Americans support "reforming the existing public school system" to "finding an alternative."[13]

Getting Rid of Taxes

Taxes are yet another area in which the approach of anti-government activists is much more extreme than that of most Americans. Most of us would like to get rid of taxes that seem clearly unfair – such as the marriage penalty in the federal income tax. And most would agree that changes need to be made when local property taxes become too much of a burden on retirees on a fixed income. But these anti-government conservatives and libertarians aren't as concerned with making the tax system fairer or more reasonable as they are with simply cutting taxes. They oppose taxes in principle – seeing them as a form of theft that penalizes hard working Americans. Many also believe that severely cutting taxes is the best way to reduce government. For many in the anti-tax movement, their ultimate goal is to get rid of as many taxes as possible, including the federal income tax, capital gains taxes, corporate income taxes, payroll taxes and property taxes. One anti-government Libertarian Party web site made the point quite succinctly: "Where do we stand on taxes? The short answer is we are against them."[14]

In enacting a series of massive tax cuts starting in 2001, President Bush and the Republican Congress insisted that they were simply giving the public what they wanted: tax relief. But poll after poll showed that this was not what the public wanted. Surveys at the time found that hardly any Americans thought tax cuts were an important priority and only 5% named taxes as the nation's "most important problem."[15] And when asked if they preferred a tax cut or to spend that money on "education, the environment, health care, crime fighting, and the military," 69% of Americans said they preferred to devote the money to these programs. Only 22% favored the tax cuts.[16] Clearly, the Republican obsession with continually cutting taxes is greatly out of step the views of most Americans.

Rolling Back the Twentieth Century

To sum up, the agenda of the anti-government coalition is a radical one – they do not simply want to reform and improve government; they want to gut it. They fundamentally oppose the basic roles and functions of government in modern society. They believe the government's power to tax, its ability to enact health, safety, and environmental regulations, and its attempts to redistribute income to provide more economic security are all basically illegitimate activities. They fundamentally oppose the modern idea of government and the role it has come to play in advanced societies. As William Greider has observed, many of the leaders of the anti-government movement feel deeply uncomfortable with the expansion of government power and programs that took place during the New Deal and the Great Society and are nostalgic about earlier times when government played only a very minor role in society.

> The movement's grand ambition is to roll back the twentieth century, quite literally. That is, defenestrate the federal government and reduce its scale and powers to a level well below what it was before the New Deal's centralization. With that accomplished, movement conservatives envision a restored society in which the prevailing values and power relationships resemble the America that existed around 1900, when William McKinley was President. Governing authority and resources are dispersed from

> Washington, returned to local levels and also to individuals and private institutions, most notably corporations and religious organizations. The primacy of property rights is re-established over the shared public priorities expressed in government regulation. Above all, private wealth – both enterprises and individuals with higher incomes – are permanently insulated from the progressive claims of the graduated income tax.[17]

Out of Step with Other Democracies

For much of the twentieth century, most Americans welcomed the growing power of the federal government and its ability to effectively address the serious economic and social problems that people could not solve on their own. In fact, much of that growth came from *public demands* that the government tackle pressing issues like economic depressions, tainted food, environmental pollution, and unsafe workplaces. But while this more positive view of the state has been fading in the United States, it still remains alive and well in many European countries. The state-hating views of American conservatives seem especially strange when compared with the way most citizens in these other advanced Western countries look at government. T. R. Reid, a reporter who lived in Europe for many years, has observed with some surprise that the term "welfare state" is not a pejorative one there. They don't say "welfare state" with that sneer in their voice that we usually hear in the States. In fact, he found that most Europeans are very proud of their welfare states and they like to brag about public programs like their universal healthcare systems.[18] Typically, Europeans believe that the government should take a much greater responsibility for helping people with their lives than we do here in United States. For example, when asked, "How much responsibility does the government have for seeing to it that everyone who wants a job can have one?", an average of 91% of the citizens in Germany, Great Britain and Italy said that this was either an essential or important responsibility of the government. Ninety-five percent believed that the government had an important or essential responsibility to provide citizens with good medical care; and 89% thought that providing adequate housing was an important or essential responsibility of government.[19] Such views must surely make American minimal-government crusaders cringe. Perhaps more surprising, however, is that the anti-government attitudes of American conservative leaders are not only alien to most citizens in other Western countries; they are even out of step with *conservative movements* in these countries. A passionate hatred of government and the desire to dismantle it is unique to U.S. conservatives. John Micklethwait and Adrian Wooldridge work for the British magazine the *Economist* and have written an insightful history of conservatism in the United States, *The Right Nation*. One of their central points is how exceptional American conservatism is. "Most Americans still do not realize how extraordinary their brand of conservatism is. ...The American Right exhibits a far deeper hostility toward the state than any other modern conservative party. How many European conservatives would display bumper stickers saying 'I love my country but I hate my government'?"[20] The answer, presumably, is very few. Because while conservatives in other countries champion the benefits of the market system and disagree with their liberal opponents over how extensive social programs should be, most do not deny the importance of these programs or that the government has a responsibility to play an active role in meeting the needs of its citizens. So the extreme government bashing that we see here is really an exclusive sport of American conservatives.

Beneath the Surface: Surprisingly Strong Support for Government

Of course, most conservative ideologues in American are hardly bothered by the fact that their movement is exceptional among Western countries in its strong distaste for government. In fact, they take pride in this. They often argue that their anti-state views merely reflect the broader "exceptionalism" of American political culture – that Americans just have a more intense dislike for the state than do citizens in other Western cultures. But this is highly misleading. In reality, the American public is very much of two minds about government: we both dislike and like government. It depends a lot on how we are asked about it. When asked about government in general, Americans usually react negatively. They say that government is inherently wasteful and incompetent, and that they have little confidence in it. The number of people who say they trust the federal government to do the right thing most of the time declined from a high of 62% in 1964 to 40% in 2000.[21] And people usually rate politicians at the bottom of the list of occupations in terms of integrity and honesty – right next to used car salesmen. From this it is easy to conclude that most Americans really don't like government at all. But questions about government in the abstract are exactly those that are likely to trigger the negative stereotypes of government that are so close to the surface in many of our minds – corrupt politicians, wasteful bureaucracies, etc. However, if we begin to probe beneath these initial, knee-jerk attitudes towards government, we begin to see something else. If we go beyond questions about government *in general* and begin to ask more *specific* questions about this institution, we get a very different reaction from most Americans. For instance, most people rate Congress quite low as an institution, but when they are asked about their own particular congressperson – who they usually know fairly well – they routinely give their own representative very high marks. More importantly, when pollsters ask Americans to think about how much responsibility government should have in specific areas like jobs, housing, and health care, you get some unexpected answers. Our answers are not as pro-government as those of the European citizens noted above, but a surprising number of us believe that government should play a large role in addressing these pressing social problems. 71% of Americans believe that the government has an important or essential responsibility for seeing to it that anyone who wants a job can have one. 63% believe that the government has an important or essential responsibility to provide citizens with adequate housing; and 78% of us think that the government has an important or essential responsibility to provide citizens with good medical care.[22] These are hardly the answers of a people who want to drastically reduce government's role in society. One social scientist, looking at the figures, commented that "Rather than a confirmation of American individualism, the results ... are better understood as an indication of the surprisingly strong support for government social responsibility that exists in this land of 'rugged individualism.'"[23]

We find similarly strong public support for government when we ask people whether we should be spending more money or less money on programs that care for the elderly, protect the environment, support education, etc. Large majorities actually say they like these programs and want the government to spend more money on them – not less. Table 6 shows the typical results of one of these surveys. As the results clearly demonstrate, very few people actually think the government should spend less on Social Security, crime, the environment, health, parks, education, highways, etc. The only areas where a substantial number of people want less spending are welfare (35.3%), foreign aid (55.3%), and defense (42.4%). In almost every other issue area, *less than 10% of the public want to cut spending*. More importantly, in every single one of these areas, a majority of Americans want the government to keep spending at least the same amount. And in the areas of the environment, health, crime, education, childcare, and Social Security, a majority thinks the government should spend more. This evidence clearly shows that while we don't seem to like *the idea* of government, we do like what it does for us *in reality*. So the conventional wisdom about Americans uniformly hating government – the view assumed and promoted by anti-government conservatives – is in fact wrong. Most of us have enough common sense to strongly support the vital government programs that are working to improve our lives.

Table 6: Public Attitudes Toward Spending on Government Programs.

	Should Spend More	Spending About Right	Should Spend Less
Protecting the environment	65.6%	23.5%	8.1%
Protecting our health	74.6%	17.6%	4.7%
Halting the rising crime rate	59.9%	24.5	6.8%
Improving the educ. system	70.4%	23.1%	5.4%
Social Security	59.6%	30.1%	5.5%
Childcare subsidies	50.6%	35.6%	6.2%
Highways and bridges	45.3%	41.8%	9.5%
Military, arms, and defense	23.4%	30.3%	42.4%
Foreign Aid	11.7%	25.9%	55.3%
Welfare	25.0%	34.7%	35.3%
Parks and recreation	30.4%	61.8%	5.3%
Mass transit	46.6%	38.7%	7.6%

Source: National Opinion Research Center, "General Social Survey Codebook 2008." (Table does not include respondents who answered "Don't know.")

No Turn to the Right in Public Opinion

Another striking finding of the polls cited above is that Americans' positive attitudes toward many key government programs have held steady *for the last three decades.*[24] Since the 1970s, our strong support for these programs has hardly wavered at all. This comes as a surprise to many people, especially those on the right. Minimal government activists like to argue that their attempt to cut programs is simply a reaction to the public's increasing conservatism and hostility toward government. They suggest that there has been a general turn to the right in American politics in response to the liberal excesses of the

Great Society in the 1960s, and this includes an increasing public opposition to big government. But no such "right turn" has taken place. As numerous studies have shown, "there is virtually no compelling survey evidence that more Americans have actually embraced conservatism since the 1960s."[25] Surveys that ask people to position themselves on a conservative—liberal continuum have found that the number of people calling themselves "conservative" has increased by a mere 2% since the 1960s. And a study of the public's view of left-right issues conducted by Morris Fiorina concluded that "Americans are about as conservative or liberal as they were a generation ago."[26]

Polls also reveal that negatives attitudes toward government have not increased across the board during the last decades – and some have even decreased. In 1972, when asked if government was "too powerful," 49% of Americans said yes. But that figure was down substantially in 2002 – to 39%.[27] And when asked whether they wanted to cut government services or to provide more services (even if that required raising taxes), Americans were evenly divided in 1992. By 2000, however, more than twice as many wanted to increase services (39%) than wanted to cut them (18%).[28]

Something *has* turned sharply to the right in the last 30 years, but it has not been the public. It has been the conservative leadership. A generation ago, most Republican politicians were actually moderates, in the mold of Dwight Eisenhower, Nelson Rockefeller, Richard Nixon and Gerald Ford. Nixon was probably the most conservative of these four, but he often embraced government and expanded its powers and programs when necessary to deal with a variety of problems. He signed into law the Clean Air Act and the Environmental Protection Agency, he helped to implement Affirmative Action, and he supported passage of a national health insurance plan. More new federal regulations were adopted under Nixon than under Lyndon Johnson. And he approved the largest increases in domestic spending since the New Deal. Hardly the policy record of someone who thought that we had too much government.

But conservative leaders began to veer sharply to the right in the 1980s, as Jacob Hacker and Paul Pierson have documented in their book, *Off Center: The Republican Revolution and the Erosion of American Democracy*. They show, for example, that the median Republican in the U.S. House of Representatives is now 73% more conservative than their counterpart in the 1970s. They also cite studies that examine how the political views of core Republican activists compare to those of independent voters. These studies show that in the 1960s Republican activists were only about 20% more conservative than independents, but that by 2002, they had become 40% more conservative.[29] Hacker and Pierson conclude that "Republican activists are not only far to the right of independents, they are also far to the right of ordinary voters within their own party. And they have been heading ever more sharply right since the 1980s."[30]

Part of this increasing gap between conservative leaders and many independent and conservative voters can be seen in their diverging attitudes towards the value of government programs. This is clearly evident in the results of the polls cited earlier on how much the public supports spending on various government policy efforts. These surveys reveal that those who oppose the conservative leadership's agenda of cutting vital government programs are not just liberals – they include many independents and conservatives as well. Only about 20% of the electorate identify themselves as liberals; and yet the figures in Table 6 show that upwards of 90% of Americans believe we should not be cutting spending on health, education, environmental protection, and so on. This means that very large numbers of people who see themselves as moderates or independents support these government programs. And since over 30% of Americans identify themselves as conservative, clearly many of them too do not want to see cuts in these areas of government responsibility. In fact, when Republican lawmakers proposed in 2011 to cut spending on Medicare and Medicaid, polls showed that a whopping 70% of Republicans and 80% of registered Tea Party voters actually opposed those cuts – much to the shock of many conservative pundits.

But such grassroots conservative support for large government programs should not be shocking. Many conservative citizens benefit greatly from these programs. Also, it is certainly possible to be a social conservative who is strongly anti-abortion and anti-gay, and yet who also strongly supports spending on health care and environmental protection. In any case, these poll figures provide more evidence that the anti-government movement's policy agenda of slashing funding for many big-government programs is not only at odds with the views of most Americans, it is out of touch with the views of many conservatives as well – a good indication of just how extreme this agenda really is.

An Undemocratic Movement

The anti-government movement represents a deeply disturbing development in American politics: a group of political activists imposing their radical policy agenda on a public that does not support it. There is not, and has never been, a widespread public demand to drastically reduced government in the United States. This movement has not been an example of democracy at work. It has been an example of special interest politics at work – it has been an attack on democracy. The demand for smaller government has come primarily from those wealthy individuals and powerful business interests who would most directly profit from lowered taxes and less regulation. As I describe in the previous chapter, it is these very interests that have provided the billions of dollars of support that has enabled this movement to grow in political power. The success of the anti-government movement in this country has not been the result of a shift to the right in public opinion, but the result of a shift to the right in political influence – a product of the ever-increasing power of affluent interests in our political system. But the undemocratic nature of this anti-government crusade and its lack of popular support have not discouraged it most ardent promoters.

---

1 Barry Goldwater, quoted in the Cato Institute, "The Paradox of the Statist Businessman" http://www.cato.org/pubs/policy_report/pr-ma-pa.html, June 19, 2006.

2 See the work of Professor Richard Epstein of the Chicago Law School. Also, see Epstein's views described in William Greider, "The Right and U.S. Trade Law: Invalidating the 20th Century" Nation, October 15, 2001.

3 Jacob Hacker and Paul Pierson, *Off Center: The Republican Revolution and the Erosion of American Democracy* (New Haven: Yale University Press, 2005), p. 34.

4 Meg Bostrom, "By, or For, the People? A Meta-Analysis of Public Opinion of Government," August 26, 2006, p. 33. http://www.demos.org/pubs/ByOrForthePeople20050426.pdf

5 Charles Murray, *Losing Ground: American Social Policy, 1950-1980* (New York: Basic Books, 1995), p. 227.

6 California Governor Ronald Reagan in the Sacramento Bee, April 28, 1966.

7 Metrotimes, "Dubious Achievement Awards, 2005," June 20, 2006 http://www.metrotimes.com/editorial/story.asp?id=7162.

8 Daniel Schorr, "Bush's Social Security Plan Carries Ideological Underpinnings," *All Things Considered*, March 7, 2005.

9 Quoted in Earthworks Action, *50 Simple Things You Can Do to Fight the Right* (Ashland, OR: Earthworks Press, 2006) p. 103.

10 People for the American Way, *The Voucher Veneer: The Deeper Agenda to Privatize Public Education* (Washington DC: People for the American Way, 2003) Appendix 1.

11 Quoted in Earthworks Action, *50 Simple Things You Can Do to Fight the Right* (Ashland, OR: Earthworks Press, 2006) pp. 103-04.

12 "Action for All: The Public's Responsibility for Public Education," a report of findings from a nationwide survey sponsored by the Public Education Network and Education Week, April 2001, p. 9.

13 People for the American Way, *The Voucher Veneer: The Deeper Agenda to Privatize Public Education* (Washington DC: People for the American Way, 2003) p.3.

14 Libertarian Party of New Hampshire, "Key Issues." http://www.lpnh.org/issues.htm

15 Hacker and Pierson, p. 50.

16 Ibid. p. 50.

17 William Greider, "The Right's Grand Ambition: Rolling Back the 20th Century" May, 12, 2003, The Nation, p. 11.

18 See T.R. Reid's discussion of Europeans' positive attitudes toward the welfare state in *The United States of Europe* (New York,: The Penguin Press, 2004), p. 149.

19 Martin Gilens, *Why American's Hate Welfare* (Chicago: Chicago University Press, 1999), p. 26.

20 John Mickethwait and Adrian Wooldridge, *The Right Nation: Conservative Power in America* (New York: The Penguin Press, 2004), p. 11, 13.

21 The National Election Studies, http://www.umich.edu/~nes/nes guide/toptable/tab5a_1.htm

22 Gilens, p. 26.

23 Gillens, p. 27.

24 Marc J. Hetherington, *Why Trust Matters* (Princeton, NJ: Princeton University Press, 2004) Chapter 3.

25 Hetherington, p. 45.

26 Cited in Jacob Hacker and Paul Pierson, *Off Center: The Republican Revolution and the Erosion of American Democracy* (New Haven: Yale University Press, 2005), p. 39.

27 Hacker and Pierson, p. 40.

28 Ibid. p. 40.

29 Ibid. pp. 28, 27.

30 Ibid. p. 28.

CHAPTER 14

Starving the Beast

For decades, a key goal of anti-government agenda conservatives has been to substantially cut spending on social and regulatory programs. But they have faced a difficult and tricky obstacle. Most Americans actually like these programs. As seen earlier, most of us would like to increase – not cut – spending on social programs like health care and education. And we greatly appreciate the job being done by regulatory agencies that protect the environment, consumers, and workers. So how can these valued programs be cut without invoking the wrath of the public?

The answer the Republicans found is to attack these programs indirectly. The weapon of choice? Tax cuts. The idea is simple: if we keep cutting taxes, eventually there won't be enough money to spend on these programs and they will have to be reduced. If there simply is not enough money in the budget, even liberal supporters of these programs will have to reluctantly concede that cuts are necessary. Conservatives call this tactic "starving the beast." Taxes are what nourish government. Take that source of nourishment away and government must inevitably shrink. For anti-tax advocates like Grover Norquist, this is the ultimate purpose of tax cuts: "The goal is reducing the size and scope of government by draining its lifeblood."[1]

Milton Friedman, the arch-conservative economist, speaking of ways to limit or reduce the size of government, offered this prescription: "How can we ever cut government down to size? I believe there is only one way: the way parents control spendthrift children, cutting their allowance. For the government, that means cutting taxes. Resulting deficits will be an effective – I would go as far as to say, the only effective – restraint on the spending propensities of the executive branch and the legislature."[2]

So underneath all the Republican rhetoric about cutting taxes – all the talk about stimulating the economy and giving money back to hardworking Americans, there is another, deeper and more disturbing political goal: to strangle government social and regulatory programs. But this is rarely acknowledged publicly. Conservatives focus the public's attention on what they will gain from the tax cuts, not what they will lose by reducing social programs.

This strategy was first tried in the Reagan administration. He came into office in 1980 promising to balance the federal budget. But he quickly cut taxes and raised military spending, creating huge budget deficits. (Sound familiar?) This made little sense to many people at the time and was not understood until Reagan's budget advisor, David Stockman, later revealed that this was a conscious effort to "starve the beast" – a phrase he is reputed to have coined.[3] The idea was to put increasing financial pressure on the government's budget in order to make it easier to cut spending on programs. And indeed, it had some effect, with domestic discretionary spending falling from 4.5% of the economy in 1981 to 3.3% in 1988.[4]

A series of massive tax cuts during the George W. Bush administration revived this strategy and implemented it in a much more extensive way. These tax cuts cost the federal government over two trillion dollars ($2,000,000,000,000) in lost revenue from 2001 to 2010 alone.[5] As economist Paul Krugman observed at the time, "'starving the beast' is no longer a hypothetical scenario. It's happening as we speak. For decades, conservatives have sought tax cuts, not because they're affordable, but because they aren't."[6]

The Deficit Trap

There is an obvious problem with this starving the beast strategy. On the federal level, cutting taxes does not necessarily require spending cuts: the government may simply borrow money and increase its debt to continue spending. And this is exactly what happened during the Bush administration. Along with his tax cuts, Bush also oversaw some large increases in government spending – mostly in the area of defense. The wars in Iraq and Afghanistan cost an estimated 900 billion dollars between 2001 and 2009. This combination of increased spending and huge tax cuts caused budget deficits to soar. This led some conservatives to complain that Bush had abandoned the idea of limited government. David Brooks concluded in one of his *New York Times* columns that all this spending and the growing deficits heralded "the death of small government conservatism."[7]

But these accusations were misplaced. They ignored one key fact: growing deficits were entirely consistent with the long-term plan to reduce government. The hope was that soaring deficits and a rapidly growing national debt would eventually force policymakers to reduce government spending – whether they liked it or not. From its very first days, the Bush administration embraced deficits as a good way to reign in government. In August of 2001, as the federal budget surpluses began to disappear and new deficits began to loom, the president had an unusual fit of candor and described these developments as "incredibly positive news," arguing that this would now put Congress in a "fiscal straitjacket."[8] The Republicans in Congress also came around to this point of view. As conservative Rick Santorum explained it, he first hated deficits, but then came to like them because they made it harder to pass any new spending bills. "I came to the House as a real deficit hawk but I am no longer a deficit hawk. I'll tell you why. ...Deficits make it easier to say no."[9]

More importantly, the Republicans knew that if the deficits and public debt continued to grow, eventually there would be no choice but to initiate deep cuts in mandatory spending programs like Medicare, Medicaid, and Social Security. As Paul Krugman explained in 2003, if the Bush tax cuts continued and no effort was made to increase revenues, the crunch would eventually come. "We're not talking about minor policy adjustments," said Krugman. "If taxes stay as low as they are now, government as we know it cannot be maintained."[10] He predicted that we could end up with large cuts to many central government programs: "Social Security will have to become far less generous; Medicare will no longer be able to guarantee comprehensive medical care to older Americans; Medicaid will no longer provide basic medical care to the poor."[11] In fact, eight years later, the Republicans were to propose radical cuts to Medicare and Medicaid.

The election of Obama in 2008 was the signal for conservatives to spring the deficit trap. They immediately turned from being deficit lovers into being deficit haters. All of a sudden they claimed that deficits were the number one problem facing government and that we needed to begin drastically cutting domestic spending. Matters were made worse when the severe recession started in 2008. It necessitated large bailouts to key financial institutions and billions in stimulus funds to prevent the economy from sinking into a depression. The recession also dramatically lowered federal tax revenues and made the deficits even worse. All of this played right into the hands of conservatives, who blamed these increased deficits on "out of control government spending." The only question that remained was how far the Republicans would go in their proposals to dramatically reduce government. It turned out they wanted to go farther than most Americans would have imagined.

The Goal: Massive Cuts in Federal Programs

In the spring of 2011, Rep. Paul Ryan introduced the Republican budget proposal and it was passed by the House of Representatives with enthusiastic GOP support. It proposed unprecedented and drastic cuts to a wide variety of government programs – reducing spending by $4.5 trillion (that's $4,500,000,000,000) over the next decade. In essence, this proposal amounted to nothing less than fundamental effort to dismantle the basic programs of the social welfare state that were established in the New Deal of the 1930s and the Great Society of the 1960s. For example, the Republicans wanted to end Medicare and Medicaid as we know them. The successful Medicare program would be phased out and instead the elderly would be issued limited vouchers to help them buy increasingly expensive private health insurance. As the years went by, the vouchers would have paid for less and less of the cost of medical care. It has been estimated that by 2030, the vouchers would have covered only a third of the cost of health care currently provided by Medicare.[12] So once again, seniors would have to make tragic decisions about whether to spend money on health care, rent or food.

The plan also called for Medicaid spending to be capped and handed off to state governments, whose chronic budget problems would encourage them to cut spending on this program. It is estimated that Medicaid spending would be cut in half by 2030, thus ripping a huge hole in the medical safety net for poor Americans who are least able to deal with the large and rising costs of medical care.[13]

These attacks on Medicare and Medicaid were just the tip of the iceberg. The Ryan budget plan also required massive cuts to virtually all social and regulatory programs. Take, for example, the Environmental Protection Agency. The Republicans wanted to reduce funding for the EPA by a third – $3 billion – *in 2012 alone*. This would have crippled the ability of this agency to enforce pollution regulations. Polluters would have been able to flout regulations needed to protect the quality of our air and water. The agency would also have been unable to fund needed projects like replacing broken and ineffective water treatment facilities. Illnesses and deaths caused by pollution would have inevitably risen. In a similar vein, the Republican plan also called for tens of billions of cuts to other regulatory agencies whose job it is to protect workers, consumers, and investors.

The Republican budget plan also mandated severe reductions in public investment efforts in the United States – cutting them by $1.4 trillion in the next ten years. A report by the Center for American Progress found that the plan would have cut money for education and job training by 53%, transportation infrastructure by 37%, and science and technology research and development by 28%.[14] These kinds of public investments are important for economic growth. They create a more talented workforce, spur technological advances, cut costs for businesses, and increase productivity. If we want a healthy economy we need to be investing hundreds of billions of dollars into improving education, replacing and improving our infrastructure system, encouraging clean energy technologies, etc. The Republican plan would have sharply reduced these crucial investments at a time when we needed to be increasing them.

A look at some numbers reveals just how extreme this proposal to shrink government really was. A study of the Republican budget plan by the non-partisan Congressional Budget Office found that it would have reduced government spending to 20% of gross domestic product by 2015 and to 14.75% of GDP by 2050 – a level not seen since 1951, before the existence of Medicare and Medicaid.[15] The CBO pointed out that the amount allocated for spending in 2050 would only be enough to fund Social Security, health care programs, and defense spending – and nothing else. Virtually all other federal programs would have to disappear! Could it be that the Republicans had simply failed to accurately forecast the dire long range consequences of their radical budget cutting plan? Hardly. Consider this: along with the Ryan budget, the Republicans introduced a Constitutional amendment to balance the budget that was just as radical. As a *New York Times* editorial described it:

> The amendment would hold annual spending to 18 percent of the previous year's gross domestic product, a formula that works out to about 16.7 percent in the proposals early years, according to the Center on Budget and Policy Priorities. This is a level last seen in 1956 – a time before Medicare, before the interstate highways, when many baby boomers were not yet born, never mind aging into retirement.[16]

"This is not a budget," said Rep. Ryan when he introduced his plan, "This is a cause." No truer words were ever spoken. His plan made clear the radical ideological cause lurking under the GOP budget proposals: to defund and dismantle large parts of our basic social safety net programs and public regulatory protections. For many in the anti-government movement, this is the eventual goal of their crusade, and they see the political struggles over budgets and deficits as the ultimate battleground in this war on government.

Reducing Government as a Form of Class Warfare

This starving the beast plan to radically reduce government is also extremely unfair and regressive. It is designed to make the rich richer and the poor poorer. For example, a report by the Center for Budget and Policy priorities found that the Ryan budget cuts targeted those Americans who could least afford them. Two-thirds of the $4.5 trillion in cuts over the next ten years would have come from programs aimed at helping people of limited means: Medicaid, food stamps, low income housing, Pell grants for poor students, etc.[17] Food stamps alone would have been reduced by $128 billion, inevitably increasing hunger and malnutrition among the poor.

Even worse, the Republican plan would have handed out trillions of dollars to the richest Americans. One trillion in tax breaks would have gone to the wealthiest 2% of Americans. Tax rates for the rich would have been reduced to their lowest rates since the 1930s. Taxes for corporations would have been greatly reduced as well. In short, the Republican budget was a plan to transfer trillions in wealth from the poorest of Americans to the richest. As budget expert Robert Greenstein described it:

> [Ryan's budget plan] proposes a dramatic reverse-Robin-Hood approach that gets the lion's share of its budget cuts from programs for low-income Americans – the politically and economically weakest group in America and the politically safest group for Ryan to target – even as it bestows extremely large tax cuts on the wealthiest Americans. Taken together, its proposals would produce the largest redistribution of income from the bottom to the top in modern U.S. history, while increasing poverty and inequality more than any measure in recent times and possibly in the nation's history.[18]

In essence, the Ryan plan was a form of class warfare – a blatant and unconscionable attack on the interests of the less well-off in our society. And the tax cut portion of the Republican budget plan also made it clear that they cared more about helping wealthy Americans than about deficit reduction. A CBO analysis revealed that because of these tax giveaways to the rich, this plan would have actually *increased* the deficits and debt over the next ten years.[19]

As the next chapter, "The Deficit Scare: Myth vs. Reality," will make clear, our deficit and debt situation is not nearly as dire as Republicans would have us believe. And there are ways to address these financial issues without putting our social safety net programs in jeopardy.

But unfortunately, many policymakers, including some Democrats, have fallen for these deficit scare tactics and have been insisting on severely reining in domestic spending.

Fortunately, the Ryan budget proposal did not pass. But in the summer of 2011, as this book went to press, the situation took a turn for the worse. The House Republicans insisted that massive budget cuts must be made or they would refuse to raise the federal debt limit and create financial chaos in an already weakened economy. The Democrats gave into this irresponsible threat and agreed to $2.5 trillion in budget reductions over the next ten years, $1.5 trillion of which would be decided by a joint House and Senate committee. Under discussion were large cuts to Medicare, Medicaid and Social Security. Other likely targets included environmental protection, student aid programs, education programs, scientific research, and infrastructure investment. And this may just be the beginning. Republicans said that they would again take the country hostage and insist on even more budget cuts every time the debt limit must be raised. If this ruthless tactic works, the Republicans may actually succeed in their goal of crippling regulatory agencies and shredding our social safety net.

Starving the States

If you want to get a sense of what we have in store for us as a nation if the Republican's starving the beast strategy works, you need only look at what is happening in some states. Many state governments today are already suffering from the results of this conservative strategy. In large part, this is due to an enormous advantage that anti-government activists have on this level of government: virtually all states are legally required to balance their annual budgets. So when revenues fall or expenses increase, these governments cannot borrow to make up the difference; they must either cut programs or raise taxes. Conservatives have often been successful in blocking tax increases, which has meant that states have had no choice but to reduce spending on social programs.

During the recession that began in 2008, most states cut their social spending – often in disturbing ways. Many of these cuts fell on these states' most vulnerable residents. Several states cut reimbursements to nursing homes or made it more difficult for the elderly to qualify for nursing home care. Twenty-one states implemented cuts that restricted low-income children's access to health insurance. Services for the elderly and disabled were cut in 22 states. Educational spending also took big hits, with state aid for K-12 education reduced in 24 states. Funds were also cut for higher education in 32 states, forcing some to raise tuition by more than 10%.[20]

Clearly, the decline in state revenues caused by the recession played a large role in these budget cuts. But that is not all that was going on. Many states have had ongoing fiscal problems, and in many cases those problems have been caused or exacerbated by conservative forces who have undermined the abilities of states and local governments to raise needed taxes. For example, the foundation for many states' fiscal problems was laid in the 1990s when state-level anti-government groups waged successful campaigns to reduce taxes. Between 1994 and 2001, under political pressure from conservatives, 44 states passed significant tax cuts. The effects of these cuts were masked at first by the stock market boom that increased the states' returns on investments in the late 1990s. But now, with the stock market boom long gone, those cuts have come home to roost and are costing the states an estimated $40 billion or more a year in lost revenue – a significant cause of the long-term fiscal difficulties in many states.[21]

Conservatives have also been successful in several states in installing caps on certain tax rates. In Massachusetts, for example, local property taxes cannot be increased by more than 3.5% a year. In many years, city expenses have risen faster than that rate and tax revenues have not kept up. This has forced many cities to repeatedly cut public school budgets – firing teachers, reducing course offerings, eliminating sports, and increasing class sizes. Cities have also been forced to reduce fire and police staffing and limit essential public services like snow plowing and road repair.

Fourteen states also now require supermajorities for the raising of some taxes – and this has become particularly problematic. Supermajorities require that 60%, 67%, or even 75% of the legislators must agree before taxes can be raised – rather than the simple majority of 50% plus one that applies to other kinds of legislation. This allows an anti-tax minority to block majority rule. In some states, for instance, a majority of citizens in local school districts has often voted to raise taxes to help fund education – but they have been frustrated because they couldn't marshal the needed two-thirds majority. Statutory requirements like supermajorities and tax caps are the some of the best political weapons used by anti-government forces because they make it all but impossible to raise taxes and this forces state and local governments to cut spending on programs.

Making matters even worse, conservatives are now pushing efforts to establish constitutional caps on state government expenditures – plans that would limit spending growth to the rate of inflation plus population growth. The first state to adopt this approach, Colorado in 1992, saw its public services deteriorate significantly. For example, it dropped from 35th to 49th in K-12 spending as a share of personal income, and from 35th to 48th in higher education funding a as share of personal income.[22] In 2005, citizens in Colorado voted to suspend this amendment for five years so that they can restore needed funding to vital services. The disastrous results in Colorado have not stopped anti-government activists from launching campaigns to pass similar amendments in 15 other states.

The Case of California

The severe and ongoing budget problems in California are a good example of the kind of damage that anti-government activists can do on the state level. During the recent recession, the state ran into billions of dollars of deficits and was forced to make draconian cuts in state programs and services. The main problem was not excessive spending but excessive restrictions on the taxing ability of the state, which made it all but impossible for it to raise taxes to deal responsibly with its fiscal crisis.

The problems for California began decades ago when obstacles to tax increases were introduced into the state constitution by an anti-tax campaign. Proposition 13 was passed in 1978 and capped property taxes at ridiculously low levels. Cities and counties were then forced to try to raise other assessments and fees in order to continue to supply basic public services. But anti-tax zealots were then able to pass Proposition 218, which prevented cities from raising those fees without the approval of two-thirds of the voters – usually an impossible barrier to overcome.

This left localities no choice but to go begging to the state government for needed revenues. But Proposition 13 actually worked to restrict this source of funds as well. It mandated that the state could not increase taxes without the approval of two-thirds of both houses of the legislature. This anti-democratic arrangement has allowed a minority of tax-hating lawmakers to frustrate the majority and consistently block any efforts to raise needed revenues.

Faced with these anti-tax restrictions, the state had no choice but to institute a series of very damaging cuts in state services. Severe cuts were made in aid to K-12 school systems. California's public schools already ranked 34th among the states in per-pupil expenditures and 49th in teacher-student ratio – a disgraceful situation that could only be worsened by new budget cuts. Millions of children have been denied medical coverage. Large cuts have also been made in many other essential programs, including mental health services, mass transit, home health care, food stamps, prisons, and aid to the blind and disabled. State colleges and universities have become more expensive and less accessible.

The Effects of Starvation on Education and Infrastructure

Sometimes the effects of starving the beast are serious, but not immediately obvious. Some vital public sector programs have been reduced so gradually that the effects may not be clear to many in the public. Two examples of this are the effects of funding cuts on higher education and infrastructure development.

In recent years, spending for state higher education institutions has taken a hard hit. States have been cutting budgets for public colleges and universities – which produce three quarters of all degrees in the United States. Teaching positions are being cut, class sizes are spiraling, and needed maintenance is being neglected. Some colleges are now unable to provide students with the required courses they need to finish their degrees. In addition, states have been raising their tuitions and cutting financial aid. A study by the National Center for Public Policy and Higher Education gave the public college and university systems in 43 states a grade of "F" for affordability.[23] This means that many low and middle-income students simply cannot afford college anymore – in one year alone a half million were turned away for lack of money.[24]

Crucial infrastructure spending is also being neglected. A study by the American Society of Civil Engineers found that America's infrastructure is in terrible shape and blamed low levels of investment by state and federal governments. They estimated that over the next five years it would take at least $2.2 trillion to bring our national infrastructure into an acceptable state.[25] Some excerpts from the report:

- Roads and transit systems are in peril. Thirty-three percent of our roads are in poor or mediocre conditions. Funding at the federal, state and local levels is in danger of drying up and citizens are failing to invest in their communities' futures. The nation is failing to even maintain the substandard conditions we currently have, a dangerous trend that is affecting highway safety, as well as the health of the economy.
- 27.5% of the nation's bridges (162,000) were structurally deficient or functionally obsolete.
- The nation's 16,000 waste water systems face enormous needs. Some sewer systems are 100 years old and many treatment facilities are past their recommended life expectancy. Currently, there is a $12 billion annual shortfall in funding for these infrastructure needs.
- Due to either aging, outdated facilities, severe overcrowding, or new mandated class sizes, 75% of our nation's school buildings

> remain inadequate to meet the needs of schoolchildren. While school construction spending has increased, the cost to remedy the situation remains more than $127 billion.

A recent report by CNN found that in 2001 the United States was ranked 6th in infrastructure in the world by the World Economic Forum. Ten years later we were ranked 23rd and falling. Clearly this failure to invest in our infrastructure is a very serious problem – one that can only be addressed with higher taxes and more spending on the state and federal level. But as was noted earlier, the Republican budget plan for the next decade actually calls for hundreds of billions in cuts for highways, bridges, mass transit and other infrastructure developments.

Conservative Responses to the Fiscal Crisis in the States

Seeing the wide spread negative effects – and human costs – of all of these cuts in services, programs, and investments on the state level, you might expect that conservatives would have second thoughts about their anti-tax and anti-spending policies. But amazingly, these kinds of problems have actually been welcomed by anti-government activists. Reports indicate that the Bush White House was happy to see states and their citizens caught in a fiscal crunch and forced to cut programs, and had no desire to help bail them out. Numerous administration officials stated privately that the states' fiscal problems would play a useful role in shrinking state governments.[26] And anti-tax activist Grover Norquist has seemed almost gleeful about the fiscal troubles being faced by states, remarking that "I hope a state goes bankrupt."[27]

Another typical conservative response to the fiscal problems of the states has been to search for scapegoats – someone they can blame for these problems and thus distract the public from the role played by their anti-tax policies. Their preferred scapegoat is public employees. There has been a coordinated campaign to portray public employees as a well-to-do class who are grossly overpaid and enjoy sumptuous benefit packages. Never mind that study after study has shown that public employees are actually underpaid compared to their counterparts in the private sector.[28] Many of them do have decent pensions, but these were often won by giving up pay raises. In addition, many public employees are not eligible for Social Security, so their pensions are not as generous as they first appear.

This assault on our public employees has been widespread and surprisingly nasty. Some conservative commentators have called on them to give back part of the pensions they are living on. Republican legislators in Wisconsin passed a bill that stripped nearly all the collective bargaining rights from the state's public workers. Ohio passed an even harsher law that allows state and city officials to impose whatever contract terms they want on public employees. Similar bills are being considered in other states where conservatives hold power.

Some anti-government ideologues have actually argued that because workers in the private sector are having a tough time – high unemployment, low wages, and shrinking benefits – that public sector workers should be made to suffer as well. Conservatives are trying to provoke resentment against these workers, calling them "haves" when many Americans have become "have nots." But we should be proud that we treat our public employees decently. Undermining the economic security of public workers and making it harder for them to live a middle-class life will only create more suffering in society, not less.

There is an Alternative

It doesn't have to be this way in state governments. In fact, it hasn't always been this way. In the days before the anti-tax movement took hold in the U.S., many states had a vibrant public sector with healthy investments in infrastructure projects and adequately funded social programs for state residents. In his book, *Paradise Lost*, Peter Schrag offers the following descriptions of pre- and post-Proposition 13 California:

> California was once widely regarded as both model and magnet for the nation – in its economic opportunities, its social outlook, and its high-quality public services and institutions. With a nearly free and universally accessible system of public higher education, a well-supported public school system, an ambitious agenda of public works projects – in irrigation and flood control, in highway construction and park development – and a wide array of social services and human rights guarantees that had no parallel in any other state, California seems to have an optimism about its population, possibilities, and future....
>
> But California ... is no longer the progressive model in its public institutions and services, or in its social ethic, that it once was. California's schools, which 30 years ago had been among the most generously funded in the nation, are now in

> the bottom quarter among the states in virtually every major indicator – in physical condition, in public funding, in test scores – closer in most of them to Mississippi than to New York or Connecticut or New Jersey. The state, which had almost doubled in population since the early 1960s, has built some 20 new prisons in the past two decades, but has not opened one new campus of the University of California for nearly three decades. Its once celebrated freeway system is now rated as among the most dilapidated road networks in the country. Many of its public libraries operate on reduced hours, and some have closed altogether. The state's social benefits, once among the nation's most generous, have been cut and cut again, and then cut again. And what had once been a tuition-free college and university system, while still among the world's great public educational institutions, struggles for funds and charges as much as every other state university system, and in some cases more.[29]

Schrag laments what he has termed the "Mississippification" of California. He has nothing against Mississippi, but is simply referring to the reputation that state has for stingy social programs, abysmal schools, inadequate health care programs, and a poor quality of life. This is what could be in store for all of us if government is reduced to an emaciated state. If the anti-government and anti-tax crusaders have their way, we will all be living in Mississippi, whether we want to or not.

---

1. Paul Krugman, "The Tax Cut Con," New York Times Magazine, September 14, 2003, p. 57.
2. The Cato Institute, Cato Handbook on Policy (Washington D.C.: The Cato Institute, 2005) p. 113.
3. See William Greider, "The Education of David Stockman," Atlantic Monthly, December 1981.
4. Krugman, "The Tax Cut Con."
5. Urban Institute, "Bush Tax Cuts," January 16, 2008. http://www.urban.org/decisionpoints08/archive/01bushtaxcuts.cfm
6. Paul Krugman, "Maestro of Chutzpah," New York Times, March 2, 2004, Page A23.
7. David Brooks, "Reinventing the GOP" The New York Times, August 29, 2004.

8. Paul Krugman, "The Tax Cut Con," New York Times Magazine, September 14, 2003, p. 57.
9. Ed Kilgore, "Starving the Beast," Blueprint Magazine, June 30, 2003.
10. Paul Krugman, "The Tax Cut Con," New York Times Magazine, September 14, 2003, p. 56.
11. Ibid. p. 56.
12. Dean Baker, "Representative Ryan Proposes Medicare Plan Under Which Seniors Would Pay Most of Their Income for Health Care," Center for Economic and Policy Research, April 6, 2011, http://www.cepr.net/index.php/blogs/beat-the-press/representative-ryan-proposes-medicare-plan-under-which-seniors-would-pay-most-of-their-income-for-health-care
13.January Angeles, "Ryan Medicaid Block Grant Would Cause Severe Reductions in Health Care and Long Term Care for Senior, People with Disabilities, and Children," Center for Budget Priorities, May 3, 2011, http://www.cbpp.org/files/5-3-11health.pdf
14. Center for American Progress, "Divesting in America." http://www.americanprogress.org/issues/2011/04/disinvesting_america.html
15. Robert Greenstein, "CBO Report: Ryan Plan Specifies Spending Path that would Nearly End Most of Government other than Social Security, Health Care, and Defense by 2050," Center for Budget and Policy Priorities, April 7, 2011, http://www.cbpp.org/cms/index.cfm?fa=view&id=3453
16. "Dangerous Games," *The New York Times*, Saturday, April 23, 2011, p. A16.
17. Robert Greenstein, Chairman Ryan Get's Nearly Two-Thirds of His Huge Budgets Cuts from Program for Lower Income Americans," Center for Budget and Policy Priorities, April 20, 2011, http://www.cbpp.org/cms/index.cfm?fa=view&id=3451
18. Center for Budget and Policy Priorities, "Statement of Robert Greenstein on Chairman Ryan's Budget Plan." http://www.cbpp.org/cms/index.cfm?fa=view&id=3452
19. Brian Beutler, "CBO: GOP Budget would Increase Debt, Then Stick It To Medicare Patients," TPM, April 5, 2011, http://tpmdc.talkingpointsmemo.com/2011/04/cbo-gop-budget-would-increase-debt-then-stick-it-to-medicare-patients.php
20. Center for Budget and Policy Priorities, "At Least 39 States Have Imposed Cuts that Hurt Vulnerable Residents," June 29, 2009. http://www.cbpp.org/cms/?fa=view&id=1214
21. Center on Budget and Policy Priorities, "A Brief Update," p.1.

22. Center for Budget and Policy Priorities, "TABOR: A Threat to Education, Health Care, and Social Services. http://www.cbpp.org/sssl-series/thm. May 20, 2006.
23. National Center for Public Policy and Higher Education, "Measuring Up 2006: The National Report Card on Higher Education. http://measuringup.highereducation.org.
24. "The College Aid Crisis," New York Times, May 25, 2004, p. A26.
25. American Society of Civil Engineers, "Report Card for America's Infrastructure: 2009 Progress Report," http://www.infrastructure reportcard.org/
26. David Firestone, "Does Pain Makes States Stronger?" New York Times, April 27, 2003, p. 4.
27. Ibid.
28. Center for Economic and Policy Research, "State and Local Workers Earn Less than Private Sector Workers, Even Factoring in Benefits," September 15, 2010, http://www.cepr.net/index.php/press-releases/press-releases/state-local-workers-earn-less-than-private-sector
29. Schrag, p. 7-8.

CHAPTER 15

The Deficit Scare: Myth vs. Reality

In recent years, a new and dangerous front has opened up in the conservative war on government: the battle over deficits and debt. The anti-government forces have tried to portray their position as merely one of fiscal common sense. They say that it is simply a matter of not spending more money than one earns. But make no mistake: this anti-debt crusade is a highly politicized effort to fundamentally undermine liberal programs and progressive government in this country.

If the deficit hawks are successful, they will do major damage to society and the economy. They are promoting a deficit hysteria in an effort to force the government to enact deep cuts in vital social programs like Social Security, Medicare, and Medicaid. This fiscal austerity movement would also prevent the government from using deficit spending to speed the recovery of the economy when it is in recession. And it would inhibit us from making the crucial public investments in education, technology, energy, and transportation that are necessary to improve society and lay the foundations for future economic growth.

The Anti-Deficit Campaign

First, let's be clear on the terminology. The "deficit" is the yearly difference between the money the government takes in and what it spends, while the "national debt" is the accumulation of the yearly deficits. The debt is funded by the federal government selling Treasury securities like T-bills, notes, Treasury Inflation-Protected securities, and savings bonds to the public.

Since the election of President Obama, the Republicans have been working diligently to whip up public panic about growing deficits and the debt. Conservative commentators like Glenn Beck have been pushing this issue hard in their daily tirades against overspending "socialist" government. These ideologues maintain that deficits hurt economic growth and that the national debt is putting an unfair burden on the future generations. The only answer, they argue, is to reduce government, rein in public spending, and to move toward balanced budgets.

Also leading the charge to alarm the public has been private-equity billionaire Peter G. Peterson. For 25 years he has been warning that the growing national debt would lead the economy into a disastrous collapse – even during the Clinton administration when many economists predicted many coming years of budget surpluses. In recent years he has pledged to spend a billion dollars to convince lawmakers that we must drastically curtail spending and reduce Social Security and Medicare benefits. He has funded a foundation dedicated to this cause, produced a documentary shown on PBS, and created an on-line newspaper, *Fiscal Times*, to spread his alarmist point of view.

Despite the fact that Peterson's anti-deficit arguments rely on highly questionable predictions and fuzzy math (more on that later), he has been effective in his efforts to woo lawmakers to his cause, even some Democrats. And all these conservative propaganda efforts are having an effect on public opinion, with more Americans saying that deficits are one of the most serious problems facing our country.

Clearly this anti-deficit campaign is part of the larger "starving the beast" strategy that was discussed in the previous chapter. But deficits and debt are complicated topics that merit some analysis on their own. This chapter takes on the "deficit hawks" and critically examines their arguments. It will show that (1) Republicans only care about deficits when the money is being spent on liberal programs; (2) our current large deficits have not been caused by overspending by the Obama administration; (3) deficit spending is an essential tool for combating economic recessions and depressions; (4) public debt can fuel vital public investments in education, technology, and infrastructure that lay the groundwork for future economic expansion; (5) the inflated and misleading right-wing rhetoric about deficits and debt is distracting from a more rational and helpful discussion of the financial problems that we do face as a nation.

Deficit Hypocrites

Before considering what exactly is wrong with the conservative critique of deficits, it is first useful to see just how hypocritical many of them are about this topic. In reality, most conservative politicians don't care nearly as much about deficits as they claim. Consider the evidence: most Republicans in Congress did not become deficit hawks until *after* President Obama was elected. During the previous administration they were busy helping President Bush turn the budget surpluses of the Clinton era into large deficits. Most conservatives did not see this rapid increase in the national debt as a problem at all. Vice-President Cheney blithely dismissed those issues at the time by saying, "Reagan proved deficits don't matter."

So clearly many Republicans think deficits are just fine when they are spending the public's money on their own political priorities. It didn't bother them to fund the wars in Iraq and Afghanistan by massive deficit spending. And they were all too glad to add hundreds of billions to the national debt by passing several enormous tax cuts – money that went largely to the wealthy. The Center for Budget and Policy Priorities has estimated that those wars and tax cuts will eventually contribute a whopping $7 trillion to federal deficits by 2019.[1]

Many Republicans know – or should know – that almost all the projected deficits in the coming years have nothing to do with "out of control and irresponsible spending" by the Obama administration. Consider, for example, the projected deficit for 2013 of $962 billion. A study has shown that 42% ($402 billion) of that deficit will be due to the Bush-era tax cuts. Costs of the Bush initiated wars in Iraq and Afghanistan will account for 16% ($153 billion). Another 41% ($395 billion) of the deficit will be caused by the economic downturn that began in 2008.[2] This last figure includes lost tax revenues, money for the bailout that was necessary to prevent a complete economic meltdown, and money for an economic stimulus package to speed economic recovery. All these factors together will amount to 99% of the deficit in 2013! But this reality is being ignored by Republican politicians who continue to erroneously claim that Democrats and their policies are the main cause of our deficit problems.

Further evidence of Republican hypocrisy about deficits can be found in the way they ignore obvious ways of addressing this problem. If they really cared about reducing deficits, they would be enthusiastic about letting the Bush tax cuts expire. This would be the single most immediate and effective way to help rein in deficit spending. But instead, in 2010 they refused to extend unemployment benefits to millions of Americans until the Democrats agreed to extend all of these tax cuts – thus adding hundreds of billions to the national debt. Apparently, preserving low taxes, especially for the rich, is the real number one priority for Republicans, not cutting the deficits.

As their behavior indicates, many Republicans are not in principle against deficits, only deficit spending they don't agree with. It is only when the Democrats want to spend money on things like making health care more accessible, improving education, or extending unemployment benefits that suddenly deficits matter and we are "broke" and "can't afford" these "irresponsible" expenditures.

The Real Reasons the Republicans are Pushing Deficit Reduction

If deficit reduction isn't a matter of principle for many Republicans, what are the real reasons they are pushing this issue so hard? There are two. First, conservatives believe that deficits make a good campaign issue. They need something to rile up people – something to fan their anger and resentment against government – and deficits fit the bill. Unfortunately, it seems to be working. Polls find increasing numbers of Americans are mentioning deficits and the national debt as one the most important problems facing our nation.

However, the main reason the Republicans have seized on this issue is that it is a good way to reduce government or at the very least prevent its expansion. Efforts to rein in the budget have long been a part of their "starving the beast" strategy that was described in a previous chapter. That is why Republicans have no interest in one of the obvious ways to approach this problem: raising taxes so government does not have to borrow so much money to pay for necessary programs. In their view, there is only one way to addresses deficits: cut spending. Of course this could eventually necessitate cutting back on many of the established liberal programs – like Medicare and Medicaid – that Republicans have never liked. In fact, the Republican budget proposal in 2011 actually called for ending Medicare and Medicaid as we know them. In the end, this renewed conservative concern about deficits is simply a new way to pursue their real goal – reducing big bad government.

Deficits Are Good During Recessions

But irrespective of their motivations, aren't Republicans right that deficit spending is a terrible idea and we must stop doing it? Aren't balanced budgets just a matter of common sense? The answer is "No." In fact, a good case can be made that deficit spending is an indispensable government tool in addressing serious economic problems.

For example, most economists agree that deficit spending during a recession, especially a severe one, is a very good thing to do. Even though tax revenues are decreasing, the best thing for the economy is for the government to keep spending money, and even increase spending. When consumer and corporate spending are swooning, only the government is in the position to spend money and stimulate economic activity. The market will not take care of this problem, so the government must step in.

Government spending has a *multiplier effect* that provides a large economic boost during recessions. If it spends money on building schools and roads, for example, that money first helps construction companies. These companies in turn will hire more workers who will then spend more money on goods and services, thus helping other businesses. The construction companies will also purchase more tools and materials from other businesses, who will then hire more workers, and so on. In this way, deficit spending spreads through the economy, lessening the impact of recessions and helping to speed economic recovery. And as the economy rebounds, this produces higher tax revenues, which eventually lessens the need for deficit spending.

Contrary to the wildly erroneous claims of the political right, most economists agree that the deficit spending and economic stimulus programs of the Obama administration provided enormous benefits. A 2010 study by Alan Blinder of Princeton and Mark Zandy of Moody's Analytics found that the combined effect of the fiscal stimulus package, TARP, and the actions of the Federal Reserve Board raised real GDP 11% over where it would have been, saved an estimated 8 million jobs, and probably averted deflation and a depression. They concluded: "It is clear that *laissez faire* was not an option; policymakers had to act. Not responding would have left both the economy and the government's fiscal situation in far graver condition. We conclude that Ben Bernanke was probably right when he said that 'We came very close in October [2008] to Depression 2.0.'"[3]

The worst thing the federal government could have done was to listen to the deficit hawks and curtailed spending in the face of a severe recession. To see why, you simply need to look at state governments that did this in recent years. As their economies were tanking, many state governments – which are constitutionally required to balance their budgets – had to lay off workers, cut benefits to individuals, and curtail purchases of goods from the private sector. This simply made a bad economic situation worse. It created a kind of reverse multiplier effect, taking money and jobs out of the economy and lowering demand for goods and services in an already weak economy. Instead of speeding an economic recovery, this kind of frugal spending policy actually slows it down. It hardly makes sense to kick the economy when it is down, but this is what happens if governments are forced to balance their budgets every year.

If the Republicans continue to be successful in blocking further stimulus spending, this will only hurt the economy. At best, it will delay recovery from the recession, and at worst, it might actually precipitate a dip back into more severe recession. Either way, this will only add up to more suffering for millions of American workers. Chronic long term unemployment has reached heights not seen since the Great Depression of the 1930s. This is the real crisis facing many Americans. They are out of a job, out of savings, and losing their house. Their American dream is fading fast. Only the government is in the position to help – to stimulate the economy to produce more jobs. And yet the Republicans keep insisting that budget balancing must be our first priority – thus leaving millions of jobless working class and middle class Americans hung out to dry.

Bogus Math and Questionable Estimates

Peterson and many other fiscal austerity zealots rely primarily on highly questionable predictions that budget deficits and the debt will soar to unimaginable heights several decades from now. They predict economic doom as interest rates soar and investment grinds to a halt. But as numerous critics have pointed out, predictions that extend out several decades are extremely unreliable and depend entirely on the assumptions one uses. For example, slight changes in his assumptions about the rate of economic growth or key tax rates would mean that none of his dire predictions about soaring debt would actually come about.

Robert Kuttner is particularly critical of the misleading calculations in Peterson's analysis:

> The Peterson Foundation's central claim of over $50 trillion in unfunded liabilities is arrived at by miscounting apples and oranges. The only true figure for debt—that is, debt on which actual interest is paid by taxpayers—is the public debt held by the public, estimated as of January 12, 2009, according to the Treasury, is $7,781,352,915,790.80.
>
> The Treasury Department's figure for public debt is about 54 percent of GDP, a far smaller portion of GDP than at any time during the quarter-century after World War II, a period of record economic boom. The rest of the Peterson Foundation's fanciful arithmetic is derived by adding debt that one government agency owes to another (another roughly $4.5 trillion) as well as the projected seventy-five-year deficits for Social Security, Medicare, and Medicaid, using worst-case scenarios.[4]

Social Security is a good example of just how questionable Peterson's alarmist analysis really is. There is clearly no immediate crisis and not a likely long-term problem either. The Social Security payroll tax was hiked in the 1980s to handle the increasing number of baby-boomers retiring now. As a result, the program's trust fund is projected to grow steadily, with a surplus lasting until at least 2027. After that, some very small modifications in income or payouts could return the system to surplus. Even if that wasn't done, the program will still be able to pay 100 percent of benefits until 2041.[5]

The only way that Peterson can make Social Security look like a problem is if he projects the program out 75 years, and assumes very low rates of economic growth and wage increases. Slightly more optimistic economic assumptions would mean that Social Security would be quite viable for the foreseeable future. So to whip up public panic about the Social Security system, as Peterson and his allies have done, is simply irresponsible.

Deficits and Debt can Encourage Economic Growth

Conservatives are also wrong when they argue that deficit spending and a large national debt will inevitably undermine economic growth. To see why, we need to simply look back at times when we have run up large deficits and increased the national debt. The best example is World War II when the national debt soared to 120% of GDP – nearly twice the size of today's debt. This spending not only got us out of the Great Depression but set the stage for a prolonged period of sustained economic growth in the 50s and 60s. Massive investments were made in science and technology, American workers were re-trained and re-employed, private investment was encouraged, and consumer purchasing power was increased. That 25-year post-war economic boom, with the most rapid increase in living standards in our history, would not have happened without the stimulus of all this deficit spending.

History also shows that balancing the budget does not necessarily ensure a spurt of economic growth. In fact, in most periods when we have not had deficits, such as the 1990s, this was followed by an economic recession.[6] So there is clearly little historical evidence to show that deficits and debt inevitably hurt economic growth.

But what about the conservative argument that public spending "crowds out" private investment, to the detriment of economic growth? They maintain that if the government is borrowing a lot money, that is money that the private sector cannot invest to increase its production and productivity. This has to undermine economic growth, right? The answer is "No, not necessarily."

As most economists point out, government spending also has a "crowding in" effect that actually encourages more private investment. That is because much of the money that the government borrows and spends goes to the private sector. Private industry must then prepare to provide the various goods and services demanded by the government – such as weapons systems, green energy systems, new roads and schools, etc. In order to do this, these businesses must invest in new production facilities and greater productivity. This "crowding in" effect thus helps to mitigate any negative effects that public borrowing has on the private sector by indirectly encouraging more private investment and business growth.

Investing in America's Future

But there is even a more important issue here – one often brought up by Joseph Stiglitz, a Nobel Prize winning economist. He argues that deficit spending, when it is done right, can be a major stimulus to economic growth and actually lower long term government debt.[7] When economic growth is back on healthy terms, this leads to increased tax revenues, which eventually lessen the need for government to borrow money. For Stiglitz, the key is to spend that deficit money on things like education, technology, and infrastructure that lay the groundwork for future economic expansion. We will not remain competitive with other countries for long if we don't have decent roads, efficient airports, adequate clean water supplies, and sufficient school facilities. Recently the American Society of Civil Engineers estimated that over the next five years it would take at least $1.6 trillion to bring our national infrastructure into an acceptable state. These are huge investments that the private sector is unwilling to make. Going into debt to pay for these things is a good investment in our collective futures.

We also need government to invest in emerging technologies that are vital to our economic prospects. We are falling behind many other countries in our public investments in high-speed rail, modern telecommunications technology, and an advanced electricity grid. Another area that will drive economic expansion in the future is green technology and alternative energy. Left to itself, the market has not been leading us in that direction. Several other countries, including China and Germany, have been spending billions in public funds to encourage consumers and industry to jump on the green technology bandwagon, and they are already beginning to reap the economic rewards of this strategy. We are trailing badly in this vital economic area and we are unlikely to catch up without substantial investments by our government.

Who Really Cares about Our Children?

One of the most common Republican complaints about deficits is that they will ruin our children's future. We are saddling them with this enormous debt that they will have to repay – presumably to their great detriment. So if we care about future generations, we must severely cut spending to rein in this increasing debt. "Do it for the kids," say the deficit hawks.

The main problem with this argument is that it focuses only on the *costs* of deficit spending for future generations, and completely ignores how that spending would actually *benefit* them. Would you be a good parent if you considered only the costs of buying braces for your child and not the benefits they would enjoy for the rest of their lives? Similarly, we must not just think about the national debt that we are handing down to our children, but consider also all of the valuable assets, projects, and programs that could be financed by that debt. Those benefits could make future generations much better off.

It all depends on what the deficits are spent on. If we are simply going into debt, as we did in the Bush era, to pay for tax cuts for the rich and wars like those in Iraq and Afghanistan, this will do little to help our descendants. But what if some of that deficit spending goes to make higher education more affordable? A study by the National Center for Public Policy and Higher Education gave the public college and university systems in 43 states a grade of "F" for affordability. This means that many kids who do go to college end up saddled with enormous student loans that will detract from their standard of living for years. More importantly, many low and middle-income students simply cannot afford college anymore – hundreds of thousands of kids are being turned away every year for lack of money. In contrast, public investment by many countries in Europe has made higher education there low cost or free. Whose kids are better off?

In addition, we are not doing our offspring any favors if they inherit a country whose infrastructure is in disastrous condition. They will not enjoy balanced budgets if that means living in a world of bad roads, dangerous bridges, failing sewer systems, questionable drinking water, and congested airports. Future generations might also be thankful if we spend some money now on lessening the potentially disastrous impacts of climate change. Global warming is already beginning to do enormous harm with unusually intense droughts and floods. If we do nothing now, the impacts on our children and grandchildren will be much more severe.

Finally, as noted earlier, government spending can be crucial for ensuring a prosperous and growing economy. A large part of the economic growth in the last twenty years has been fueled by various kinds of private sector economic bubbles. This is hardly desirable or sustainable. In the 1990s, there was a large technology bubble that created billions in apparent investment profits. Later, it was the housing bubble which encouraged consumers to borrow and spend much more money because of the rapidly increasing value of their homes. When these bubbles burst, they took the economy down with them. Today, we need a more stable and reliable way of encouraging economic growth. Public investments in emerging technologies, like alternative energy, could prove to be a valuable part of that economic strategy. If we can leave our children a sustainable growing economy, this could be their greatest inheritance.

Our Real Financial Concerns

All of this is not to say that there are not some serious financial concerns looming on the horizon. But they are all solvable. The challenge is to do so in a way that does not shred our social safety net or prevent us from engaging in the kind of public investment that we so crucially need.

The main problems we face are with Medicare and Medicaid. Without any reforms, Medicare will go into deficit by 2020, and benefits will have to be reduced. This is due to the fact that that health care costs in this country are already high and rising even further. Why are costs so high? Because we have one of the most inefficient health care systems in the world. We pay almost twice as much per person for health care compared to many other advanced countries, and we often provide worse care (and a lower life expectancy). The main culprit is the commercial domination of our health care system. We rely primarily on private, for profit, insurance companies and healthcare companies. Many other countries have more streamlined, government-run, single-payer systems that provide high quality care at much lower costs.

In the long run, then, solving the financial problems of Medicare and Medicaid require some basic reforms in our health care system. As Dean Baker, one of the most thoughtful economists analyzing government debt has explained it, the best way to address our debt is to "fix health care, fix health care, fix health care." The health care reforms passed in 2010 have some promise to slow down growing costs. But the health care system remains the hostage of the private, profit-making, health care industry. Many analysts believe that additional major reforms must take place if we are truly to rein in rising medical costs. The crucial importance of doing so was made clear in a report by Our Fiscal Security, which concluded: "The rapidly rising cost of private health care—doctor's visits, prescription drugs, procedures—is the only truly unsustainable part of the long-term budget. If U.S. health care costs were growing at the rate of other wealthy countries, we would have no long-term debt problem."[8]

A Crucial Part of the Solution: Raising Government Revenue

Baker and other progressive economists have also been promoting another approach to long-term debt reduction: raising more revenue. For example, Robert Kuttner has proposed a series of tax changes that could bring in an addition $800 billion a year into the federal coffers.[9] These include:

- A tax on Wall Street financial transactions. This would have the added benefit of discouraging short term speculative trading and encouraging more stable longer term investments.
- Crack down on off-shore tax havens. Estimated to bring in at least $100 billion a year.
- End the deferral on foreign source dividend income. Obama promised to close this loophole, which also would discourage shifting jobs overseas.
- Eliminate deductibility of interest payments on corporate mergers. Should bring in at least $50 billion a year and discourage abusive takeover attempts.
- Raise taxes on short term capital gains. These gains should be treated as ordinary income, as they were before the Reagan era.

None of these additional revenue sources would have much of an effect on 90% of Americans. More importantly, they would enable us to stabilize and perhaps even expand our crucial safety net programs and also to pay for vital public investment projects, such as alternative energy and infrastructure improvements.

Other analysts have argued that much of the needed money for social programs and public investments could easily come out of the defense budget. If one considers how much countries spend on defense, the U.S. heads that list by a very wide margin. In fact, we spend more money on defense than the next nineteen countries on that list combined. Our navy alone has the capability of the next eight countries navies combined – many of which are our allies. So there is a lot of room to downsize without undermining our security. A bipartisan group, the Project on Defense Alternatives, has done an analysis that found we could cut a trillion dollars out the defense budget in the next ten years without compromising our military superiority.[10] That kind of money would go a long ways toward solving our fiscal problems.

The Real Battle

In the end, the political battle over deficits and the national debt is really just a proxy for the more basic ideological struggle over the proper role of government in a modern society. The Republicans want to use fear-mongering over these alleged financial problems to advance their political vision of the minimal state. They promise Americans a future of balanced budgets, reduced spending, and lower taxes. But what they don't tell us is that this would also be a future in which most people would be on their own to try to deal with serious economic, social, medical, and environmental problems that face our country. The jobless would be left to fend for themselves during serious recessions. Basic safety net programs like Social Security and Medicare would be cut back and/or privatized, and scores of other unmet human needs would be neglected due to lack of sufficient taxes and public funds. It would be a world where infrastructure would continue to crumble and we could not afford to make the necessary investments in education and growth-producing technologies.

Of course there is another possible scenario: a much more positive one in which we all worked together through government to address our common problems. It would be a future in which active government used all of the tools at its disposal – including taxation and deficit spending – to improve the lives and security of average Americans. Where the government would step in vigorously to reduce the impact of recessions and to promote job creation. Where the government would make the necessary investments to shore up vital safety net programs, and to update and improve our educational and infrastructure systems. In this scenario, we would also have a society that was made more sustainable and livable by public spending to encourage alternative energy and other green technologies.

But it is exactly this future that will be denied us if we fall prey to the deficit hysteria being manufactured by the anti-government forces in this country.

1. Kathy Ruffing and James Horney, "Critics Still Wrong on What's Driving Deficits in Coming Years," June 28, 2010, Center for Budget and Policy Priorities. http://www.cbpp.org/cms/index.cfm?fa=view&id=3036
2. Kathy Ruffing and James Horney, "Economic Downturn and Bush Policies Continue to Drive Projected Deficits," May 10, 2011, Center for Budget and Policy Priorities. http://www.cbpp.org/cms/index.cfm?fa=view&id=3490
3. Alan Blinder and Mark Zandy, "How the Great Recession was Brought to an End," July 27, 2010. http://www.economy.com/mark-zandi/documents/End-of-Great-Recession.pdf
4. Robert Kuttner, "Progressive Revenue as the Alternative to Caps, Commissions, and Cuts," February 25, 2010. http://www.scholarsstrategynetwork.org/pdfs/Progressive_Revenue_as_the_Alternative-Robert_Kuttner.pdf
5. David Knox, "Social Security More Solvent that Most American Realize," August 24, 2008 http://www.ohio.com/news/american_dream/27325314.html
6. Ezra Klein, "Galbraith: The Danger Posed by the Deficit is Zero," May 12, 2010, "http://voices.washingtonpost.com/ezra-klein/2010/05/galbraith_the_danger_posed_by.html
7. Joseph Stiglitz, "The Dangers of Deficit Reductions." March 5, 2010. http://www.sfbg.com/bruce/2010/03/05/stiglitz-dangers-deficit-reduction
8. Our Fiscal Security, "The Budget Deficit and Debt: What You Need to Know," September 2010, http://www.ourfiscalsecurity.org/deficit-101
9. Robert Kuttner, "Progressive Revenue as the Alternative to Caps, Commissions, and Cuts," February 25, 2010. http://www.scholarsstrategynetwork.org/pdfs/Progressive_Revenue_as_the_Alternative-Robert_Kuttner.pdf
10. Project on Defense Alternatives, "Debt, Deficits, and Defense: A Way Forward," June 11, 2010, http://www.comw.org/pda/

CHAPTER 16

Stealth Deregulation: The Untold Story

The enormous ecological and economic damage in the Gulf of Mexico caused by the British Petroleum oil spill is just one telling example of the breakdown of regulation and oversight by the federal government. There are many more. Consider the 2009 outbreak of salmonella in several peanut butter factories. And of course it is now clear that the lack of government oversight of the financial sector was a major cause of the mortgage loan crisis and the severe economic recession that it triggered.

Some people have blamed such regulatory lapses on the inherent incompetence of the federal government. But these failures have little to do with incompetence and everything to do with the rise of a conservative, anti-government ideology that has been fundamentally hostile to regulation. "Deregulation" was the mantra of President George W. Bush and his Republican predecessors, and many of the problems we are now facing are the predictable result of this failed political philosophy. Importantly, these conservatives not only undermined federal oversight of the energy industry, the food system, and the financial sector, they also worked to reduce broad protections for consumers, workers, and the environment.

One particularly glaring example of this atmosphere of deregulation: the Minerals Management Service (MMS) of the Department of the Interior, the agency charged with overseeing oil operations in the Gulf of Mexico. During the Bush administration, the staff of MMS frequently partied with oil company representatives and accepted expensive gifts from them. In return, British Petroleum got a waiver from conducting an environmental impact analysis and no inspections were conducted of its blowout preventers. In addition, BP was allowed to not use an advanced blowout prevention technology (one that is required by many other countries) because the MMS agreed with the company that it would be too expensive. Not surprisingly, Randal

Luthi, MMS director under Bush, eventually was rewarded with a well-paying job as head of the National Oceans Industries Association, a private trade group that focuses on creating "a favorable regulatory and economic environment for the companies that develop the nation's valuable offshore energy resources."

Most Americans still do not know the full story about this Republican effort to weaken and dismantle regulatory protections for the public. Indeed, most were not even aware that it was happening on such a wide scale. That is because much of this deregulation was accomplished behind closed doors, deep in the bowels of the federal bureaucracy where it got little attention.

This chapter will bring to light how this strategy of stealth deregulation was pursued in the administrative branch under George W. Bush. It is a story of devious appointments, slashed budgets, weakened rules, and relaxed enforcement. I will also discuss what needs to be done to solve the problems caused by this era of runaway deregulation.

The Attack of the Anti-Regulators

Imagine the following scenario: a new president comes into office and announces that he will appoint a dedicated pacifist to head the Department of Defense and a mafia lawyer as Director of the FBI. What would be the reaction? Many in the public would be outraged and the media would go into a feeding frenzy. In short, all hell would break loose.

In reality, of course, the chances of a president getting away with such ridiculous and disruptive appointments would be slim to none. And yet President George W. Bush did essentially the same thing: he routinely appointed officials whose political priorities ran exactly counter to the missions of the agencies they were charged with running. And many of these appointees worked for or represented the very industries that these agencies were supposed to be policing. For example, important posts in the Food and Drug Administration were filled by people who had careers working for the drug industry.

Exhibit One is Daniel Troy, who Bush appointed to be Chief Counsel for the Food and Drug Administration. Previously, as a lawyer, he filed a number of lawsuits against the FDA arguing against its right to regulate drug companies. Once in office, he stalled efforts to investigate the problems surrounding ephedra - a dietary supplement implicated in the deaths of more than 100 people. Amazingly, in a speech he gave to drug industry lawyers after his appointment, he offered the help of the government in defending these companies against lawsuits by consumers, such as those claiming that medications caused devastating side effects. Not coincidentally, enforcement actions against improper drug advertising went down dramatically after his appointment.

J. Steven Griles was another example of a Bush appointment that seemed designed to sabotage the agency to which he was appointed. He served as Deputy Secretary of the Interior in Bush's first term. He worked previously as a high-paid lobbyist for the coal and oil companies – the very industries he was then put in charge of regulating. Not surprisingly, the National Mining Association celebrated his appointment, lauding him as "an ally of the industry." And to top it off, while working for the government, he still received $284,000 a year from his former lobbying firm that continued to represent those industries.

This strategy of handing over regulatory bodies to the industries they are supposed to regulate has been dubbed by critics as "foxes guarding the henhouse." Among some of the other more obvious foxes in the Bush administration:

> **Eugene Scalia**, appointed to be Labor Department Solicitor. Scalia's sympathies were unlikely to be on the side of labor since his previous job was specializing in anti-labor law and representing the management side in labor disputes. He also represented many of the companies that were opposing the new ergonomic rules that were later abandoned by the Department.
>
> **Jeffrey Holmstead**, who became the EPA's assistant administrator for Air and Radiation. How protective could he be of the environment when he formerly worked as a lawyer representing numerous corporations seeking to block environmental regulations? He eventually headed the administration's efforts to relax clean air requirements for coal-fired power plants – a move that Sen. James Jeffords called "the biggest rollback of the Clear Air Act in history."
>
> **Marianne Horinko,** Asst. Administrator for the Office of Solid Waste and Emergency Response – in charge of the Superfund program to clean up toxic waste sites. Before this, she worked as an attorney representing the industry side in Superfund suits. The rate at which Superfund sites were being cleaned up fell dramatically under the Bush Administration.
>
> **Michael F. Duffy**, Federal Mine Safety and Health Review Commission. His primary experience was working as an

attorney for the National Mining Association and the American Mining Congress.

Chuck Lambert, United States Department of Agriculture official in charge of regulating the meat packing industry. His previous job was working for a lobbying group for the National Cattlemen's Beef Association. He was just one of a dozen people with ties to the meat industry who were appointed to the USDA, leading one consumer advocate to observe that "the USDA gives the impression of being a wholly owned subsidiary of America's cattlemen."[1]

And these are just a few examples. An investigative reporter for the Denver Post found that over 100 of the high level officials appointed by President Bush in this first term of office were "overseeing" the industries they used to represent as lobbyists, employees, or lawyers. As Maria Weidner of the Earthjustice Legal Defense Fund observed at the time: "They are lawyers and lobbyists who build their careers by helping industry get out of … regulations. Now they will be doing the same things, only the taxpayers will be paying for it."[2]

The Deregulation Playbook

Once these anti-regulatory ideologues and industry representatives were in place, they were free to begin to impede the regulatory process and to undermine regulations passed by Congress. The specific tactics varied, but included:

Stalling. Agency personnel routinely and systematically delayed in formulating and issuing regulations mandated by law. For example, even though the Bush administration promised to act quickly to devise urgently needed rules to protect the right whale from extinction, it took the maximum time allowed by law, then refused to issue the rule, in violation of the law, for an additional 453 days.[3]

Cutting Their Own Budgets. Remarkably, Bush appointees routinely tried to cut the budgets of their own agencies – making it more difficult for them to do their job. The budget for mine safety inspections, for instance, went from $139 million in 2001 to $118 million in 2006.

Inactivity. Administrators simply ignored emerging problems. In the area of workplace safety, despite evidence of a number of threats to Americans on the job, the Bush Occupational Safety and Health Administration largely sat on its hands during its entire tenure – issuing only one significant new regulation in eight years. Also, for years, Bush environmental officials refused to admit that global warming was a serious issue that merited immediate action.

Reducing Enforcement. Regulations are only effective if they are enforced vigorously. Bush appointees routinely worked to weaken enforcement. For example, they cut the civil penalties that polluters had to pay by half – weakening the incentives to comply with environmental protection rules. Another example was the reduction of inspectors and inspections in areas like food safety and mine safety. In 2003, the FDA conducted over 11,000 inspections a year for food safety – a figure that fell to 6,000 by 2007.

"Relaxing" Rules. Bush officials would look for opportunities to create exceptions or loopholes to rules so that various businesses could escape regulation. For example, they relaxed nationwide permit rules so coal companies, developers, and others could fill in thousands of streams, swamps, and other wetlands, without public notice or comment.

Listening Only to Industry. Many Bush appointees met routinely with business lobbyists interested in deregulation, but met only rarely or never with representatives of public interest groups. For example, Dick Cheney and other officials on the Energy Task Force met dozens of times with business leaders from the oil, gas, coal, and nuclear industries. Only one meeting was held for environmental groups – it lasted just one hour and much of that was taken up with introductions of the participants.

Refusing to Fill Appointments. Bush often took an inordinate amount of time filling high-level management vacancies in agencies he didn't like. This left these agencies adrift, often run by temporary appointments who tended to not be very aggressive in pursuing the mandate of these organizations.

Ignoring Expert Advice. When research produced results that the Bush administration did not like, administration officials often ignored it and refused to act on it. A particularly egregious example was the suppression of scientific research about the seriousness of global warming and the attempt to gag administration scientists who tried to speak out on this issue.

Embracing "Voluntary" Regulation. Abandoning aggressive approaches to regulatory enforcement – like the use of the courts to force compliance – the Bush administration favored "voluntary" compliance schemes which often had little effect. The SEC, for instance, relied heavily on voluntary regulation of financial institutions. After the financial meltdown in 2008, the Chairman of the SEC admitted that this approach was "fundamentally flawed from the beginning … because investment banks could opt in or out of supervision voluntarily."

The Secret Office of Deregulatory Affairs

Just in case some federal administrators forgot what administration they were in and became too enthusiastic about initiating regulatory protections, the Bush White House vigorously employed the oversight powers of the Office of Information and Regulatory Affairs. Created in the Reagan administration, this little-known 50-person unit is buried in the Office of Management and Budget. In conservative administrations, the job of the OIRA is to review every proposed regulation and see if it may be too costly, particularly to business. If so, it is sent back to the particular agency for review or repeal. For much of the Bush administration, this agency was run by John Graham – a well-known opponent of much federal regulation. In the past, he had written that efforts to regulate such things as nuclear power and PCBs were simply a product of "a hypochondria raging among various consumer advocates and public interest groups."[4]

Graham was particularly enthusiastic in using his unique administrative powers to frustrate regulation. During the eight years of the Clinton Administration, the OIRA sent back only 16 proposed regulations. In his first year alone, Graham sent back 19 regulations. And in his second year, his office identified 326 regulations for possible rejection or softening. Not surprisingly, many of these regulations were specifically targeted by various business interests and right-wing think tanks. In fact, when Graham entered office, he secretly surveyed business groups in order to compile a hit list of regulations they considered too onerous. The list included a wide variety of environmental, health, and safety regulations, including some addressing pesticide use, coal-mine ventilation, air and water quality, lead paint disclosure, toxic-release reporting, and family and medical leave. According to one lobbyist, "This was hush-hush, behind closed-doors stuff." For business interests, this process showed them that Graham was on their side. As another lobbyist observed, "With Graham in that job, we figured we could get whatever we want."[5]

New (Anti) Regulatory Philosophies

Anti-government ideologues in the Bush administration were not only trying to relax regulations and their enforcement, they were also trying to change the way administrators *think* about regulations. They were promoting new "regulatory philosophies" that primarily functioned as rationalizations for more deregulation. One new way of thinking about regulation that proved particularly dangerous to the public and the environment was cost-benefit analysis. The Bush administration acted vigorously to impose strict cost-benefit tests on all new proposed regulations, insisting that the benefits of new rules outweigh the costs. One of the chief promoters of this approach has been none other than John Graham, the one-time head of the Office of Information and Regulatory Affairs discussed earlier – a man who believes America has become highly over-regulated. At first glance, cost-benefit analysis sounds pretty reasonable – no one wants regulations that create more harm than good, right? But the problem is that there is a strong anti-regulatory bias in this analytic process.

Consider this: it is usually much easier to calculate the costs of regulations than it is to quantify the resulting benefits for society. For example, one can easily find out how many millions it would cost a utility to install a scrubber on a coal burning utility plant; but how much is it worth in dollars to save a life, or to reduce disease, or to have cleaner air? There are no markets for such things, and so they are difficult to "monetize." This means that many benefits will always seem less important than the costs of the proposed regulations. The Bush administration admitted as much in 2004 when it deleted 55 pages describing benefits of a program to save an endangered species, leaving only the sections describing the costs to industry. An official explained that it was "too difficult to monetize the value of a species" – and the agency then used the amended report to justify cutting back the amount of protected habitat.[6]

Consider also what happened when the EPA proposed new regulations to limit runoff from construction and development sites, the largest source of pollution in coastal waters and estuaries in the U.S. During construction and development, massive amounts of sediments are carried into our water systems, and these activities also greatly increase storm water runoff that contains pollutants like pesticides, oil, grease, and fertilizers. But officials in the Bush White House gutted the proposal because the EPA was not able to put a dollar figure on the benefits the new regulations would produce for natural ecosystems and human health.[7]

Stealth Tactics Designed to Undermine Accountability

For conservatives, one of the main advantages of these kinds of deregulation tactics was that they took place deep in the bowels of the federal bureaucracy and so these decisions often flew underneath the public radar. Republicans were well aware that most Americans actually wanted more regulation, not less, in many areas like the environment and health care. For example, 60% want the government to spend more money on environmental protection. And only 7% of Americans want less regulation of pharmaceutical and drug companies, while 57% want more. And when conservatives tried to roll back these kinds of regulations in Congress during the 1990s, the public quickly found out and reacted very negatively. So to avoid this kind of public backlash, conservatives turned to "stealth tactics." Once they had control of the presidency, they largely abandoned attacking consumer, environmental and workplace regulations in Congress where everyone could see what was going on, and instead turned to undermining these regulations in the dark halls of the federal bureaucracies. The idea seemed to be this: what people don't know about, they are unlikely to get upset about.

What Can Be Done

While few Americans knew about all of these deregulation efforts, we are all now painfully aware of many of their disastrous consequences. People do tend to notice when tens of millions of gallons of crude oil spread over the Gulf of Mexico, when their food makes them sick, or when their retirement funds are cut in half. Clearly many of us are now outraged by the results of runaway deregulation, but what can we do about it?

First, the public must reject the conservative philosophy that fueled the deregulation fervor in the first place: the belief that the best market is an unregulated one. By now it should be abundantly clear that unregulated markets are prone to any number of problems and that there are legitimate reasons for government to step in to regulate them for the public interest. (For a description of the numerous failures inherent in a free market economy, see the chapter "Capitalism Requires Government.") It should also be evident that we cannot always trust businesses to do the right thing since they have to put corporate profits before the public interest.

Second, we must elect leaders who appreciate the importance of regulation as a way of protecting the public interest. Fortunately, President Obama understands this point and has pledged to use the administrative powers of government to actively protect consumers, workers, and the environment. He has appointed regulators who not only have expertise in the areas of their responsibility, but who also have pledged to vigorously enforce the rules and regulations of their agencies. The

President has also promised that science and research will once again play a respected role in the formation of regulatory policies. Reports on his first two years in office found that many agencies have been much more diligent in their enforcement of regulations. For instance, Occupation Safety and Health Administration inspectors increased the number of citations for health and safety violations, and the agency shifted its attention toward high-risk sectors and repeat violators.

We must also insist that Congress step up to bat on these issues – something it has not always done, even when Democrats have been in control. It needs to ensure that agencies have the funds necessary to do their jobs effectively. In 2009, for instance, Congress passed a bill increasing the funding for the Consumer Product and Safety Commission, which should now allow this agency to increase a staff that had been reduced to almost half of what it was in the early 1980s. Increased budgets for other key agencies are also needed. Further, Congress needs to increase its oversight of these agencies and not wait until some disaster has struck before it calls hearings about a malfunctioning agency.

All of this recent activity to begin to revitalize our regulatory system is a good sign. But this should not be taken to mean that conservatives have given up on their efforts to promote deregulation. In 2010, for example, the Republican leadership called for a complete moratorium on new regulations – at a time when polls showed that a majority of Americans wanted increased regulation of the energy industry, health care companies, and the financial industry. Conservatives will try to return to their anti-regulatory agenda whenever they can – especially if the Republicans are able to gain control of the presidency and the administrative branch once again. And they made their intentions clear after taking over the House of Representatives in the 2010 elections. Who did the Republicans name to chair the House committee in charge of regulation of the financial sector? Rep. Ron Paul, who once observed: "I don't think we need regulators."

---

1. Anne C. Mulkern, "When Advocates Become Regulators," May 23, 2004, Denver Post.
2. Earthjustice and Public Campaign, "Paybacks: Policies, Patrons, and Personnel," September 2002.
3. This and many of the other examples in this section come from *The Bush Legacy: An Assault on Public Protections*, a highly information 2009 report put out by OMB Watch. http://www.ombwatch.org/node/3877

4. Carl Pope, *Strategic Ignorance* (San Francisco: Sierra Club Books, 2004) p. 52.
5. Michael Grunwald, "Business Lobbyists Ask to Discuss Onerous Rules," *Washington Post*, December 4, 2001.
6. Sherry Devlin, "Feds: Benefits of Bull Trout too Hard to Put a Value On," *The Missoulian*, April 7, 2004.
7. "Special Interest Takeover: The Bush Administration and the Dismantling of Public Safeguards" (Washington, D.C.: The Citizens for Sensible Safeguards Coalition, 2004), p. 54.

CHAPTER 17

The Courthouse Crusade Against Government

The more radical elements of the anti-government movement face a serious problem. They would like to eliminate or drastically reduce many of our basic progressive social programs, like Social Security and Medicare; and they also want to curtail many of the federal government's regulatory programs. But broad public support for such programs makes it difficult to attack them effectively through the legislative process. So some anti-government activists have turned to the federal courts in an effort to construct a constitutional assault on these programs. Conservative and libertarian judges and legal scholars are promoting a radical reinterpretation of the Constitution that would severely constrain the powers of the federal government. They are attempting a legal end-run around the democratic process to impose their small government views on all Americans.

Anti-Government Extremism in the Courts

Judge Janice Rogers Brown could serve as the poster-child for the anti-government movement's efforts in the third branch of government: the judiciary. Now a member of the United States Court of Appeals for the District of Columbia, Brown is a jurist intent on radically reinterpreting the Constitution in order to undermine the power of the federal government. For example, she has asserted that the states should not be subject to the Bill of Rights – a view that most legal scholars see as virtually indefensible. In the past, she has also argued for overturning established precedents in cases involving the government's authority to regulate corporations and supported the idea of striking down health and safety laws that might infringe on the rights of business. Even more strangely, she has also attacked the 1937 decisions by the Supreme Court that upheld much of the legislation of the New Deal, calling them a "disaster" that marked "the triumph of our socialist revolution."

Brown's legal opinions are largely informed by a deep and abiding contempt for government and its role in modern society. She has commented that "where government advances – and it advances relentlessly – freedom is imperiled; community impoverished; religion marginalized and civilization itself jeopardized...."[1] She expanded on these ultraconservative views in a speech she gave in 2000 to the Federalist Society, a leading conservative legal group:

> Where government moves in, community retreats, civil society disintegrates and our ability to control our own destiny atrophies. The result is: families under siege; war in the streets; unapologetic expropriation of property; the precipitous decline of the rule of law; the rapid rise of corruption: the loss of civility and the triumph of deceit. The result is a debased, debauched culture, which finds moral depravity entertaining and virtue contemptible.[2]

It is sobering that President Bush believed that someone with such a radical and paranoid view of government would be qualified to render decisions in one of the highest courts in this country – one often considered a stepping stone to the Supreme Court. Not surprisingly, over 270 law professors opposed the nomination of Judge Brown to the federal bench. Several Democratic senators were outraged enough by Brown's nomination to organize a successful filibuster to block her appointment. However, in 2005, the Senate Republicans threatened the "nuclear option" – to take away the Democrats' right to filibuster – if they did not agree to procedures to approve several Bush appointees to the bench, including Brown. The Democrats were forced to capitulate in the face of this outrageous tactic and Brown was appointed. She was even talked about as a possible appointee to the Supreme Court. The case of Brown shows just how far conservative administrations are willing to go to put people in the federal courts who are loyal soldiers in the war on government.

Unfortunately, Judge Brown is but one example of Bush's appointment of conservative and libertarian judges with an anti-government political agenda. Another is former Alabama Attorney General William Pryor. One legal scholar described Pryor as a man who "was against almost every progressive reform of the past half-century."[3] The *Atlanta Journal-Constitution* editorialized that Pryor was "the perfect Christian right extremist." He was, for example, the only attorney general in the 50 states who argued for striking down the Violence Against Women Act maintaining that it was a problem that did not have any national impact. He testified in Congress urging the repeal of provisions of the Voting Rights Act. He filed a brief in support of Nevada's effort to block remedies for violations of the Family and Medical Leave Act. He also argued against federal enforcement of civil rights and worker protection laws. And again he was the only state Attorney General who challenged significant portions of the Clean Water Act and the Endangered Species Act. He also filed a brief with the Supreme Court, arguing that the Constitution's Commerce Clause doesn't give Congress the authority to protect endangered species. Clearly Pryor has a deep hostility toward the federal government and its regulatory efforts to protect, women, minorities, and the environment.

As with Judge Brown, several Democratic senators were appalled by Pryor's extremist legal views and organized a filibuster to block his appointment. But like Brown, Pryor was eventually elevated to the bench when the Republicans threatened to revoke the Democrats' right to filibuster. Pryor and Brown were merely two of over a hundred nominees to federal district and appellate courts – many of whom also had ultra-conservative legal views – that were approved in the first Bush administration alone.

The Rise of Activist Conservative Judges

The federal courts have now become a major battleground in the effort to weaken government and reduce its powers. The courts are arguably the most powerful branch of government; they are the final decision-makers in many policy areas – abortion, the death penalty, environmental protection, civil rights, gun control, and gay rights, to name just a few. There is virtually no way to overturn their decisions. And unlike with our elected officials, the public has no way to get rid of these policymakers. So this is the high ground in American politics and well worth fighting for.

Some history is useful here. For decades, conservatives have railed about the abuses of liberal "activist" judges and justices. They have complained that these jurists have stretched their interpretations of the Constitution to support wrong-headed liberal policies like abortion, school busing, and affirmative action. So from the Reagan administration onward, conservatives have been appointing so-called "strict constructionists" to the federal courts – judges pledged to stick to very narrow and limited interpretations of the Constitution.

But all the attention being paid to the notion of strict constructivism and to hot-button issues like abortion has obscured something else that has been going on in the courts. In recent years, a new conservative legal philosophy has emerged – one that few Americans are aware of. Conservatives are no longer content with strict constructionism but have moved on to promote an intentionally *activist* orientation. But now it is a *right-wing* activism. Now it is many right-wing judges who are striving to stretch and radically reinterpret the Constitution to promote their own political agenda. Supreme Court Justice Antonin Scalia once stated candidly that "I am not a strict constructionist, and no one ought to be."[4] One of the main goals of these judicial activists is to limit the scope and power of the federal government. They want to both rein in the power of the federal courts and also to launch an attack against the power of Congress and its ability to pass regulatory laws. This new conservative, anti-government judicial activism, if successful, could have profound and widespread political implications.

The Federalist Society

To understand where this new conservative activist approach in the courts has come from, we need to step back for a moment and consider the role that the Federalist Society has begun to play in judicial politics in United States. The Federalist Society is a loose network of law school professors, law students, lawyers, and judges who are all interested in actively promoting a more conservative/libertarian legal philosophy. The Society has attracted little public attention, in part because it has tried to keep a low profile, preferring to describe itself as an innocuous and powerless "debating society." But in reality it is an increasingly powerful organization that is helping to push the law and the judiciary to the far right and in the process is beginning to reshape the legal landscape in United States. The Society is generously funded by Richard Mellon Scaife and other wealthy conservative patrons who fully appreciate its potential impact of the judiciary and on American law.

Many of the Society's members espouse a new constitutional philosophy that goes far beyond strict constructionism. These Federalists are not content to simply reverse the rulings of liberal activist courts – they want to impose their own form of conservative and libertarian activism on the courts. For instance, they not only want to broadly limit the power of the courts, they also want to drastically limit the role of the federal government in society and they have begun to attack the legal and constitutional underpinnings of much of modern government. They believe the federal government has exceeded its constitutional powers in establishing the social welfare policies and regulatory policies of the New Deal and the Great Society. (It is revealing that one of their forums had the title "Rolling Back the New Deal.") They would not hesitate to overturn decades of precedent and settled law in order to undermine many of the laws and regulations that currently protect our environment, health, and workplaces. For example, in some of their forums and publications, members of the Society have called for such things as the abolition of the Securities and Exchange Commission and for the drastic limitation of the regulatory powers of the Environmental Protection Agency and the Occupational Safety and Health Administration – all proposals that are very far from the mainstream political ideas of most Americans.

The reach of the Federalist Society was particularly clear in the administration of George W. Bush, in which many of his appointees were active members. During his first term, these officials included:

Attorney General John Ashcroft
Secretary of the Department of Energy Spencer Abraham
Secretary of the Department of Interior Gale Norton
Solicitor of Labor Eugene Scalia
General Counsel of the Department of Education Brian Jones
Deputy Attorney General Larry Thompson
Solicitor General Ted Olson
Assistant Attorney General for Legal Policy Viet Dinh
Inspector General of Department of Defense Joseph Schmitz
Asst. Attorney General for Environment and Natural Resources Thomas Sansonetti
Principal Deputy Solicitor General Paul Clement
Associate Deputy Attorney General Ted Cruz
Director of National Institute of Justice Sara Hart
Deputy White House counsel Timothy Flanagan
Associate White House counsel Brett Cavanaugh
Associate White House counsel Bradford Berenson
Assistant White House counsel Noel Francisco
General Council Department of Energy Lee Liberman Otis
Deputy Secretary Department of Agriculture James Moseley
Assistant Secretary Department of Agriculture William H. Lash III
General Council Department of Education Brian Jones
Assistant Secretary Department of Education Gerald Reynolds
General Council Department of Health and Human Services Alex Azar III

Clearly membership in this club functioned as a passport to power in the Bush administration. But more important than these administrative appointments were the Federalists tapped for judicial appointments. Soon after his first election, George Bush organized the judicial selection committee made up of White House and Justice Department lawyers, most of whom were members of the Federalist society. Not surprisingly, 17 of the first 20 candidates that President Bush nominated to the federal judiciary were recommended by the Federalist society.[5]

Given this kind of reach, the Federalist Society might seem to some people like some right-wing legal cabal, but it is too open and too loose a network to really fit that description. It is interesting, however, that the conservative activist Grover Norquist once wryly commented that "If Hillary Clinton had wanted to put some meat on her charge of a 'vast right-wing conspiracy,' she should have had a list of Federalist Society members and she could have spun a more convincing story."[6]

The Takings Movement

How far are these right-wing activist judges willing to go to stretch and distort the Constitution in support of this anti-government ideology? Consider the disturbing implications of the "takings" legal movement. The Fifth Amendment has a "Takings Clause" that stipulates that the government must pay private property owners if it "takes" or expropriates private land for public use. A typical example is when a government takes property by eminent domain to use for a freeway or for an urban renewal project. The meaning of this clause has always been quite specific and very narrow – if the government physically takes your land, it must pay you. But libertarian and conservative legal scholars have tried to extend the idea of takings to mean that the government must pay private property holders, such as corporations, for complying with regulations. They argue, for instance, that if complying with an environmental regulation limits the way a business can use its land, that is a "taking" of the land and the government must compensate them.

The political intent of this radical reinterpretation of the Takings Clause is to make government regulation of business so expensive as to be impractical. If a government had to pay businesses to comply with regulations it would soon go bankrupt – so if this interpretation became common, governments would have to drastically reduce their regulatory efforts, particularly as they affect land use. As William Greider has explained:

> Because any new regulation is bound to have some economic impact on private assets, this doctrine is a formula to shrink the reach of modern government and cripple the regulatory state – undermining long-established protections for social welfare and economic justice, environmental values, and individual rights. Right-wing advocates frankly state their objective – restoring the primacy of property against society's broader claims.[7]

Let's consider a specific example of how this works. In 1994, the Florida Rock company sued the federal government because the U.S. Army Corps of Engineers denied them a permit to mine limestone from 1,500 acres of wetland in the Everglades.[8] The Corps argued that pollution from the mining would destroy large amounts of wetlands that filter water for the Biscayne aquifer and would severely damage critical habitat in the Everglades ecosystem. They also pointed out that even with these restrictions, the company had received offers for the land that were twice the price it had paid. And yet the Federal Circuit court ruled that a "partial takings" of the land had taken place and required the government to pay tens of millions of dollars to Florida Rock for these damages. In one fell swoop, this decision effectively abandoned over a hundred years of the courts' traditional interpretation of the Takings Clause. This ruling was described by one law professor as "an extremely destabilizing decision, exposing all wetlands regulations, indeed all environmental and land use regulation, to compensation claims."[9]

The intellectual godfather of this "takings" attack on government regulation is Professor Richard Epstein of the Chicago Law School. His views make clear just how wide-ranging and revolutionary this constitutional reinterpretation really is. He has written that extending the Takings Clause renders "constitutionally infirm or suspect many of the heralded reforms and institutions of the twentieth century: zoning, rent control, workers' compensation laws, transfer payments, [and] progressive taxation. ... It will be said that my position invalidates much of the 20th century legislation, and so it does."[9] In an interview, he justified this extreme position by arguing that "Most of economic regulation is stupid ... What possible reason is there for regulating wages and hours? If my takings doctrine prevails, you have no minimum wage laws. That's fine. You'd have an OSHA a tenth of the size. That's fine too. You'd have no antidiscrimination laws for privileged employees, which would be a godsend."[11] This notion of "regulatory takings" is so peculiar that even some conservatives have backed off from it. One pre-eminent conservative legal scholar, Robert Bork, has complained that Epstein's views are "not plausibly related to the original meaning of the takings clause."[12]

But the absurdity of this idea has not stopped many right-wing groups from proselytizing for its use. The Federalist Society is very active in recruiting and training lawyers to pursue takings cases in the courts; and several conservative foundations have contributed large amounts of money to further these efforts. Also, the Foundation for Research on Economics and the Environment has sponsored all-expenses-paid seminars on the new takings legal philosophy that have been attended by thousands of federal judges.[13] Even more troublesome is that Supreme Court Justice Antonin Scalia has expressed sympathy for this notion of "regulatory takings" and some legal experts have estimated that four of the nine current Justices agree with at least parts of this highly questionable legal theory.

Back to the 1930s

Currently, the top priority of anti-government legal activists is a constitutional challenge to President Obama's health care reform bill. Several suits have been brought in the federal courts alleging that the bill's requirement that all individuals have health insurance violates the Constitution. One federal district court judge has already ruled in favor of this argument and it seems inevitable that this challenge is headed to the Supreme Court. But while this legal challenge has garnered a great deal of publicity, what has often been ignored is that this particular effort is only the tip of a very deep iceberg. Conservative legal activists have been mounting a wide-ranging constitutional attack on the powers of the federal government, an assault that could undermine much of the progressive legislation passed during the last 75 years.

For some years now, right-wing legal scholars and conservative judges have been trying to reinterpret parts of the Constitution in their efforts to undermine the regulatory powers of the federal government. Their main target has been the so-called "Commerce Clause" of the Constitution, the passage that empowers the federal government to regulate commerce between the states. Before the New Deal, the federal courts had a very strict interpretation of this clause that confined Congress to regulating only those activities that directly involved interstate commerce. However, a 1937 Supreme Court decision – Wickard v. Filburn – created a broader interpretation of this clause that gave Congress the power to regulate many activities located within states, such as factories and employer-employee relations.[14] This has been the conventional interpretation of this clause for over 70 years and it is the constitutional basis for many modern federal laws, including environmental regulation and much of the legislation that protects the rights of women, workers, and minorities.

Anti-government judicial activists are now committed to overturning this interpretation of the Commerce Clause, and with it many of the elements of the New Deal. Specifically, by returning to the narrow pre-1937 interpretation, they hope to overthrow such programs as federal minimum wage laws and requirements that employers participate in Social Security.[15] Despite the radical nature of this plan, it is clear that these conservatives have some sympathizers in the federal judiciary and that they are making some progress in their efforts. One federal district judge blocked the federal government from enforcing toxic waste cleanup requirements, because he decided that the chemical manufacturing site involved was really just a local real estate matter, not an economic activities subject to federal control. In 2003, U.S. Court of Appeals for the 9th Circuit issued three decisions that gradually narrowed what was constitutional under the Commerce Clause.[16] Also, the Supreme Court itself has declared that the Gun Free School Zones Act exceeds Congress' constitutional powers.

On the Supreme Court, Justice Clarence Thomas has often expressed sympathy with this revisionist attempt to severely restrict the powers of the federal government. In three separate cases he has argued that the federal government's attempts at regulation are "at odds" with the Constitution. If his views were to become common on the court, this would put in jeopardy a wide range of current laws, including the Americans with Disabilities Act, the federal minimum wage, bans on child labor, and anti-discrimination legislation.

Many legal scholars and political commentators find this a very disturbing trend. Adam Cohen, for example, has criticized what he has called "the campaign to undo the New Deal."

> [C]onservatives are making progress in their drive to restore the narrow view of federal powers that predated the New Deal – and render Congress too weak to protect Americans on many fronts. ... In pre-1937 America, workers were exploited, factories were free to pollute, and old people were generally poor when they retired. This is not an agenda the public would be likely to sign onto today if it were debated in an election. But conservatives, who like to complain about activist liberal judges, could achieve their anti-New Deal agenda through judicial activism on the right. Judges could ... declare laws on

workplace safety, environmental protection and civil rights unconstitutional.[17]

The Tort Reform Sham

There is another legal strategy being promoted by government haters that is very different from the ones just described. It is a strategy of limiting public access to the courts. It is really a very clever idea: instead of trying to limit the power of the courts, you simply block people's access to that power. Without access, the power of the courts cannot be used in ways that conservatives oppose. A good example of this attempt to deny access to the courts has been the intense and widespread political campaign to pass legislation on the federal and state levels to limit citizens' right to sue businesses – under the rubric of so-called "tort reform." A particular effort has been made to limit people's abilities to participate in class-action suits. These suits have been one of the most important and useful tools employed by citizens to fight the abuses of business and other institutions. Because of the high expense of litigation and the enormous legal resources of big business, individuals are often not in a position to successfully sue. Class action suits allow harmed individuals to band together and more effectively seek justice. As former United States Supreme Court Justice William O. Douglas has explained: "the class action is one of the few legal remedies the small claimant has against those who command the status quo."[18]

Class action and other suits have a long history of helping the average American get justice and compensation for wrongs committed against them. They have been successfully used by people in neighborhoods poisoned by toxic waste spills, patients prescribed medicines with undisclosed dangerous side effects, employees who have been victims of systematic racial or sexual discrimination, consumers who have been seriously hurt by defective and dangerous products, people who have lost their savings to fraudulent investment practices, and consumers who paid greatly inflated prices because of monopolistic and unfair business practices. And many people not even directly involved in these suits have greatly benefited from them. Thousands of dangerous products have been removed from the marketplace, thus preventing future injuries and the medical costs associated with them. Our cars and hospitals are much safer due to citizen suits. Millions of dollars have been recovered in suits over various consumer fraud schemes. Perhaps more importantly, fear of lawsuits has prompted many businesses to produce safer products and to behave in more responsible ways to their consumers and their employees. In short, citizen lawsuits have helped to protect us all.

Not surprisingly, however, the business community does not like class-action suits and it has organized a well-funded and highly coordinated campaign to promote legislation that would limit the ability of people to file these kinds of lawsuits. This is how one consumer group described this extensive political effort:

> The huge corporate campaign against consumer access to the courts is approaching its 25th year. [It] includes the creation of new trade associations of companies pushing for state as well as federal legislation to limit consumer rights, hundreds of lobbyists pressuring congressional and state lawmakers, the creation of front groups across the country called citizens against lawsuit abuse (whose members are actually businesses), new think tanks such as the Manhattan Institute who hire authors to write books and reports attacking the civil justice system, and strategic television and radio advertising at the state and national level.[19]

The Republican Party signed onto this effort to limit the public's ability to sue, especially through class-action suits. In the mid-nineties, Congress passed legislation limiting the courts' ability to hear class action suits by immigrants seeking to fight against deportation. Another bill limited the abilities of legal services lawyers to bring class actions suits on the behalf of their poor clients. And in 1995, the Republicans passed the Private Securities Litigation Reform Act, over the veto of President Clinton. This law severely restricted investors' ability to sue companies for securities fraud. In doing so, it greatly undermined the ability of investors to hold corporate officials, accountants, and auditors accountable for such activities as deceptive bookkeeping, lying to investors about profits, and other forms of investor fraud. With little threat of investor suits, and with the SEC essentially asleep on the job, it is little wonder that more and more corporate officials soon felt free to cross the line over into illegal and fraudulent behavior. Eventually a whole host of companies, including Enron, WorldCom, ImClone, Global Crossings, Adelphi Communications, Xerox, Merck, Bristol-Myers Squibb, and Qwest were caught engaging in just these kinds of investor frauds – costing their investors billions of dollars in losses.

Unsatisfied with these political victories, the business community and the Republican Congress then set its sights on a higher goal: reining in class action suits across the board. They introduced a bill to do just that in 2004. It was entitled, with typical cynicism, as the "Class Action Fairness Act." But its intent was far from fair. It would forbid citizens from filing major class action suits in state courts, and force them into the already overburdened federal courts. Moreover, federal judges do not usually certify cases that are based on state consumer protection laws, which means these cases would be blocked. Public Citizen President Joan Claybrook commented that "This is an issue of basic fair play. The American Revolution was fought, in part, over no access to the civil courts so that citizens could redress their grievances. This is a right that is essential in a democracy. But this right will, in many cases, literally be taken away by this legislation."[20]

Over eighty different consumer, senior, environmental, labor, and civil rights organizations worked against the bill. Several state and federal judge associations and many state attorneys general opposed it as well. *The New York Times* eventually weighed in with an editorial sharply condemning the bill:

> Under the phony banner of "tort reform," this act is a legislative gift to wealthy special interests. It would make it harder for Americans to win redress in court for corporate violations of state civil rights, health, consumer and environmental protection laws. The act's core provisions would permit big polluters and other companies to delay justice, or even escape justice entirely, by moving most class-action lawsuits from state courts to the overburdened federal courts, which are less familiar with the disputed legal and factual issues. The act would also impose new litigation hurdles and burdens on plaintiffs.[21]

But powerful forces were amassing to pass the bill. The Chamber of Commerce made passage of this bill their number one priority in 2004 and literally hundreds of business lobbyists were pressuring Congress to pass it. Also, an official of the National Association of Manufacturers stated that this bill was "the biggest thing in years."[22] With all of this lobbying pressure and the dominance of Republicans in Congress, it was only a matter of time until this bill was passed. After the bill passed in early 2005, *The New York Times* observed that "Having spent tens of millions of dollars lobbying for this bill, the United States Chamber of Commerce and allied business groups are understandably pleased. They got what they paid for."[23]

The conservative effort to deny court access to citizens is particularly galling when considered along with their efforts to weaken and roll back the regulations that are supposed to protect the public. When government fails to protect us from cars that roll over, water that poisons our children, and drugs that make us sick, then people can only resort to lawsuits to defend themselves. Conservatives have been aghast when shareholders have sued corporations because the illegal and unethical actions of company officers have cost investors their life savings. But this happened because the Securities and Exchange Commission has been asleep on the job, ignoring these problems. Tort reformers also bemoaned the way lawyers quickly jumped in to sue the makers of the drug Vioxx when it was shown that it caused thousands of unnecessary deaths. But those suits would not have been necessary if the FDA had been on the job and noticed those dangerous side effects sooner. If conservative administrations are going to neglect to protect citizens through vigorous regulation, then it is doubly unfair to also deny them the ability to seek justice in the courts. Citizen lawsuits are not the "plague" that conservative propaganda would have us believe. They are a form of citizen power – and the more we are denied their use, the less powerful and less safe we all become.

Irreversible Decisions

What we are witnessing today is nothing less than a conservative campaign to radically change the law and the legal system of the United States in a way that greatly reduces the power of government and citizens. The political right has engaged in a relentless effort to appoint libertarian-leaning judges and justices that adhere to a minimal-government philosophy. Fortunately, these appointments have come to an end, at least temporarily, with the election of President Obama. But the damage has already been done. These "radicals in robes" have been appointed for life, and many are in their fifties and likely to stay on the job for several more decades. The public is powerless to replace them or to overturn their decisions. There is no democratic accountability here. We will have to live with their legal rulings – and their assaults on government – for the many years to come.

---

1 Janice Rogers Brown, "Hyphenasia: the Mercy Killing of the American Dream," Speech at Claremont-McKenna College (Sept. 16, 1999), p. 3.

2 Janice Rogers Brown. "A Whiter Shade of Pale," Speech to Federalist Society (April 20. 2000).

3 Herman Schwartz, Right Wing Justice: The Conservative Campaign to Take Over the Courts, (New York: Nation Books, 2004) p. 252.

4 Dana Milbank, "Scalia Showing His Softer Side," The Washington Post, March 15, 2005; Page A02.

5 Herman Schwartz, Right Wing Justice. (New York: Nations Books, 2004), p. 197.

6 Thomas Edsall, "Federalist Society Becomes a Force in Washington," the Washington Post, April 18, 2001 page A04.

7 William Greider, "The Right and U.S. Trade Law: Invalidating the 20th Century," The Nation, October 15, 2001.

8 See a description of this case in Sharon Buccino, et al., "Hostile Environment: How Activist Judges Threaten our Air, Water, and Land," Natural Resources Defense Council, July 2001, p. 12.

9 Ibid. p. 12.

10Richard Epstein, Takings: Private Property and the Power of Eminent Domain (Cambridge: Harvard University Press, 1985), p. X.

11 Greider, "The Right and U.S. Trade Law."

12 Buccino, "Hostile Enviroment," p. 2.

13 Herman Schwartz, Right Wing Justice, p. 221.

14 Adam Cohen, "What's New in the Legal World? A Growing Campaign to Undo the New Deal," New York Times, December 14, 2004, p. A30.

15 Cohen, "What's New in the Legal World? p. A30.

16 Jacob Sullum, "Pot Luck: A victory for federalism," ReasonOnline, December 19, 2003, http://www.reason.com/sullum/121903.shtml

17 Cohen, "What's New in the Legal World? p. A30.

18 About Class Action, p. 1.

19 Promoters, p. 3.

20 Joan Claybrook, "Business-Backed Class Action Bill Locks Consumers Out of Court," Common Dreams Progressive News Wire, Feb. 7, 2005 http://www.commondreams.org/news2005/0207-11.htm

21 New York Times, October 22, 2003.

22 Common Dreams,

23 "A Dismal Class-Action Finale, New York Times, February 12, 2005, p. A30.

CHAPTER 18

Why Government Becomes the Scapegoat

In the summer of 2011, the U.S. economy was still suffering from the lingering effects of the Great Recession that began in 2008. Economic growth was anemic, a double dip recession was a very real possibility, and unemployment remained disturbingly high. While serious analysts debated about how to best revive the economy, Republican members of the U.S. House of Representatives came up with a novel approach to this problem: they passed a bill that curtailed thirty-nine environmental regulations. As Rep. Mike Simpson explained: "Many of us believe that overregulation from the EPA is at the heart of our stalled economy."[1] Not to be outdone, Rep. Michelle Bachmann came up with her own pet theory about how government had to be the cause of our economic woes. She argued that health care reform was the reason we had such high unemployment. She seemed to forget that the major components of that bill were not scheduled to take effect for several years.

These examples of bizarre reasoning should really have surprised no one. They are typical of what has become an ongoing and central political strategy of anti-government conservatives: to blame the government for just about every problem we have as a society. But this kind of bizarre reasoning should really have surprised no one. It was just another typical example of what has become an ongoing and central political strategy of anti-government conservatives: to blame the government for just about every problem we have as a society. This idea has always been popular in conservative circles, but it received a major boost from Ronald Reagan's first inaugural addressed in which he famously quipped that "Government is not the solution to our problem. Government is the problem." It was an argument that resonated deeply with most conservatives, and they have engaged in a continuous campaign to make the government the scapegoat for virtually all of society's ills.

This chapter will reveal exactly what is wrong with this effort to use government as a scapegoat. It will first show that government policy is usually *not* the cause of our country's problems. Second, it will answer an intriguing question: why do conservatives and the business community continually insist on blaming government even when their arguments make very little sense? The answer, it turns out, has to do with the way that this scapegoating serves to distract Americans from the real causes of their problems.

The "Blame Government" Strategy

Using the government as a universal scapegoat is very clever political strategy on the part of conservatives. It plays directly into a traditional American distrust of government. And if people can be convinced that "the real problem in the United States is the same one being recognized all over the world: too much government," then little else need be said to get them to support reducing government.[2] And it seems that there are certainly many Americans who are willing to buy this "blaming government" argument. One poll found that 70 percent of Americans believe that "government creates more problems than it solves."[3] And another found that a very large majority of Americans (71%) blame government for stagnant wages.[4] To the extent that people can be made to believe such things, the easier it becomes for anti-state conservatives to reduce government. It just makes common sense to try to reduce the cause of your problems, doesn't it?

Now there is no denying that sometimes government policies cause problems or make the problems they are addressing worse. Given thousands of policies, inevitably some of them will fail in this way. A good example of this is our federal "War on Drugs" policy. Many political commentators on both the left and right have now concluded that approaching drugs as a crime problem and relying on police efforts to solve it has not worked well. Indeed, this approach has had a lot of unintentional and bad consequences: it has created a more lucrative black market in drugs, increased drug-related violence and crime, and filled our prisons to overflowing with drug users and small-time dealers. You could make a good case that this drug policy has created more problems that it has solved – which is exactly why most other Western countries have abandoned it in favor of an approach that emphasizes decriminalization and drug treatment programs. But such policy failures are hardly evidence that "government is the problem." They don't indicate that government is flawed, just that particular policies are flawed. And they don't mean that we should have less government, just that we need different and better policies in some areas.

Besides, policy failures like these are not really what conservatives are getting at when they say the government is the problem. What they mean is that misguided government policies are actually *causing* many of our social and economic problems. Is the economy stagnant? It is because of government over-regulation of business. Are you having trouble paying your bills or sending your children to college on your current wages? It is because government takes so much of your salary in taxes. Concerned about the persistent level of poverty in this country? It is due to overly generous welfare programs that make government handouts more profitable than working. Are your kids misbehaving and defying authority? It's the fault of the public schools for not teaching them the right values. You didn't get that job or that promotion? It is probably the fault of government promoted affirmative action programs. Upset about the rising divorce rate and the continuing demise of the traditional family? It's because government has made divorce too easy. Are you worried about promiscuity among young people and teenage pregnancy? Blame the sex education programs in our public schools. Do you not have enough money for retirement? It's the fault of government for not letting you invest your Social Security money in the stock market. Did your job go overseas? It's because your local government didn't do enough to keep the business in your city. And so on. For many conservatives, government has become a one-size fits-all explanation that can be stretched to fit just about every problem in this country.

The Big Lie

The main problem with this blame-the-government tactic – and with all attempts at scapegoating – is that it is based on a distorted vision of reality. The reality of government is exactly the opposite of what conservatives contend: it is rarely the cause of societal problems and typically functions as a solution to problems. As we saw in an earlier chapter, "The Forgotten Achievements of Government," modern American government has taken on a series of large and difficult problems and has in most cases made significant progress in addressing them. And there is actually little evidence that the government is the direct cause of most of the serious social and economic problems we face as a nation. This is why one political commentator, Charles Noble, has called the conservative blame-the-government campaign "the big lie."

Some of these lies about government are not even very plausible. In the mad rush by anti-state conservatives to blame government for everything, reason and common sense are often thrown out the window. Witness, for example, Reagan's 1983 confident pronouncement that "We think there is a parallel between federal involvement in education and the decline in profit over recent years."[5] No one has yet to make much sense out of this contention.

Other government critics have even tried to blame it for our many environmental problems. The official position of the libertarian Future of Freedom Foundation makes it perfectly clear where they think the fault lies: "Governments are the great destroyers of the environment. In fact, most environmental problems can be traced to public, not private, ownership of resources."[6] And Dick Armey has written that our current health care crisis is entirely the fault of federal tax policy and programs like Medicare and Medicaid. He suggests that if only the government would get out of the way then private health insurers would make sure that nearly everyone, including the poor and elderly, had affordable health insurance – and the cost of health care would be lowered in the process.[7] Clearly, no one but a hard-core, right-wing government hater would put much credence to any of these bizarre theories.

But while many of these conservative charges against government are easily dismissed, not all of them are. Some of their accusations have the semblance of plausibility and are taken seriously by many people in the public and the press – and these demand a more detailed refutation. Of course there is not enough room in this chapter to take on all of these blame-the-government theories – but let's take a look at one of them. Let's consider a charge against the government that conservatives believe is particularly strong – where they are convinced that they are right about government being at fault and where they have successfully convinced many others of this as well. It is the contention that misguided government policies are one of the main reasons so many people remain poor in this country.

Does Welfare Cause Poverty?

Poverty has been a remarkably persistent problem in our society. In 1970, the poverty rate was 12.6 percent and in 2008 it was 13.2 percent. So why won't this problem go away? Most conservatives have put the blame on government policies. In 1984, Charles Murray published *Losing Ground* in which he argued that welfare policies, while intended to alleviate poverty, have in fact just made it worse. Welfare payments were so high that they discouraged people from getting jobs. It became economically beneficial to stay on welfare rather than to take a low paying job. Overly generous welfare payments were making people dependent on these programs and trapping them in poverty. His solution: get rid of the major source of the problem. Cut back drastically on welfare, thus forcing people to get jobs and work their way out of poverty.

When the Republicans took over Congress in the mid-1990s, one of their first priorities was to "reform welfare" along these lines. In a landmark 1996 bill, welfare was declared to be no longer an entitlement, and strict time limits and work requirements were imposed on recipients – all designed to discourage people from staying on welfare and forcing them onto the job market. This legislation has come to be celebrated by conservatives as one of the most successful policies coming out of that period. They point out that between 1996 and 2003, the number of people on the welfare rolls dropped by over 60%.

This is pretty impressive. But unfortunately, the effect of this reduction of the welfare rolls on the poverty level was not what Republicans had predicted. If welfare was actually a major cause of persistent poverty, then we should have also seen a dramatic decrease in poverty as millions of people were forced off welfare and onto the job market. But this is precisely what did *not* happen. The poverty rate did not fall by 60% or 50%. Not even by 40% or 30%. Not by 20%, nor even by 10%. It fell by a measly 8% — from 13.7% to 12.5% from 1996 to 2003.

How can this be explained? It is simple. Conservatives were wrong about poverty being largely caused by government welfare programs. First, they ignored the fact that most poor people aren't even on welfare – and that many of them work already. Second, as many scholars of poverty have pointed out, the major causes of poverty in this country are mostly in the economic system. Most people are poor for two reasons: (1) there is a chronic lack of jobs, and (2) many low-level jobs pay wages below the poverty level.

If you can't get a job, your chances of being poor are quite high. And there is a persistent lack of full-time jobs in our economy. The unemployment rate has traditionally hovered around the 5% to 7% in the U.S. – and of course it is much higher during recessions. But this does not count those who have become so discouraged they are no longer searching for jobs. Moreover, it has been estimated that unemployment would have to fall to around 2% for there to be enough jobs for everyone who wants one.[8] So chronic unemployment in our economy remains one of the main causes of poverty.[9]

But beyond the obstacle of lack of jobs, there is the problem of the quality of jobs that many people do get – and that mire them in poverty. Many workers are trapped in part-time or part-year jobs that do not pay enough to raise them out of poverty. Millions more work at full-time jobs that pay wages so low that they also remain poor. An embarrassing large percentage of American workers, at least 25 percent, receive wages that do not allow their families to enjoy a decent standard of living. One poverty researcher, Mark Rank, found that almost a third of heads of families in the workforce in 1999, in the midst of a strong economy, earned less than $10 an hour, barely enough for a full-time worker to maintain a family of four above the official poverty line.[10] In terms of poverty, then, the basic problem has been the chronic inability of our economy to provide the kinds of employment opportunities necessary for people to work their way above the poverty line. As Gordon Lafer has concluded: "There simply are not enough decently paying jobs for the number of people who need them."[11]

Given the real causes of poverty in this country are located in the economy, it is not hard to see why the Republican effort to slash government welfare rolls has had little impact on this problem. Since Republican lawmakers had the wrong diagnosis of the poverty problem, their policy prescription was misguided as well. Kicking people off of welfare does nothing to create the additional jobs or the better paying jobs that would actually enable people to escape poverty. Interestingly, poverty rates did dip a bit during the economic boom of the late 1990s, when unemployment declined and wages rose a bit. But since 2000, a sputtering economy has meant that the poverty rate has gone back up every year – ballooning to 14.3% in 2009, a result of the severe economic recession that began in 2008. This is just another indication that it is the failures of our economic system, not government welfare policies, that are at the heart of our continuing poverty problems.[12]

Why Conservatives Must Scapegoat Government

While the "welfare-causes-poverty" theory was completely mistaken, it at least had some semblance of plausibility about it. But as we saw earlier, many of the charges that "government is the problem" are not only untrue; they are hardly plausible at all. Who in their right mind would believe, for instance, that the government is the main cause of environmental problems? But if this is the case, why do anti-government conservatives insist on making so many of these kinds of questionable arguments? The answer is not necessarily obvious. It is not just that they want to take every possible opportunity to criticize government. Something else is also going on here. To fully understand what it is, you need to understand the underlying political purpose of scapegoating. Scapegoating involves more than blaming an innocent group for society's problems. It also functions to distract attention away from the *real* causes of these problems – and that is what is so important for many anti-government conservatives. That is the reason they must engage in the scapegoating of government, no matter how implausible their arguments. Because to acknowledge the real causes of many of our social and economic problems would simply be too threatening to their ideology and interests.

Ordinary Americans are facing an ever increasing number of financial and economic difficulties: their wages have stagnated, many people have little money for retirement, jobs have been downsized and outsourced, rising costs have put college out of reach for many, the gap between rich and poor has increased, health care costs have continued to rise for millions, and so on. And all of this was before the recent deep recession. The American dream just isn't what it used to be; and faced with these mounting difficulties and risks, many Americans are anxious and angry. And they are looking for someone to take it out on. But the problem for conservatives is this: the causes of virtually all of the serious problems just mentioned are located in the private sector. The workings of the free market and the decisions of business leaders are largely responsible for low wages, high medical costs, increasing economic inequality, stock market crashes, and so on. These are some of the downsides of a modern capitalist market economy. But of course conservatives cannot admit this. They must find a scapegoat on which to deflect this public anger – and government is the perfect one.

Increasingly, most anti-government activists have embraced a kind of "market fundamentalism." They have a blind faith in the perfection of the market and a strong belief that if markets are left alone, they will solve most problems and produce the best of all possible worlds. So these people desperately need someone or something else they can blame for the economic problems being experienced by many Americans. They have to blame government, because the alternative – admitting to the imperfections of market capitalism – is unthinkable. That is why they are forced to try to blame virtually all of society's problems on government – no matter how absurd and how unfounded most of these accusations actually are. This seemingly irrational display on the part of free-market conservatives actually begins to make more sense once we realize that they really have no choice. Once they are committed to believe in the perfection of the market, they must also then believe that the government is the source of our problems. So it is not just that they *want to* blame government for our problems; they *have to* blame government, no matter how ridiculous this might be in many cases.

Why Business Must Scapegoat Government

Free-market conservatives must scapegoat government in order to protect their ideological illusions. But the business community has a very different reason for doing it – they need to protect their own economic interests, their own bottom lines. If business could not get us to blame government for our economic difficulties, then we would be much more likely to turn our anger toward them. The last thing businesses need is an increasing number of Americans pointing their fingers at them and the free-market economy as the source of their problems. This would inevitably lead to demands that the government do something to address these problems – and these government solutions would in many cases restrict the freedom of businesses and hurt their profits.

Consider the public debate that took place after the financial crisis that began in 2008. Business was unable to blame government for the mortgage loan mess and the resulting economic meltdown. So public discussion focused on what was wrong with the financial system and the malfeasance of financial companies. Many people aimed their anger at Wall Street, and there was a great deal of resentment about the enormous corporate profits and huge executive bonuses that were being amassed as these institutions drove the economy to the brink of ruin. There was talk about limiting executive compensation and reining in the speculative business model that brought millions in profits to these financial firms.

Imagine if the same shift in public discussion were to happen with other economic problems – say with poverty and low wages. What if the target for people's wrath became the private sector and companies like Wal-Mart that continue to prosper by paying their workers low wages, denying them benefits, and preventing unionization? The public would be more likely to band together politically to demand legislation that would ensure that all people be paid a living wage or that all workers be free to unionize. But this is precisely the kind of political development that many companies would find very threatening. So to deflect criticisms and protect their bottom lines, businesses have an incredibly strong motivation to blame government for economic problems that would otherwise end up on their doorstep.

The 800-Pound Capitalist Gorilla in the Living Room

Just to be clear: I am not suggesting that all of America's problems are caused by free-market capitalism. Nor do I want to substitute capitalism for government as a public scapegoat. Clearly many of our problems – including terrorism, teen pregnancy, drugs, AIDS, and so on – are not the fault of the market. And certainly misguided government policies do at times make problems worse rather than better. But all of this should not obscure the fact we do suffer from a substantial number of serious problems that *are* caused or exacerbated by the workings of our free-market economy. If we look at capitalism objectively, we see an economic system with enormous economic advantages – incredible productivity, enormous wealth generation, great economic efficiency, and high degrees of technological innovation – but we also see a system with large numbers of limitations and disadvantages. Many of the built-in problems of capitalism were discussed in some detail in the earlier chapter, "Capitalism Requires Government." A short list includes economic bubbles, environmental pollution, uncontrolled resource depletion, high degrees of wage and wealth inequality, poverty, economic depressions, abuses of corporate power, unsafe workplaces, dangerous products, monopoly and price-fixing, etc. This doesn't mean that capitalism is bad and that we should get rid of it; it just means that unrestrained capitalism is an imperfect system that creates a great deal of problems that we must deal with – usually through government.

But this is exactly what many conservatives do not want to admit. Free market capitalism has become the 800-pound gorilla in our living room that they are desperately trying to ignore. The critical discussion about financial markets that followed the economic meltdown of 2008 is a perfect example of what conservatives and the business community want to avoid. Many political pundits and commentators began to question the value of unregulated financial markets and laissez-faire capitalism itself. There was talk of adopting a more European approach where there are much more extensive public controls over markets and business. However, if conservatives can keep people convinced that government is really the cause of most of our economic problems, then these kinds of disturbing discussions about the problematic nature of our economic system would not have to take place. Business can go on as usual. What gorilla?

But Why Do We Believe This Stuff?

It is easy enough to understand why free-market fundamentalists and business interests believe that "government is the problem" – it is in their ideological and economic interests to do so. But why do *we* believe it? Why do so many average, non-ideological Americans accept these arguments – arguments that often make very little sense? Polls show, as noted earlier, that a very large majority of Americans (71%) blame government for stagnant wages – a problem that clearly has it causes in the private sector, not the government.[13] It would make much more sense for those angry about stagnant wages to focus their attention on businesses who continue to prosper by paying their workers low wages and who refuse to let their employees unionize.

Or consider the issue of globalization and other long-term changes in our economy. The political scientist Joseph Nye, Jr. has noted that many of these changes are causing problems for an increasing number of Americans, even many in the middle-class. As problems like increased job insecurity, lower wages, downsizing, job stress, and higher unemployment have multiplied, many people seem determined to blame government for these things. As Nye explains:

> Many of the people being laid off today are middle-class holders of white-collar jobs – something that was not as prevalent in the past. We are seeing the "democratization of insecurity." This produces a "politics of the anxious middle." In the long run the country may profit from this creative destruction, but in the interim people feel insecure and anxious and then blame the government rather than the deeper economic and historical forces.[14]

Susan Tolchin has noticed the very same phenomenon: "Today, when middle managers and blue-collar workers lose their jobs, they blame government even though, when pressed, they cannot think of what specific role government played in influencing decisions by Xerox, or Mobil, or IMB to downsize their workforces or move factories to Mexico."[15] So as financial problems and anxieties rise for many Americans, instead of getting angry with businesses or capitalism, they get angry with government. But why is this so? Why do so many Americans – even those who are not conservative – take their anger out on government when it is not the cause of many of their problems?

Powerlessness and Kicking the Dog of Government

The main reason that the public tends to go along with the right's efforts to scapegoat government is the sense of powerlessness that most people feel when it comes to trying to control what is going on in the private sector. Many people believe they have little or no influence over business decisions or the workings of the market economy. This creates the conditions for the emergence of what psychologists call "displacement." Displacement is a psychological defense mechanism in which feelings of anger and frustration are displaced or redirected from the real causes of those feelings onto an innocent third party. The typical example is a man who feels harassed by his boss at work, who then comes home and yells at his wife. The worker is powerless to take his frustrations out on his boss, so he redirects it at another person over which he has some power.

This is exactly what often happens when citizens are confronted with serious problems over which they feel they have little or no control – they take their frustrations out on government and officials over which they have at least some control. Take the deeper social forces at work in the family. Divorce rates are up and traditional families are on the wane. Yet there is little that people can do about these larger social changes, so they turn to blaming government officials and schools for not emphasizing "family values."

But again, it is especially when people are confronted with economic problems that they tend to feel powerless to respond. It is not a coincidence that the classic example of displacement involves a man who feels unable to directly address problems in his workplace and so takes it out on his family at home. People feel that there is little they can do about economic problems – such as low wages, joblessness, boring work, rising health care costs, loss of pensions, etc. – that are generated in the private sector. Even though they often have some idea that these problems are caused by decisions made in the economic system, they also realize that they have no power to directly affect those decisions. So they tend to take it out on a group over which they *do* have some power – politicians and the government. These officials can at least be booted out of office. Blaming government is a way for the public to express their anger and resentment and to act upon it – even if the target is ultimately the wrong one.

Susan Tolchin remarked on this process in her book, *The Angry American*. She noted that people concerned about the loss of family farms often tend to direct their anger at government and blame land-use regulations such as those designed to protect wetlands.

> Why blame the government? Far more family farms are gobbled up by the forces of agribusiness, timber, and mining interests than by wetlands legislation. Why isn't Weyerhauser as tempting a target as the Interior Department? Probably because people can do something about government, whereas it is virtually impossible to vote out the chairman of the board or change corporate policies.

Living in a capitalist society, we often have little control of what is happening in the private sector. So we take our frustrations out on the public sector. Ironically, of course, we take them out on the very public institutions that have enough power to actually allow us to exert some more democratic control over the private sector decisions and the market forces that shape so much of our lives. But if we are busy blaming government, we are less likely to think about how we could use this form of collective power to make private sector decision makers more accountable to the public.

A New Acceptable Form of Scapegoating

Scapegoating is certainly nothing new in American politics. It has been particularly common among extreme right-wing populist groups throughout our history. The Know Nothings of the 19th century heaped blame on Catholics and immigrants for society's problems. In the twentieth century, the Ku Klux Klan pointed the finger at blacks and Jews. Today, instead of targeting and demonizing a particular religious or ethnic group, the target has often become politicians, bureaucrats, judges and the institutions of government itself.

This new target has a number of advantages for conservatives. First, it plays on traditional American distrust of government and politicians. Second, and more importantly, blaming the government seems to be a more sanitized and acceptable form of scapegoating. Those who do it cannot be charged with being racist or xenophobic. Most people today would not tolerate an effort to make racial or religious groups the scapegoats for society's problems. But many are willing to stand by as the very same vicious tactic is used against government officials and politicians. This "sanitizing" of scapegoating has allowed it to become more widespread. This is the other thing that is new about this kind of political scapegoating – it has gone mainstream. This tactic is no longer limited to ultra right-wing kooks, but is now used by a major political party and by large numbers of average Americans. Targeting government has become the political witch-hunt that the whole family can enjoy.

The Mobilization of Hatred

But while targeting government may seem like a less pernicious form of scapegoating, it is not. It is still a malicious, misleading, and destructive process. As Chip Berlet and Matthew Lyons have explained, scapegoating is not a dispassionate attempt to understand the real sources of society's problems, but a tactic that inevitably relies on the encouragement and exploitation of dangerous emotions. "Scapegoating [is] the social process whereby the hostility and grievances of an angry, frustrated group are directed away from the real causes of a social problem onto a target group demonized as malevolent wrongdoers."[16] Anger and demonization are in integral part of any scapegoating strategy. It relies on the mobilization of popular hatred against its target. You can see this in the kind of inflammatory rhetoric used by right-wing pundits, such as Rush Limbaugh, Ann Coulter, Glenn Beck, and others, when they attack government. They do not simply argue that certain policies are bad, they also try to demonize the policymakers, especially liberal, pro-government politicians. They vilify these government officials as "idiots," "slime balls," "Nazis," "communists," "traitors," and "tyrants." Sometimes the demonization is quite literal, as when liberal politicians are referred to as "evil leaders," "agents of the devil," and people "in league with the Antichrist." The clear intention of this kind of talk is to fan the flames of anger, resentment, and hatred. Most Americans would not stand for it if this same kind of vicious language was aimed at a racial or religious group – if, for example, Jews were constantly disparaged as "idiots," "traitors" or "agents of the devil." But when these terms of vilification are aimed at government officials, many people simply turn a blind eye. That has to stop – we must oppose scapegoating and demonization no matter what group it is being aimed at.

The politics of hatred is a dangerous politics. It breeds irrationality and ultimately carries with it the threat of violence. We need not look too far to find examples of this violence. When President Clinton was elected in the 1992, the Republicans ramped up their virulent verbal attacks on government. Not long after, in 1995, two men associated with an extremist militia movement chose to act on their fears of government. The target of their political rage was the federal building in downtown Oklahoma City. They detonated a bomb that killed over 100 government employees and many of their children.

In recent years, we again have seen conservatives intentionally encouraging more hatred and resentment against government. Not surprisingly, death threats leveled at President Obama increased by 400% over those aimed at President Bush. And there have been incidents of violence aimed at government officials. In 2009, Richard Poplawski killed three police officers in a paranoid fit about what he thought were President Obama's anti-gun plans. In 2010, John Patrick Bedell, a rabidly anti-government libertarian, shot two police officers outside the Pentagon. Then in 2011, Jared Lee Loughner shot Congresswoman Gabrielle Giffords and 18 others in Tucson

Arizona. Six people were killed, including a federal judge and a child. Republicans and Tea Party supporters were quick to argue that Loughner was simply a disturbed and paranoid individual and these murders had nothing to do with politics. But clearly there is a pattern here. Anti-government forces have actively encouraged paranoia about government. They argued that health care reform would create "death panels" that would kill innocent Americans. They warned that the government would soon be invading people's homes to seize their guns. Some suggested that Obama was the "anti-Christ," and others maintained that he wanted to establish a communist or fascist dictatorship in this country. When such paranoid fantasies are being promoted by elements of the political right, it gives disturbed people a ready target for their own paranoia. Loughner may have been living in his own fantasy world, but it was informed by the real world of anti-government activists who were feeding his political hallucinations.

Shooting Ourselves in the Foot

Ultimately, however, the biggest problem with scapegoating government is that it makes it much harder to solve our pressing social and economic problems. Whipping up feelings of anger and resentment against the government only encourages irrational thinking and distracts us from understanding the real causes of our problems. As the hatred of government grows, it pushes out reason and common sense. People caught up in these powerful emotions rarely stop to think clearly about whether government is really to blame or to consider alternative causes of our problems.

And when blaming government obscures the real sources of our problems, this makes it much more difficult to develop effective solutions. We will never have a more effective approach to lowering our poverty rate, for example, if we persist in the delusion that government policies are what are keeping people poor. And finally, scapegoating government not only distracts us from developing better solutions to our problems, it also works to delegitimize the only institutions that are large enough and powerful enough to successfully take on many of these social and economic problems. Blindly accepting the idea that "government is the problem" only undermines and weakens the very democratic political institutions that we must rely on to actually develop and implement the solutions we need. We are just shooting ourselves in the foot.

1. Leslie Kaufman, "Republicans Seek Big Cuts in Environmental Rules," New York Times, July 27, 2011.
2. David Boaz, *Libertarianism: A Primer* (New York: Free Press, 1997) p. 12.
3. Derek Bok, *The Trouble with Government* (Cambridge: Harvard University Press, 2002), p. 43.
4. Cheryl Simrell King and Camilla Stivers, *Government is Us* (Thousand Oaks, CA: Sage Publications, 1998) p. 24.
5. President Ronald Reagan, quoted in *USA Today*, April 26, 1983
6. The Future of Freedom Foundation, "What is Libertarianism?" http://www.fff.org/aboutUs/whatIs.asp August 9, 2005.
7. Dick Armey, *The Freedom Revolution.* (Washington, D.C.: Regnery Publishing, 1995) p. 212-213.
8. Philip Harvey, "Combating Joblessness: An Analysis of the Principal Strategies That Have Influenced the Development of American Employment and Social Welfare Law During the 20th Century," *Berkeley Journal of Employment and Labor Law* 21 (2000), pp. 679n3, 682, 705-709.
9. Timothy Bartik, "Poverty, Jobs, and Subsidized Employment," *Challenge* 45 (No. 3, May-June, 2002), pp. 100-111.
10. Mark Robert Rank, *One Nation, Underprivileged: Why American Poverty Affects Us All* (New York: Oxford University Press, 2004), p. 59.
11. Gordon Lafer, *The Job Training Charade*, (New York: ILR Press, August 31, 2004) p. 3.
12. The economic causes of poverty also explain why liberal anti-poverty programs have failed to make much of a dent in anti-poverty rates. Welfare and food stamps do nothing to increase the number of jobs available to the poor or to raise the wages of those jobs. In this sense, they were not intended to fix the problem of poverty, only to lessen the suffering of those who were poor. And in this effort they were very successful.
13. Cheryl Simrell King and Camilla Stivers, *Government is Us* (Thousand Oaks, CA: Sage Publications, 1998) p. 24.
14. Joseph Nye, Jr., et al, editors, *Why People Don't Trust Government* (Cambridge: Harvard University Press, 1997, p. 12.
15. Cited in King, p. 24.
16. Chip Berlet and Matthew N. Lyons, *Right Wing Populism in America* (New York: The Guilford Press, 2000), p. 8.

PART III

REVITALIZING DEMOCRACY AND GOVERNMENT

CHAPTER 19

What is Really Wrong with American Government

While it is crucial to acknowledge all that is right with American government, we must not turn a blind eye to what is wrong with it. Although government on the whole is good, there are things wrong with government – things that need to be fixed. And fixing those problems is necessary if we are to revive Americans' support for government. The better we can make government, the more we can expect citizens to oppose efforts to undermine this vital institution.

Readers of the previous chapters might have gotten the impression that I was suggesting that there are no serious problems with American government. But my argument has not been that there is nothing wrong with this institution – only that it is not what *conservatives* say it is. It is simply not the case that government grossly overtaxes us, or that bureaucracies are incredibly wasteful, or that Big Brother is constantly threatening our freedoms. What is wrong is something altogether different – and something more disturbing. The main fault of our government is that it is not as democratic as it should be. We have what some have called a "deficit of democracy."

The problem is that American government is now increasingly responsive to special interests and not the public interest. This is why many people are frustrated and disappointed with our political system. Instead of a democracy where all citizens have an equal say in the governing process, some organizations and individuals have a disproportionate and unfair influence over what the government does. The result is that the power and greed of the few too often win out over the needs of the many.

This problem is getting worse and it is increasingly limiting how good government can be in the United States. The less responsive a government is to its citizens, the less liable it is to act in the public interest. The more it favors the interests of the few over the interests of the many, the less likely it is to do all the good things it could do.

Most of the substantial achievements of government described in this book have occurred because it was reacting to demands made by the public to deal with serious social and economic problems. So if we want our government to live up to its potential as a force for good in society, we need it to be as democratic as it can be. That is why it is crucial to understand exactly why our democracy is falling short, and what can be done to fix that.

The Public's Disappointment with American Democracy

While many politicians ignore our democratic deficit, most Americans are painfully aware of it. Surveys find that they are increasingly concerned that their democratic government is not working for them the way that it should. In the last ten years, the number of people who say that "public officials don't care about what people like me think" has ranged from 50% to 75% – up from 36% forty years ago. Polls show that many in the public also have a very clear sense of who really is influencing what government does. A clear majority now says that "the government is run by a few big interests looking out only for themselves."[1]

This perception – that government is working for the few, not the many – is part of what fuels public hostility toward politicians and government in general. A 2000 survey found that over 60% of respondents cited the undue influence of special interests as a reason for not trusting government.[12] The less democratic a government is, the less legitimate its actions are and the more alienated the public becomes. In this book, I have been arguing that much of modern cynicism about government is unfounded – but in this case, it is not. It makes a great deal of sense to be cynical about a government which seems to consistently favor special interests over the public interest. When people feel that they have little say over what government does and see that their government is not working democratically, it is only natural to be distrustful of that institution.

The Real Problem: The Mal-Distribution of Private Power

But while it is natural to lay the blame for our unresponsive public institutions at the doorstep of politicians and the government itself – this is a mistake. Undemocratic government is just the symptom. The ultimate source of this political illness lies in society at large – in the private sector. The real problem is that private economic power – primarily money – is not distributed equally among all citizens. Some people and organizations have very large financial resources that they can then turn into political influence. Private economic power too easily becomes public political power, and this is what is undermining the conditions of political equality that are so essential to a well-functioning democracy.

For a society to be truly democratic, political power must be shared by all – it must be distributed relatively equally among all citizens. All citizens must have a voice in determining government policy. This principle is what lies at the heart of a democracy. And this is what Lincoln was getting at when he described democratic government as being "of the people, by the people, and for the people." Americans understand this principle very well. In surveys, as many as ninety-five percent of them endorse the idea that "every citizen should have an equal chance to influence government policy."[3]

If we all have the same basic amount of political power, then government will respond to what most people want – and its actions are more likely to be in the public interest. That is why elections are so crucial to democracies – why they are defining characteristics of democracies. Ideally in elections, we all have the same exact amount of power: our one vote. A suburbanite does not have more votes than a farmer, and a rich person can't vote more often than a poor one. So the vote is the ultimate form of equal political power. And if it were the only form of political power, our democracy would not be in so much trouble.

But the vote is just one among many other sources of political power. And many of these other sources are located in the private sector where they are distributed very unequally. The result is that instead of being responsive to average Americans, our government is primarily reacting to a powerful elite. And this is undermining the promise of American democracy. The political dangers of this situation were recently highlighted by a task force of distinguished political scientists put together by the American Political Science Association. They issued a disturbing report entitled: *American Democracy in an Age of Rising Inequality.*[4] They concluded that despite efforts to ensure that all citizens have an equal voice in our political system, increasing levels of economic inequality in the United States are threatening this democratic ideal:

> Generations of Americans have worked to equalize citizen voice across lines of income, race, and gender. Today, however, the voices of Americans citizens are raised and heard unequally. The privileged participate more than others and are increasingly well organized to press their demands on government. Public officials, in turn, are much more responsive to the priv-

> ileged than to average citizens and the least affluent. Citizens of lower and moderate incomes speak in a whisper that is lost on the ears of inattentive government officials, while the advantaged roar with a clarity and consistency that policy-makers readily hear and routinely follow.[5]

The Worsening Problem

The report goes on to conclude that this problem is getting worse. "Recent analysis indicates that the government has become less responsive than it was several decades ago and that it is [now] particularly attentive to the views of the affluent and business leaders."[6] Two developments over the past thirty years have increased political inequality and the disconnection between politicians and the average American. First, the financial disparities between individual Americans – which were large to begin with – have been increasing. The benefits of our growing economy have been accruing disproportionately to those who are already well-off. Not only has the gap between the rich and the poor been widening, but so has the gap between the rich and the traditional white-collar and blue-collar middle class. Here are some disturbing facts about the high level of economic inequality in America and how it is getting worse, not better.[7]

Income is distributed highly unequally in this country. Over half of all income (50.3%) goes to the top fifth income class of families. The income going to the top 5% of richest families (21.7%) is twice the combined income of the bottom 40% –the 110 million Americans living on low and moderate incomes.

- Income inequality is getting worse. Between 1947 and 1979, the income for all classes of American grew at relatively the same rate. But more recently, between 1979 and 2009, the incomes for the richest 5% of families grew by a whopping 73%; and incomes for the richest 20% by an impressive 49%. But the increases for the bottom 60% of families have been pitiful in comparison – their gains were a meager 7%.
- In 1979, the average income for the top 5% was 11 times that of the lowest 20%. In 2006, that ratio had grown to 20 times – another indication of the growing mal-distribution of economic rewards.
- In 1965, CEOs made 24 times the wages of the typical worker. By 2007 that ratio had ballooned to 275 time the earnings of those workers.

- Meanwhile the value of the minimum wage continues to decline. In the late 1960s, the minimum wage was worth 50% of average worker's hourly wage. By 2007, it was worth just 33.5% of the average worker's wage.
- The inequality in wealth among Americans is even more extreme. In 2004, the top fifth richest families owned a staggering 84.7% of all the wealth of the country. The next 40% owned only 15.1% and the poorest 40% owned less than 1%. The last time the distribution of wealth in this country was this skewed was in the 1920s, right before the Great Depression.
- The top 20% of wealthy Americans own 90.7% of the stock. The bottom 80% owns a mere 9.4%. And 77% of the increased values of stocks between 1989 and 2004 went to a very few Americans – just the wealthiest 10% of households.
- Many believe that the increasing popularity of IRAs and mutual funds has given everyone in America of piece of the wealth pie – but that is wrong. The bottom half of Americans own less than 1% of the value of mutual funds, and a mere 3.3% of individual retirement accounts.
- Upward mobility, the ability to move up the economic ladder, is declining in America. Since the 1970s, fewer Americans have been able to move up and more of those at the top have stayed there.
- Not surprisingly, given all these figures, the U.S. has the highest level of economic inequality among developed countries. We are the worst in both income inequality and wealth inequality. To make matters worse, we also have the highest poverty rate and the most children in poverty.

These facts and figures graphically illustrate the growing economic divide among Americans. This situation is not simply disturbing for moral reasons, but also because of the corrosive impacts it is having on the operation of our democracy.

The second development in the private sector that is undermining political equality and democracy is the political mobilization of the corporate community. In the 1970s, the business community was reeling from legislative defeats from environmentalists, labor, and consumer protection groups. They were increasingly concerned about the costs of new regulations. Corporations that had previously been largely apolitical realized that they had to begin to devote more resources to their political efforts. And so corporate interests launched a very well-funded and well-planned campaign to increase their political power – pouring hundreds of millions of dollars into political campaigns, advocacy advertising, think-tanks, etc. This process has been well chronicled by Jacob Hacker and Paul Pierson in their insightful book, *Winner-Take-All-Politics: How Washington Made the Rich Richer – and Turned Its Back on the Middle Class.*[8]

The result has been that today business has become by far the most powerful organized interest in the United States – greatly outdistancing other large groups such environmentalists, the Christian Right, and the elderly. Labor used to be the traditional liberal counter-balance to business, but its membership has been in steady decline for decades and its political influence in Washington is now minimal. So when large multi-national businesses choose to mobilize their enormous economic resources to influence public policy, no other group in society is able to match those efforts. This doesn't mean that business wins every political fight, but it does mean that business almost always has the political advantage.

So that is the basic problem: financial inequality is the rule in the private sector, and that has been creating more and more political inequality in the public sector. A coalition of the well-off – wealthy individuals and prosperous companies – now exerts an enormous and disproportionate amount of power in our governmental system. Let's look at exactly how they manage to pull this off.

How Private Power Becomes Public Power

There are a number of troubling ways that private power is being turned into public power. Typically it involves large amounts of money. Money is the handiest and most versatile form of power because it can buy so many different forms of political influence. It can buy advantages for political candidates, fund massive lobbying efforts, and produce volumes of politically useful information and analysis. Let's consider each of these things in turn.

Financing Campaigns. Winning office today requires a lot of money, so campaign contributions now play a very crucial role in the election process. For instance, contributions help determine who can run for office in the first place. As the APSA report explains: "To win a seat in national office, the incumbent and challenger usually have to win the support of funders before they go before voters. The effect can be to discourage certain kinds of challengers who, for instance, promote egalitarian policies that would redistribute resources from affluent campaign contributors."[9] In other words, candidates who don't support the priorities of wealthy contributors often can't amass the resources necessary to make a viable run for office.

More importantly, donations can buy candidates many advantages – like larger campaign staffs, more high-priced consultants, more media time, and better ads – in their pursuit of voter support. Candidates with more money simply have a much better chance of attracting voters and beating their opponents. Contributions to campaigns, then, are an extremely important form of political influence – they play a significant role in determining who wins office. But this influence is wielded disproportionately by affluent individuals and organizations.

For instance, the campaign donations of political action committees come primarily from organizations that are financially well-off. Corporate and industry trade PACS now far outnumber and out-donate all other interest groups. In the 2008 elections, for instance, these business-oriented PACs outnumbered Labor PACs by almost ten to one and outspent them by four to one – $321 million to $73 million.[10] Or consider the uphill battle faced by grassroots interest groups like environmentalists. In 2008, environmental PACs contributed $811,000 to various races. But the PACs for several industries that often fight against increased environmental regulations (energy and natural resources, construction, chemical, and automotive) contributed 50 times that amount — $40 million.[11] It's not hard to guess which groups are more able to help elect their preferred candidates.

This corporate dominance of campaign funding was made even worse by a 2010 Supreme Court ruling that overturned the longstanding ban on corporations spending directly on political campaigns. They are now able to spend as much money as they want to defeat candidates they oppose and to threaten elected officials who don't share their political priorities.

Supporters of our current financing system like to point out that many contributions come from individuals – not PACs or corporations. This seems to suggest that it is the average American voter who is financing most campaigns. Nothing could be farther from the truth. There is a huge class bias to these donations. In 2002, 83% of all the itemized donations to campaigns were given by less than one-half of one percent of the U.S. population. And almost three-fourths of these total donations ($1.9 billion) came from a relatively small group of well-off Americans who could afford to donate $2,300 or more.[12] This is not public participation – this is rich people's participation.

Recently, some have argued that the emergence of groups like MoveOn.org has signaled a switch to a more grassroots and democratic approach to funding campaigns. And in 2008, that organization did manage to raise $38 million through the use of the internet and local meetings. But in reality, this figure is a drop in the bucket compared to the $2.2 *billion* spent by campaigns that year.

So campaign finance is a perfect example of how the concentration of money in the private sector leads to imbalances of power in the public sector. This situation directly undermines the democratic nature of elections. Who gets elected should be determined by the voters, not by well-heeled donors whose contributions give their preferred candidates large and unfair advantages over others. Wealthy individuals and organizations should not have more say over who get elected than the rest of us.

These skewed donations not only affect whose candidates win office, but the behavior of political parties as well. The Democratic and Republican parties are supposed to be rivals that represent very different constituencies. But both have become increasing dependent on wealthy donors and business PACs. This has pushed the Democratic Party farther to the right and has made it less responsive to many of its less affluent constituents, such as workers, minorities, and the poor. Not only elections, but parties are becoming less democratic as well.

Lobbying. Another major source of political influence is lobbying – organized efforts to sway the decisions of policymakers. Lobbying largely determines whose problems and concerns get the attention of policymakers, and whose arguments get a better hearing. In the last thirty years, more and more groups have established lobbying offices in Washington – groups representing environmentalists, gays, the elderly, farmers, consumers, and so on. This gives the appearance of a fair and healthy competition between all interests. But this is only an illusion.

First, not all lobbying organizations are born equal, and the competition between them does not take place on a level playing field. Again, money is what makes the difference. Some lobbies have much larger and more reliable sources of funds, and this tilts this political process in favor of these more wealthy interests. Interests with more money can, for instance, create more lobbying groups to promote their cause. It is hardly a coincidence that the majority of organizations lobbying in Washington, D.C. are corporations. Many of these firms also enjoy multiple avenues of representation. Most businesses, for instance, belong to trade groups who also lobby in Washington. General Electric belongs to over 80 trade organizations – most of which also have lobbying arms. If you add together all the corporations, trade groups, and well-off professional organizations (doctors, lawyers, etc.), they make up over a staggering 75% of all lobbying efforts. In contrast, public interest organizations like environmentalists, consumer groups, and civic organizations make up only 4% of lobbying groups. Even more stunning, if you add together unions, civil rights groups, the elderly, women, educational groups, farmers, and veterans, they make up less than 10% of lobbying efforts.[13]

Not only does more money fund more lobbying efforts, it also pays for larger offices with more staff and better support. More money also buys more effective and more expensive lobbyists – particularly retired members of Congress who are still friendly with their former colleagues on the hill. Money also makes is easier for some lobbyists to get direct access to policymakers. Members of Congress are very busy and can't see everyone who knocks on their door. But lobbyists with direct access to policymakers have a much better ability to make their case. Studies show that who gets in and how much time they get is often directly related to the size of their campaign contributions.[14]

Given all this, it is little wonder that two of our leading scholars on interest groups activity, Kay Schlozman and John Tierney, have concluded that the lobbying process "is skewed in favor of groups representing the well-off, especially business, and against groups favoring broad public interests and the disadvantaged."[15]

The Power of Ideas. Another way that well-off interests wield political influence is by affecting the way other people look at policy issues. Ideas, information, and analysis are important sources of political persuasion and power. They influence how we look at the world – how we see political issues, what problems are considered important, how political debates are framed, and which policies are considered justified. They are a vital form of intellectual ammunition in political fights. But here again, the competition in this area is not fair. Ideas, information and analysis are commodities – and those interests with more money can pay experts to produce more of these commodities. So this is yet another way that advantages in private financial resources are translated into advantages in political power. It is another way that the voices of affluent interests drown out the voices of average Americans.

An earlier chapter in this book, "The Anti-Government Campaign," chronicles the ability of wealthy families and businesses to funnel billions of dollars into foundations, think-tanks, and universities – the main organizations that produce and promote the work of political intellectuals and policy experts. These intellectual investments produce two kinds of political payoffs. First, these efforts are very useful in lobbying policymakers. Members of Congress can only specialize in a few policy areas, and so they are often dependent on outside sources of information to inform their votes on many complex issues. Well-funded – largely conservative – think-tanks are more than happy to oblige. They provide a steady stream of detailed studies, expert testimony, and Congressional briefings that greatly aid the lobbying efforts of well-heeled interests like big businesses.

The other target of this intellectual barrage is public opinion. There is a concerted effort to shape the public's ideas about what is desirable politically. If the public can be convinced, for instance, that "what is good for business is good for America," this provides increased legitimacy for those seeking to roll-back regulations and cut business taxes. So a great deal of money has been spent on creating a sophisticated communications system that constantly promotes the ideas of conservative intellectuals and think-tanks to the public. Materials are sent to reporters on a daily basis and frequent guest commentators are provided to network news shows. Information and analysis are also funneled through right-wing political pundits like Rush Limbaugh, Sean Hannity and Fred Barnes who then disseminate these ideas through conservative cable news channels like Fox News, right-wing internet sites, and hundreds of national and local radio talk shows.

Vastly Unequal Citizens

So what does all of this add up to? Incredible imbalances in private and public power and a political playing field that is hugely uneven. A typical non-unionized worker has her one vote, but few other ways to influence policy. Her measly $25 campaign donation is lost in the avalanche of special interest contributions. She might write a letter to her Congressperson, but it will likely be drowned out by the organized letter-writing campaigns of large lobbies. In contrast, for a corporate executive, his vote is his least important political tool. He can have much more influence by donating thousands of dollars to political action committees as well as thousands more in individual donations to specific candidates – all working to increase the election chances of his favorite politicians. And his economic interests are also much better represented in the policymaking process by the many well-healed organizations that lobby for his firm and industry. Finally, our executive is more likely to have his political and policy ideas pitched to Congress by think-tank experts and espoused to the public by media pundits. So here we have two Americans, two citizens who are supposed to be political equals, but who have vastly different amounts of power. This mal-distribution of political power cannot help but have a corrosive effect on our democracy.

The Result: Policies by and for Affluent Special Interests

These imbalances of power produce a clear bias in the political system toward the interests of affluent individuals and businesses. Policymakers are more apt to listen to these interests and design policies with them in mind. Several recent studies have sought to gauge the political clout that various economic classes had over the decisions of politicians. One found that "senators are vastly more responsive to the views of affluent constituents than to the constituents of modest means."[16] In fact, if the poor and working class support a particular policy that means that senators are actually *less* likely to vote for it. Another empirical study of public opinion and policy found that "the American political system is a great deal more responsive to the preferences of the rich than to the preferences of the poor."[17] Finally, a study found that even if a majority of Americans supports a new policy, it doesn't stand a good chance of becoming law unless it is also supported by the well-off.[18] Hardly surprising, but very disturbing none the less.

It is not hard to find specific policy examples of this political tilt toward the well-off. Tax policy is exhibit number one. In recent years, the public has not been citing tax cuts as one of their highest priorities. In fact, polls reveal that most Americans would now rather forgo more tax cuts and spend that money on areas like education and health care. And yet for over a decade, the Republican-dominated Congress continued to put tax cuts high on their legislative agenda. Such behavior by policymakers makes much more sense when it is understood that these cuts have disproportionately favored the rich and businesses – the very interests who have the dominant powerbase in our political system. It is hardly a coincidence that in the first year after the 2003 tax cuts, households making over $1 million were granted a gift of nearly $100,000 in tax cuts, while the average tax cut for a middle-class family was a paltry $217. Nor is it just a matter of luck that Congressional tax policies – under both Democrats and Republicans – have reduced the share of federal taxes paid by businesses from 20% of total federal revenue in 1975 to a mere 7% in 2003.[19] One of the most blatant examples of elite power occurred in 2010, when the Republican Party refused to allow the extension of unemployment benefits to millions of jobless Americans unless the Democrats agreed to extend the Bush tax cuts for the rich. These are just a few examples of how tax policy has produced immediate and large pay-offs for the money that affluent interests have invested in buying political influence.

This current imbalance of financial and political power not only helps to explain what Congress *does*, but also what it *does not do*. It sheds light on why Congress is so slow to act on some serious problems –

especially problems that are not of particular concern to the moneyed interests wielding the most power. Consider, for instance, the problem of unemployment. The recent deep recession has left record numbers of people without jobs. And millions who want full time work can only find part time jobs. But in the face of this unemployment crisis, Congress has largely sat on its hands and has done little to promote the creation of more jobs. Largely this is because the suffering of American workers is of little interest to the well-moneyed interests that dominate in our political system.

Or take health care policy. For many decades now, our health care crisis has been growing. Over 47 million Americans had no medical insurance. Employers were cutting back on coverage for their workers. Many middle-class families were being financially pressed by increasing medical costs. Financially strapped state governments began limiting access to Medicaid for many people living in poverty. The quality of medical care was highly uneven and we compared poorly to most other Western countries in terms of life expectancy and infant mortality. And yet in the face of all of this, Congress was reluctant to act in any vigorous or concerted way. For decades we remained the only Western democracy that did not provide some form of universal health care for its citizens. And all this despite consistent public support for major health care reform. By almost a two-to-one margin, Americans said they would rather scrap the current employer-based insurance system and replace it with a government program that would provide coverage for everyone. Three-quarters of Americans said that access to health care should be a right – not something available only to those who can afford it. And 67% said they would even be willing to pay more in taxes to make this universal coverage a reality.[20] Still, until the election of President Obama, most members of Congress – both Democrats and Republicans – adamantly refused to promote such a universal plan. Why was that the case?

The answer had to do with the imbalance of political power that has been described here. First, health care reform was not a high priority for those who are well-off in society – they had no problem affording the best medical care. More importantly, there were powerful special interests who benefited from the current system and who diligently worked against any attempts to create a universal health insurance system. A sociologist, Jill Qaudagno, has written an insightful book about this problem entitled *One Nation Uninsured: Why the U.S. Has No National Health Insurance.*[21] She showed how powerful private interests were able to block every effort in Congress to move toward a national health care program. In the 1960s, it was primarily physicians who torpedoed the attempt. In recent years, it has been insurance companies and employers. And even when health care reform was finally passed in 2010, the Republicans and their health care industry allies were able to block the most promising and wide reaching reform proposals, such as the single-payer government plan that has proved so successful in other Western democracies.

Needed: More Power to the People

It hasn't always been the case that wealthy interests have so successfully dominated our political system. There have been times in our past when Congress rose up to pass broad-based policies that greatly extended economic equality, economic security, and economic opportunity among all citizens – legislation such as Social Security in the 1930s, the G. I. Bill in the 1940s, and Medicare in the 1960s. These egalitarian policies improved the lives of virtually all American families and are widely recognized as political and moral highpoints in American politics. But today these kinds of progressive bills would face a huge uphill battle in Washington, even with the Democrats in charge. Such efforts would be quickly attacked by powerful special interests, and condemned by most conservatives as expensive and wasteful "big government" programs that would only raise taxes. The shift in political power that has taken place toward well-off individuals and corporations has made it very difficult to pass these kinds of egalitarian policies.

It is this shift in power, not a shift in public opinion, which has created the right-ward swing toward more inegalitarian policies. Most Americans still support a broadly egalitarian political agenda – higher minimum wages, more help for the poor, most affordable higher education, and so on. What has changed is not public opinion, but the distribution of power. Most Americans back more government spending on health care and education, and more regulations that protect workers and the environment. Social programs, taxes, and regulations have been cut not because the public has demanded it, but because those with the most power have demanded it. As the APSA report concluded: "Interest groups and money are tools wielded disproportionately by a small segment of American citizens to enact policies that concentrate benefits on them and to block egalitarian policies..." That, in a nutshell, is the alarming policy result of the shift in political power that is undermining democracy in the United States.

Some people believe that electing more liberal politicians, like Barack Obama, will help to solve this deficit of democracy. It can't hurt.

But a change in elected leaders can only do so much to address the undemocratic tendencies that have become deeply embedded in our economic and political systems. If we are to really remedy these problems, we need more basic reforms. To see what some of those reforms are, go to the next chapter.

---

1. Lawrence R. Jacobs and Theda Skocpol, eds., *Inequality and American Democracy* (New York: Russell Sage Foundation, 2005) p. 8.
2. Ibid. p. 8.
3. Ibid. p. 25.
4. Task Force on Inequality and American Democracy, "American Democracy in an Age of Rising Inequality," American Political Science Association, 2004. This was later published in book form: Lawrence R. Jacobs and Theda Skocpol, eds., *Inequality and American Democracy* (New York: Russell Sage Foundation, 2005).
5. *Inequality and American Democracy*, p. 1.
6. *Inequality and American Democracy*, p. 117.
7. Most of these economic facts and figures came from Economic Policy Institute, *The State of Working America*, January 2006-2007. http://www.epinet.org/content.cfm/books_swa2006; and Inequality.Org, "How Unequal Are We, Anyway?" November, 2008. http://www.inequality.org/facts.html
8. Jacob Hacker and Paul Pierson, *Winner-Take-All-Politics: How Wash ington Made the Rich Richer – and Turned Its Back on the Middle Class.* New York: Simon and Schuster, 2010.
9. *Inequality and American Democracy*, p. 115.
10. These figures come from the website Open Secrets.Org, http://www.opensecrets.org
11. Open Secrets.Org.
12. Open Secrets.Org.
13. Kay L. Schlozman and John T. Tierney, *Organized Interests and American Democracy*. New York: Harper and Row, 1986, pp. 67-68.
14. *Inequality and American Democracy, p. 116.*
15. Schlozman and Tierney, *Organized Interests and American Democracy, p. 66.*
16. *Inequality and American Democracy, p. 127.*
17. *Inequality and American Democracy, p. 127.*
18. Martin Gilens, "Inequality and Democratic Responsiveness," *Public Opinion Quarterly* 69, no.5 (2005): 778-96/.
19. *Statistical Abstract of the United States, 2004 ed. (Washington, DC: U.S. Printing Office, 2004), p. 300.*

20. This poll figures can be found in Ruy Teixeira, "Public Opinion and Universal Health Care," The Emerging Democratic Majority web site, September 16, 2005. *http://www.emergingdemocraticmajorityweblog.com/donkeyrising/archives/001291.php*
21. Jill Quadango, *One Nation Uninsured: Why the U.S. Has No National Health Insurance* (Oxford: Oxford University Press, 2005).

CHAPTER 20

How to Fix American Government and Revive Democracy

As I argued in the previous chapter, the main problem right now with American government is a deficit of democracy. Moneyed interests have too much power in our political system and the public has too little. But what can be done about this – how can we fix our government and revitalize democracy in the United States?

It is not as if this threat to democracy has gone unnoticed. Many citizens and organizations have been outraged about the rising power of affluent special interests. They have been working to address this issue of unequal power and have been pursuing several different approaches. These reform efforts fall into three broad categories. The first is to lessen the economic inequality in the private sphere that is being translated to political inequality in the public sphere. The second is to attempt to erect institutional barriers that prevent private power from being easily converted to political advantage. A third approach is to reform the voting process itself so that it becomes more democratic and more empowering to average voters. Let's look briefly at each of these alternatives.

Toward Greater Economic Equality

The first line of attack is to go straight to the heart of the problem: our large inequalities in wealth and income. If these disparities are the basic cause of political inequalities, then these private inequalities need to be lessened if we want to move toward political system where power is more widely dispersed among all citizens. So we need to produce a fairer division of the economic pie that is created by the work of all Americans. However, such changes in the distribution of wealth and income will not come about naturally through the market, but can only be enacted through various kinds of public policies on the state and federal levels. Here are some policies that would help to reduce wage and wealth inequalities.[1]

- **Raise State and Federal Minimum Wages.** This policy would immediately benefit those at the bottom of the economic ladder. During the last several decades, minimum wage has been increasingly falling behind the average wage and it needs to be increased.
- **Living Wage Policies.** Another approach to raising the incomes of the poor and working class is to pass local ordinances requiring that a "living wage" be paid by companies with government contracts or subsidies. The wage has usually been pegged to the amount that would lift a family of three or four above the poverty level. Cities like Baltimore and Los Angeles have passed living wage laws that have increased the wages of thousands of workers in those urban areas.
- **Earned Income Tax Credits.** Many liberals and conservatives agree that the EITC has been very successful in subsidizing the wages of low-income working families so that they may stay out of poverty. This program must be maintained and hopefully expanded to cover even more low income workers.
- **Full-Employment Policies.** If government policymakers were more serious about reducing unemployment to a minimum, this would reduce both poverty and wage inequality. Many people are poor for lack of a full-time job. And when the employment market is tight, this forces companies to raise wages in order to attract workers.
- **Reducing High Corporate Salaries.** Decreasing economic inequality may involve not only increasing the incomes of those on the bottom, but also putting reasonable limits on the income of those on the top. The salaries of top corporate executives have been ballooning while average wages have stagnated. U.S. CEOs currently make salaries that are over 200 times that of the average worker – a much higher disparity than we see in most other Western countries.
- **Bolstering Union Power.** Government policies to strengthen the power of unions would probably have the highest payoffs in the effort to reduce wage inequality. Many other Western countries have lower levels of economic inequality precisely because unions are more common and have more clout. Union bargaining clearly helps to increase the wages and benefits of low and moderate income workers. We could do much more to facilitate

the establishment of unions and to increase their bargaining power. For example, instead of the current lengthy process needed to establish unions, we could require instant recognition of any union that signs up a majority of workers in a workplace. We could also institute a ban on the use of permanent replacement workers – a major tool used by management to break strikes. Canada has this ban and also requires instant recognition of unions – one reason their rate of unionization is three times that of the U.S. Another change that would help unions would be to remove the ban on secondary boycotts, where workers from one company are prohibited from supporting strikers in another company – say by refusing to cross a picket line. Finally, the Taft-Hartely Act should be repealed. This act impedes workers abilities to unionize and has legitimized a wide array of anti-union activities by employers.

- **Free or Low-Cost Higher Education.** We should be increasing the number of government grants (not loans) for college students – or better yet, we should make higher education free for all Americans.[2] After World War II, the G.I Bill enabled millions of people to get a debt-free college education, which gave a significant boost to their asset-building efforts. A similar effort now would help millions attend college and ensure that they graduate without a crushing load of debt.
- **Kidsave Accounts** have been proposed that would guarantee every child $1,000 at birth and $500 per year to every child from ages one to five – all to be invested until retirement. This would significantly bolster Social Security and other retirement accounts for all Americans.
- **Progressive Taxation.** More progressive tax rates would help to even the playing field. The rich should be paying more in income taxes. Estate taxes, which currently impact only the very richest families, should be maintained. Capital gains – which disproportionately go to the wealthy – should be taxed at the same rate as wages. Finally, a direct tax on wealth, from which most Americans would be exempt, would help to undermine huge concentrations of wealth. Many European countries already have such wealth taxes.
- **Employee Ownership Plans.** Government policies should help to broaden employee ownership of businesses – the main generators of wealth in our country.[3] Policies should encourage employee stock ownership plans (ESOPs), profit-sharing plans, and widely granted stock options that would significantly

increase the stake that workers have in private enterprises.

A more equitable distribution of income and wealth would certainly be a step in the right direction in the effort to remedy the unfair distribution of political power that we have in the U.S. The goal of these policies is not to eliminate economic inequality in America; no one is arguing that everyone should make the same amount of money. The point is to begin to reduce economic inequality to a more reasonable and just level – a level at which it will no longer undermine the promise of political equality.

Public Financing of Elections[4]

Even if wealth and income remains very unequal in the United States, there are several other reforms that would help to ensure that wealthy interests do not dominate in the political system. One is to erect barriers between private power and public power – barriers that make it difficult for financial advantages to be translated into political advantages. One area where this is absolutely essential is in elections. As documented in the previous chapter, well-off individuals and organizations are now able to use their financial clout to determine who runs for office and who has the best chance to win.

In the last 30 years, many campaign finance reform measures have been adopted. We now limit the size of individual donations and PAC donations, for instance. And more recently, unlimited "soft money" donations were banned. But none of these reforms have done much to stem the tide of private special interest money into campaigns. Private money behaves like water – if you damn it up in one place, it eventually just finds its way around the barrier and into the election process. Soft money, for example, has merely been reincarnated in the form of so-called "527" groups, which pour millions into campaign ads. And in 2010 the Supreme Court struck down the longstanding ban on corporations spending directly on political campaigns, which will leave them free to spend unlimited sums defeating candidates they oppose.

This situation has led many campaign finance reform advocates to argue that the only real solution to this problem is to get private money entirely out of campaigns. They are advocating public financing of elections, so that candidates will not be dependent at all on special interest money. Sometimes called "Clean Elections," this system works in the following way. To qualify for public money, candidates must collect a number of small ($5-$10) donations from citizens – say 100 of these donations for a run at a state legislative seat. Candidates then agree to not raise or spend any private money in their campaigns. All qualified candidates then receive the same amount of public funds to run their campaign. A key provision is that if a rival candidate then spends large amounts of private money to defeat a publicly financed candidate, the latter would receive more public funds to keep them competitive.

Publicly financed campaigns are the best way to short-circuit the influence of private money in elections. They ensure that candidates are being responsive to their constituents, not to the special interest money they need to win office. And this system is not that expensive. It is estimated that all political campaigns in the United States could be publicly financed for about $10 from every citizen – a small price to pay to reclaim the democratic nature of elections.

Maine citizens used an initiative to pass a "Clean Elections Law" in 1996 and it has been a resounding success. By 2005, 83% of the State Senate and 77% of the State House were made up of legislators who ran "clean" campaigns. And this system now has broad support from candidates of all parties. Here are just a few of the endorsements by current legislators:

> "I decided to use Clean Elections because I philosophically believe in not having private funding as a big part of our election process. I want to be beholden to the people who elected me, not special interests."
>
> Sen. Beth Edmonds, (D) Freeport
>
> "Clean Elections has been great for democracy in Maine. It allows any individual with community support to run for office, it has increased voter choice, and increased competition while at the same time leveling the playing field for all candidates."
>
> Rep. Chris Rector, (R) Thomaston

Public financing not only has the advantage of lessening the political advantages that affluent interests have in elections, it also reduces their leverage in the lobbying process. Politicians who are less dependent on special interest money are also less likely to feel that they have to pay more attention to special interest lobbies. As one Maine lawmaker put it: "As a Clean Elections legislator, I find myself being lobbied a lot less than traditional candidates. It is a lot easier if someone's trying to pressure you to say, 'I owe my allegiance to the taxpayers of the State of Maine, and not to any special interest group.'"

Proportional Representation Elections: Empowering More Voters

A final approach to revitalizing democracy in the United States is to change the voting system itself – the method that determines how we cast our votes for candidates and how the winners are decided. Our current winner-take-all voting system is one of the least representative and least democratic of all forms of elections. Adopting a better voting system could go a long ways toward enhancing the political power of average citizens, and this would help to blunt the influence of private economic power.

We are so used to our current "winner-take-all" voting system that we fail to see its many problems. But most of the rest of the world consider our system to be outmoded and undemocratic, and have rejected it in favor of what are called "proportional representation" voting systems – or PR.[5] In a winner-take-all system, legislators are elected one at a time in single-member districts. We cast our vote for our one favorite candidate, and the winner is the one who receives the most votes. Only those people who vote for the winning candidate receive representation. Proportional representation elections differ from this system in two-ways. First, instead of electing legislators in single-member districts, they are elected in larger, multi-member districts where several legislators are elected at once. So under PR rules, a state legislature of 100 members might be elected in 20 five-member districts, or 10 ten-member districts.

The second difference is that who wins the legislative seats in PR elections is determined by the proportion of the votes that a party receives. So if we have a ten-member PR district in which the Democrats won 50% of the vote, five Democratic candidates would win seats. With 30% of the vote, Republicans would get three seats. If minor parties like the Libertarians and the Greens were to receive 10% of the vote each, they each would get one seat.[6] Thus, in PR, all voters win some representation – not just the majority – and all voters have someone to speak for their interests in the legislative process.

Adopting proportional representation elections in the United States would go a long ways toward ensuring that all citizens have their fair share of power in our legislatures. PR elections would create diverse legislatures that include both major and minor parties. This would ensure that all political groups – not just the well-off – would have a chance to influence legislation. PR would give more power and representation to groups who traditionally have lacked access to large amounts of private financial power. Currently, for instance, neither of the major parties are strong advocates for the interests of the working class and the poor – because both parties are largely beholden to wealthy contributors and PACs. But under PR rules, it is likely that something like a Labor Party or a Progressive Party would emerge in the U.S. – a party that explicitly champions the cause of the workers and the poor. And such a party would win seats in the legislature where it could work for policies that help that portion of our population. It is the presence of these kinds of parties in most Europeans countries – Labor Parties, Social Democratic Parties, etc. – that are largely the reason that those legislatures have passed more laws that help boost wages and provide more support for those on the lower rungs of the economic ladder.

Proportional representation elections would also encourage higher voter turnout and in this way make elections and government more democratic. The more people that participate in elections, the more representative the results will be, and the more likely that public policies will reflect the views of average Americans. One of the reasons why those who are well-off now have more political influence is that they turn out to vote in much higher numbers. Voter participation is much higher for those in the upper and middle classes than for moderate- and low-income voters. But this is understandable – given our current two-party, winner-take-all election arrangements. Those on the upper end of the economic ladder are much more likely to find candidates who support their interests. Struggling farmers and poor inner-city residents are much less likely to find a candidate or party who puts their interests first – and so they have much less reason to turn out to vote.

But as we've seen, under PR rules parties are likely to emerge to represent all economic interests – even those who are less well-off. This will encourage these voters to participate in larger numbers and thus give them more representation and influence in our legislatures.[7] It is not a coincidence that in countries that use PR, there are not the same stark differences in turnout among the economic classes. Most people vote most of time in these countries. Turnout levels often approach 80% or more, in contrast to the 40%-50% rates typical here.

In short, adopting proportional representation elections in the United States would help to equalize the current imbalances of power in our political system. All groups – regardless of their numbers or financial resources – would have their fair share of seats in our legislatures and a better chance to influence public policy decisions. And the more accurately we represent all citizens in the governmental process, the better the chance for the passage of more broadly egalitarian policies that are in the public interest.

Getting from Here to There

Obviously, using these kinds of reforms to fix the problems of unequal political power will not be easy. But there are reasons to be hopeful – reasons to believe that reinvigorating our democracy is well within our reach. For one thing, history is on our side. During the last century, modern societies have been evolving in the direction of becoming more democratic and have promoted more egalitarian participation in the governing process. All the political reforms that have just been described are not pie-in-the-sky schemes, *but real policies that are already in effect to some extent in many other Western democracies.* Most other democracies, for instance, have a substantial amount of public financing of elections. Candidates and parties get public subsidies and governments grant large amounts of free television time. Also, most advanced democracies have now abandoned winner-take-all voting systems and have embraced more proportional systems. And the few remaining winner-take-all countries, such as Canada and Great Britain, now have wide-scale political movements promoting proportional representation. Finally, virtually all Western European democracies have economic policies in place that create a more egalitarian distribution of the wealth and income. So in a very real way, those Americans who are working for these kinds of political and policy reforms are swimming with the historical tide, not against it.

But we must not be naïve about the ease of change or the obstacles getting in the way. Those who want to reinvigorate democracy in the United States will certainly get no help from anti-government conservatives. These conservatives not only ignore the threat to democracy posed by vastly unequal amounts of economic and political power, they are actually making the problem worse. Under President Bush, the Republican agenda of tax cuts for the wealthy interests and program cuts for low-income Americans only deepened the economic divide between Americans – and thus further undermined political equality as well.

But it would be a mistake to simply blame conservative politicians for ignoring the sorry state of democracy in the U.S. To a certain extent, politicians of both parties have little incentive to make democratic reforms a priority. All politicians have gained their positions of power by taking advantage of our current political and economic arrangements, and so they are unlikely to challenge them. Though there are some principled politicians who support a more equitable division of economic and political power, many elected officials simply do not want to change a system that put them into power. Few, for example, support a public financing system that would give their opponents the same amount of campaign funds that they have. This means that we cannot count on democratic reforms coming from the top-down – from our political leaders. These changes will have to come from the bottom up, from demands made by the public. Policymakers will make these changes only when they are pressured to do so by us, or when the public bypasses established politicians by using the initiative and referendum process to pass reform laws.

This is nothing new. Virtually all efforts to transform and increase democracy in the United States have come as a result of grassroots political movements. As the American historian Alexander Keyssar has explained, democracy has always been an ongoing project in this country, and our political history has been very much a struggle between grassroots groups who have sought to expand democracy and those who have tried to limit it.[8] Even something as rudimentary as expanding the right to vote to include all citizens is something that took decades of continual political struggle. It took two of the largest movements in American history — the Women's Suffrage Movement and the Civil Rights Movement – to finally ensure that this key form of political power was dispersed equally in society. Today, this same ground-up political approach must be pursued in order to take the next steps down the path of democracy – steps to reclaim our government from the moneyed interests that dominate our political system today.

Fortunately, there are already many people and groups working on these issues. Labor unions and groups like Jobs with Justice and United for a Fair Economy are struggling to increase the economic and political clout of workers and create a more fair distribution of the fruits of economic growth. Other political organizations, including the Center for Responsive Politics, Common Cause, and Public Campaign, are working on campaign finance reform. Leading the fight for election system reform and the adoption of proportional representation is FairVote – the Center for Voting and Democracy. There are several state groups as well, such as Californians for Electoral Reform, that are educating Americans about how elections can be made fairer and more democratic. The existence of such groups is another reason to be politically hopeful; but they need much more of our active support if they are to make more headway in fixing our deficit of democracy in the United States.

More Democracy, More Trust, and More Government

Certainly many Americans have a legitimate reason to feel disappointed and frustrated with government – it often isn't being responsive to their needs. Unfortunately, conservatives have been quick to exploit those feelings of alienation to further their own ideological agenda of cutting back on government programs. They argue that if government doesn't listen to us, then we should reduce it. But the real solution is to make sure that government *does* listen to us – that all of us do have an equal voice in government. As the American philosopher John Dewey explained: "The cure for the ailments of democracy is more democracy." And what really needs to be reduced is not government, but the unfair power of affluent special interests. The more we do this, the more we can begin to build back up public trust in government. As our government becomes more representative and more responsive to all Americans, we will all begin to trust it more.

Here is another key point: the more democratic government becomes, the less afraid people will be of a large and active government. The stronger our democracy becomes, the more people will see the expansion of government powers as the expansion of *their* powers. The successful adoption of a universal health care plan, for instance, will now expand the power of many citizens to protect their families against serious illness and financial disaster. Similarly, the expansion of environmental, workplace, and consumer product regulations gives us a greater ability to protect ourselves from other grave threats to our well-being. "Big government" is much more appealing when it is seen as "big democracy" – a growth in our collectively ability to better our lives. If our government is to live up to its full potential as a way for us to promote the good life in the United States, then clearly what we need is not simply *more government*, but *more democratic government* as well.

---

1. Most of the policies for reducing inequalities in wages and wealth have been adapted from Chuck Collins and Felice Yeskel, *Economic Apartheid in America: A Primer on Economic Inequality and Insecurity* (New York: The New Press, 2000).
2. For details on such a plan, see "Free Higher Education: A Campaign for Free Tuition at Public Colleges and Universities," http://www.freehighered.org/index.html.
3. For one of the best discussions of worker ownership and other ways of spreading the wealth, see Gar Alperovitz, *American Beyond Capitalism* (New York: Wiley and Sons, 2005) Chapter 1.
4. For more on the case for campaign finance reform and public funding of campaigns, see Public Campaign's web site, particularly, "Clean Money Campaign Reform," November 22, 2005

http://www.publicampaign.org/publications/factsheets/CleanMoneyCampaignReform.pdf

5. For a more detailed description of the case for proportional representation in the U.S., see Douglas J. Amy, *Real Choices, New Voices: How Proportional Representation Elections Could Revitalize American Democracy* (New York: Columbia University Press, 2002).
6. For more detail on how PR elections actually work, see Amy, *Real Choices*.
7. PR would also eliminate the "spoiler effect" that discourages people from turning out and voting for third party candidates. Under winner-take-all rules, Americans who want to support minor party candidates inevitably feel they are wasting their votes and will receive no representation. Even worse, voting for a third party candidate may create a "spoiler" – a candidate that takes enough votes away from one major party candidate to ensure the election of another. This is what Ralph Nader did in Florida in the 2000 election. He took enough votes away from Al Gore to ensure the election of George W. Bush as president. "Spoilers" are impossible under PR rules, and this gives more people an incentive to vote.
8. Alexander Keyssar, *The Right to Vote: The Contested History of Democracy in the United States* (New York: Basic Books, 2000).

CHAPTER 21

Building a Pro-Government Campaign

When Barack Obama was elected President in 2008, some had hoped that this would put an end to the government-hating politics of the Bush era. But in fact it prompted a renewed bout of anti-government rhetoric and activism. Rush Limbaugh, Glenn Beck and other right-wing commentators ramped up their shrill attacks on government, accusing the president of being a "communist" and railing against the "fascist" policies of the Democratic administration. Many Republican leaders attributed their political losses to the failure of the party to push its smaller government agenda aggressively enough. They called for a renewed commitment to slashing taxes and cutting budgets. In addition, the Tea Party movement emerged, pushing a rabidly anti-tax and anti-government message.

So instead of the war on government winding down, it has actually intensified. This means that a pro-government campaign is needed now more than ever. We need to promote a more positive view of government and to organize a pro-government political coalition that can push politicians to support the refunding and revitalization of the public sector. In this chapter, I will talk about what steps we can take to aid in this effort to build support for government – from actions that we can take as individuals to suggestions about how we can begin to build a pro-government alliance among political groups in this country.

Taking Personal Responsibility

The obvious place to begin is with ourselves. There are a number of things we can do as individuals to help to revitalizing government. We can start by not inadvertently contributing to the right-wing effort to malign this institution. For example, we all tend to promote negative stereotypes of government. I recently attended a party in which an otherwise intelligent woman confidently declared that "All politicians are corrupt." Of course this is patently absurd, but it is exactly the kind of cynical comment about government that comes naturally to most of us. As we've seen, most Americans have a love-hate relationship with government – distrustful and derogatory on the one hand and yet very positive about its programs on the other. However, it is the negative attitude that is closest to the surface and which tends to be voiced most often in public. When we are among friends and families, it is our knee jerk cynicism about government that tends to come out – even among those of us who most strongly support this institution. Who can resist a good joke at the government's expense?

But we need to stop this. We need think about how we talk about government and be aware of how we contribute to the unfair denigration of this institution. Before we make our usual complaints about taxes, we should stop and consider how our money actually contributes to a whole host of important public interest efforts – such as promoting better health and protecting the environment. And we need to make it clear that even though we may strongly disagree with the particular politicians and policies, that government itself continues to play a vital role in American society.

Another thing we can do is to confront other people about their mistaken criticisms of government. All too often, when someone is bashing government, we join in or at least acquiesce. But we should be setting our friends and relatives straight about why many criticisms of government are in fact inaccurate and wrong-headed. And we should become defenders of government in public as well. Robert Kuttner, who writes for *The American Prospect*, could serve as a good example for us all. He tells a story about being on the campaign trail when John Kerry was running for re-election to the Senate in 2000. Kuttner was on a panel with Kerry at a gathering of Democratic town committees. When a questioner asked Kerry about deregulation, he started his response by observing that "Nobody wants more regulations." But while this answer went down well with most of this audience, it did not with Kuttner. After Kerry finished, Kuttner said, "Excuse me, Senator, I want more regulations" and he then went on to mention corporate excesses such as "drug-company price gouging that were crying out for more public remediation, not less."[1]

What is unusual about this story is not simply that a liberal like Kerry so easily slipped into knee-jerk government bashing, but that Kuttner had the courage to call him on it in public. It is not easy – or cool – to be a public defender of government, but it is an important task that we all need to take up. Fortunately, when you come to the defense of government, you will find more often than not that at least some people agree with you. Consider that after Kuttner confronted Kerry, the senator quickly backed down, explaining that he meant he was opposed to regulations in the sense of red tape. On some level, most people know that government plays a very positive role in our society. And almost 40% of Americans believe that "Government does a better job than it is given credit for."[2] So there is actually a large receptive audience out there for those who are willing to stand up and defend the importance of government.

Publicizing What Government Does for Us

We also need to become more aware of what government is doing for us. Many of us rarely think about what we get for our tax dollars – the kinds of services that our local, state and federal governments are providing for us every day. Remarkably, when asked if government has had a positive effect on their lives, 45% of Americans insisted that it has not.[3] But it is revealing that when these same people were asked about *specific* government programs, a majority said that they had benefited from programs on food and drug safety, consumer protection, workplace regulations, public universities, public schools, roads and highways, parks and recreation, environmental laws, medical research, police and the courts, and social security. So when people stop thinking about government in the abstract, and are made to think of particular government programs, they are more apt to recognize their beneficial effects on their own lives.

If governments bragged about their accomplishments the way all other organizations do, it would be more difficult for people to believe that they get little for their tax dollars. In fact, there is evidence that efforts like this would help. Pollsters have found that if they first remind people of the various government programs and services provided for them, and then ask them to rate government, the results improve. "After people consider different government activities and programs, they are more likely to report that government has a positive effect on their lives."[4] Hardly surprising.

So how can we begin to make the invisible achievements of government more visible? One way for Americans to get more of this information is for government to give it to them. As Steven Hill has explained:

> Government should advertise its accomplishments just like a business does, through TV and radio ads, reminding the public of the good things it accomplishes. Corporations do this;

> why shouldn't government? A potential advertising theme could "Government is Good for You," with the ads showing the many ways that government does good things for individuals and communities, from providing direct services to producing regulations that facilitate business providing direct services. Imagine ads showing the volume of mail moved every day through the U. S Postal service; the scientific breakthroughs funded by government, the transportation and communication advances fostered by government.[5]

Governments could also learn from non-profit organizations and charities, which send out annual letters to their donors explaining all the good works that have come from their donations. Our state and local governments should be sending out "annual reports" that inform citizens of all the good their tax dollars are doing. For example, our local government should tell us how many criminals it has arrested, how many supermarket scanners and gas pumps it has checked, how many fires it has put out, how many parks it has been maintaining, how many construction sites it has inspected, how many miles of roads it has cleaned and plowed, how many gallons of clean water it has provided, how many drunk drivers it has gotten off the roads, how many restaurants it has inspected, how many people have used the public libraries, how many children it has educated, and so on. As the old saying goes, "It ain't bragging if you can do it" – and government is "doing it" for citizens every day.

Another step toward correcting our collective misperceptions of government would be for the news media to cover government in a more balanced and accurate way. The public relies on the media for their information about government, and as it stands today, most of that coverage is negative. This is to be expected from explicitly right-wing media outlets like Fox News who go out of their way to bash "big government" whenever they can. But even more mainstream and less ideological news sources – such as the major broadcast networks – feed their watchers and readers with a steady diet of negative stories about government. Political scandals, policy fiascos, and "wasteful programs" are considered news, government successes are not. When government programs work, we hear little about them – they only become front page news when they fail.

The news media need to take a more objective and even-handed view of government. No one is asking them to turn a blind eye toward the problems of government, but neither should they turn a blind eye toward its achievements. It should be part of the media's civic obligation to give the American public more accurate information about the role that government is playing in their lives. Some critics of the media have suggested that one step in the right direction would be for news organizations to make an editorial decision that for every two negative stories about government, they would offer one positive one. But given the current market-driven nature of the news media, such a change seems unlikely. There are, however, some alternatives to the mainstream media that at least give government an even break – such as *The Rachel Maddow Show* and journals like *The Nation* and *The American Prospect.* These sources of news and commentary are often hard on particular politicians and policies, but they are usually willing to acknowledge, and even praise, the vital roles played by social welfare programs and regulatory efforts.

The Need to Fight over How Government is Framed

Providing better information about government is a step in the right direction – but it is not nearly enough to turn around the negative views that many people have of this institution. It is tempting to think that if more people only knew what government was doing for them, they would cease to view it in such a negative light. But as Michael Lipsky, a scholar who has been studying the way the public views government, has observed: "Unfortunately, it is not that simple. If it were, supporters of key government programs and services long ago would have reminded people of the good things government does, and the anti-government initiatives of recent years would have been turned aside."[6]

According to Lipsky, the problem is that this approach leaves untouched the basic images or "frames" that people have about government. Frames determine how we process information and "the very meaning of new information depends upon the frame through which the information is processed."[7] This means that people who start out with a negative view of government may easily downplay or simply ignore information that contradicts that view. So merely providing more accurate information about government may do little to overturn these deep-rooted negative frames.

The situation here is similar to that of racial prejudice. We now know that if people have a strong view of racial minorities as "inferior," exposing them to information about the actual abilities and achievements of minorities does little to change that prejudiced view. They simply ignore the countervailing information that threatens their cherished beliefs, or they explain away the achievements of individual minorities as exceptions to the rule. So it is with government. If people harbor a prejudiced view of government, merely exposing them to counter-information may not win them over.

What is needed, then, is an approach that not only presents counter-information but also promotes counter-frames about government. We need to provide different and more positive images through which people can perceive government. This is the key to undermining the negative and inaccurate images of government being promoted by anti-government conservatives. As Lipsky explains it:

> Dominant frames that people draw upon are stable but they are not impervious to challenge or change. …In principle, every communication contributes to reinforcing or dissolving one or another frame. People embrace many frames at once, so there are opportunities to reinforce some frames and degrade others. Just as the right wing attack on government as inherently wasteful and inferior to market-based institutions has contributed to public skepticism about the potential of government, it may be possible to enhance other frames which hold government in a more balanced light. If communications were shaped to reinforce a frame in which government plays a constructive social role, and ceased reinforcing frames in which government is consigned a negative role, supporters of a positive role for government, acting in concert, could help shape political discourse in positive ways.[8]

Promoting different frames or images of government to replace the negative images being offered by anti-government activists is not as difficult or daunting a task at it may seem at first glance. It is not as if negative images are all that exist and we have to try to replace those images with entirely new ones. As Lipsky suggests, there are already many positive frames about government out there among the public. Most people have both positive and negative frames about government and the task at hand is to reinforce the former and thus undermine the latter.

Positive Images of Government

So what are some of these more positive frames or images of government? This is an important question that is being explored by a non-profit research group called Demos – the organization for which Michael Lipsky works. Demos is one of the few organizations that is studying the public's views of government with an eye toward reviving public confidence in this institution. One of their research projects is entitled "How to Talk about Government"[9] and its purpose has been to "find a new framework for talking about government that helps to dispel negative stereotypes and open the public to a reconsideration of the central role of an effective and supported public sector in achieving public purposes."[10]

This project has utilized surveys, interviews, and focus groups to explore the public's views of government. It has found, not too surprisingly, that the initial images that most people have of government are usually negative: wasteful bureaucracies, out-of-touch politicians, Big Brother, the Taxman, etc. But once people in these interviews and focus groups began to discuss more deeply the role that government plays in our society, more positive views soon emerged, and "there were indications that participants were beginning to adopt ways of viewing government that could lead to more public support and engagement."[11] In particular, when researchers introduced certain phrases, ideas, and images about government, these tended to trigger more affirmative and supportive views of this institution. Some of these alternative "frames" for government include:

- **Government as Watchdog or Protector**. Many people readily see government as playing a "protector" role, particularly as a provider of public safety. It is government that ensures that our streets our safe and that someone comes to rescue us and our house in case of fire. And many also acknowledge that government serves as a watchdog that protects us from abuse and harm from powerful private interests. For example, the public sees a very positive role for government in regulating business in order to protect us from unsafe products, environmental poisons, dangerous workplace conditions, etc.
- **Government as Consensus Builder.** Researchers found that Americans tend to initially see government as a bunch of bickering politicians who emphasize their partisan differences. But as study participants were asked to consider such things as how speed limits are set, how the postal service operates, and how schools are run, they began to appreciate more the consensus-building function that government provides. Democratic government is the way we come together collectively to decide what it is in our common good. Focusing only on our political divisions obscures the fact that there is often a great deal of agreement, especially on the local level, about what things are in the

public interest – things such as clean streets, good schools, a safe water supply, a prosperous downtown, and so on. Government is our primary institution for searching for what is in our common interests. In this way, our democratic governmental bodies help to tie us together as a community and enable us to build a common vision of the future.

- **Government as a Collective Public Conscience.** Interview subjects were quick to recognize that government has a unique mission in society – one not played by any other organization – that of public conscience. They recognized "that government has a constraining, conscience-like function that is missing in the realm of business. In this respect, government was cast as the collective moral conscience of the country – a role and characteristic that would be absent if the country were run by business alone."[12]
- **Government as a Provider of Public Structures.** Another positive image that emerged from these conversations was of government as a provider of essential "public structures." These structures – courts, schools, highways, regulatory systems, etc. – contribute directly to the prosperity, stability, and security we enjoy in the United States. People readily understand and appreciate the notion that "what has made America so successful is the effectiveness of our public structures" and that while "developing countries have many smart, hard-working individuals, they don't have the public structures that are essential for overall prosperity."[13]

Some Other Constructive Images of Government

Beyond the work of Demos, it is certainly possible to identify additional positive images of government. Here, for example, are several more affirmative images that were discussed in other chapters in this book.

- **Government as a Practical Problem-Solver**. While the right insists that government is the problem, it is in fact one of the main problem-solvers in our society. When faced with economic meltdowns, deadly diseases, growing crime, dirty air, etc., it is government that we turn to remedy those problems. And as we've seen in several earlier chapters, it has usually come through. Government is often the only institution in a position to fix or at least mitigate many of the serious problems we face as a society. Government is the public Mr. Fix-It.

- **Government as Righter of Wrongs**. Life is often unfair. Innocent people often fall victim to thieves, scam artists, false advertisers, etc. People and organizations with large amounts of private power can often treat us unjustly – by discriminating against us or by violating our basic freedoms and human rights. Government can be seen as often the only method that we have to collectively right these wrongs and create a more just world. It is the main institution we rely on to punish the guilty, protect the innocent, and ensure that people get what they deserve in life.
- **Government as a Moral Instrument**. Government is also a unique and powerful instrument for moral action – for doing good in the world. We often rely heavily on the public sector to feed the hungry, care for the sick, and comfort the victims of tragedies. Many Americans feel a moral obligation to be their "brother's keeper," and government is often one of the most common ways that we care for each other in this way.

Again, it is crucial to note that these kinds of positive images are not alien to most Americans. But they are currently buried beneath the surface and obscured by the constant drumbeat of anti-government criticism offered by the political right. These more positive views need to be unearthed and nurtured in order to help people reconnect with how government works to improve their lives and promote the common good. On its website, Demos has some practical suggestions for how ordinary citizens can promote these more positive visions of government. They have developed a "How to Talk About Government Toolkit" that contains sample op-ed pieces and speeches that illustrate how people can fashion messages about government that better convey how it enables us to work together to solve problems and improve the quality of our lives.

But clearly we need more than just random individuals standing up for government. We need a pro-government *movement* to spread the word about why government is good – a coalition of groups that will act to counter the negative views of government being promulgated by anti-state activists. Let us consider just what this kind of pro-government coalition could look like.

Building a Pro-Government Coalition

The battle over government is not simply an intellectual debate that can be won with more accurate information and more positive frames about government. It is power struggle – a struggle that anti-government forces have been winning for the last several decades. Reviving government means more than revising our ideas about it, it means seizing political power back from the political forces that are trying to tear it down. It means refunding and reinvigorating the essential government programs that have been undermined and cut back by conservative policymakers. But how is this going to be done and who is going to do it?

This is not the place to discuss a grand strategy for how Americans can take control of their local, state, and federal governments away from radical right-wing anti-statists. But what can be said is that any effort to recapture government from these conservatives must be grounded in a more positive view of the public sector. Part of what can bring together an anti-right political coalition is an explicit appreciation of the vital role that government plays in society. In this respect, we can learn a lot from success of the political right. Much of what has held the conservative coalition together has been an ideological opposition to government. In the same way, a commitment to a strong and active government should be part of the broader political vision that will unify and inspire a center-left coalition.

There is already a wide variety of interest groups that could form a coalition around such a positive vision of government. Environmentalists, labor, minorities, teachers, consumer advocates, and the elderly are all natural supporters of a more active and well-funded government. They rely heavily on government to support programs that serve their interests and the public interest as well. However, currently most of these groups are narrowly focused on promoting particular issues – whether those are more affordable health care, workers' rights, retirement security, or improving education – and put little energy into the broader political task of promoting stronger government. This is understandable, because most of these groups must carefully shepherd their very limited political resources – but it is a serious strategic mistake. They need to see the larger picture: that building a broader base of public support for government will eventually help in their individual policy areas as well. If, for example, we can build up a more adequate and reliable tax base, this will ensure the public resources necessary to fund the programs dear to the heart of these organizations. Conservatives realized long ago that if they can delegitimize government in general, this will aid them tremendously in their efforts to cut specific government programs. In the same way, an effort to relegitimize government will generally help to promote many specific government programs. Some groups have begun to come around to this realization and coalitions are already developing to collectively fight against attacks on government, especially efforts to keep cutting taxes. But much more work has to be done to bring together all these various interest groups to promote a broad, pro-government political vision.

However, it is important to think beyond interest groups and consider the role that social movements could play in promoting a more healthy and active government. It is hardly a coincidence that broad-based social movements played key roles in every era in our history that saw a major expansion of the mission and reach of government in the United States. During the late 19th and early 20th centuries, the Progressive movement was responsible for the first major government interventions in the market to curb corporate abuses. Working with the labor movement, Progressives helped push through legislation to break up corporate trusts and monopolies, to regulate the purity of food products, restrict child labor, and institute industrial accident insurance. The next big expansion in the role of government took place in the 1930s. The severe depression and the rising power of the labor movement forced policymakers to pass many path-breaking social welfare programs, including Social Security, unemployment insurance, and the first forms of welfare assistance. Protection for workers also increased dramatically when government capitulated to labor demands for the right to unionize and for the eight-hour day. Social movements also played key roles in the next great expansion of the responsibilities of government in the 1960s. The civil rights movement forced the passage of anti-discrimination laws, voting rights legislation, and affirmative action policies. The Women's Movement pushed through a number of measures that decreased discrimination against women – especially in the private sector. The consumer movement, led by Ralph Nader, encouraged the government to move into a number of new areas, including stricter product safety requirements, truth in lending, automobile lemon laws, and so on. And of course the environmental movement was responsible for creating an entirely new and important mission for government: protection of the human and natural environments.

Remnants of these movements are around today, but primarily in a much weaker form – as interest groups. Some labor and environmental groups seem primarily oriented toward raising money so that they can build up their staffs in Washington, D.C. and lobby for particular pieces of legislation. In contrast, social movements usually emphasize grass-roots organizing and try to mobilizing large numbers of the public into their cause. They rely on "people power" rather than "money power." Movement strategies are also often different from interest groups, emphasizing a whole variety of direct action political tactics – strikes, boycotts, demonstrations, non-violent resistance, etc. – to put pressure on lawmakers. More importantly, social movements usually have a broader political vision, seeking to make society and the political system more just and more democratic. They often want to redistribute power from the private sector – which is producing the pollution, the workplace discrimination, the low wages, and the dangerous products – to the public sector, where we are better able to protect the interests of average Americans. So this broader political vision includes a very positive role for government – one that recognizes that most social and economic problems can only be solved through the actions of an energetic public sector.

For some time now, there have been discussions among those in environmental, labor, and civil rights groups about the need to reconstitute themselves as social movements. As individual interest groups, they have had few major legislative victories in the last several decades. One idea is to form a large "progressive" movement that would serve as an umbrella for workers, minorities, environmentalists, women, the poor, etc.[14] If such a united progressive movement were to emerge, this would be good news for those who also want to revitalize government in the United States. It would serve as a major political platform to pursue pro-government ideas and agendas.

Other Parts of a Pro-Government Coalition

There are other institutions and groups that would be natural participants in a pro-government coalition. These include non-profits, foundations, think tanks, public intellectuals, and public officials.

Non-Profits. These organizations could provide vital support in the effort to revitalize government. They include charities, hospitals, human service groups, museums, and community foundations, and they represent a significant sector in American society. Traditionally, many of these groups have been thought of as *rivals* to government programs – providing health care, support for the arts, disaster relief, and services for the needy that the government does not provide. However, the decline of government and cutting of government programs is having several negative effects on these organizations. First, government actually provides a substantial amount funding for many non-profit efforts. This is particularly true of many private human service organizations. For example, Catholic Charities USA, which provides emergency food and shelter to the poor, gets 65% of its budget from the government.[15] So as taxes are cut and budgets slashed, there is less money to support the efforts of these private charitable groups.

Another problem is that as government programs themselves are cut, non-profits are being asked to take up the slack. Yet there is usually little chance that private donations will increase to enable them to do take on these added responsibilities.[16] Workers for non-profits usually have a strong passion for their missions – whether that is to promote the arts or care for the needy. But the attack on government is also an attack on those valued missions and an attack on the clients that they care about and serve. For this reason, non-profit organizations should become major players in the effort to restore trust in government and to fight the conservative campaign to cut vital government programs.

Foundations, Think Tanks, and Public Intellectuals. These are the groups in the best position to bring a more accurate and positive vision of government to the public. They can do much to reframe the public discussion of government in a way that emphasizes the beneficial roles played by the public sector. Although right-wing foundations are more numerous than those on the left and the center, well-funded organizations like the Ford Foundation could become more influential players in the pro-government coalition, if they chose to do so. Several foundations are already supporting the work of Demos – the pro-government group whose efforts were described earlier.

In recent years, several progressive think-tanks have emerged and are vigorously promoting new and innovative government policies that will promote the public interest in many vital areas. Good examples include the New America Foundation, the Economic Policy Institute, and the Center for American Progress. Most of these organizations, however, are primarily policy-oriented and could do more to explicitly promote a positive vision of government itself.

Public intellectuals are thinkers who spend much of their time writing and speaking to the public about political issues. Some write books, some are opinion columnists, others work for think tanks, and many are academics. Foundations on the right are famous for their direct and indirect support of conservative intellectuals. Consider the career of Charles Murray. His rise from obscurity to become one of the most influential public intellectuals in this country was made possible by continuous support from right-wing funding groups. The Bradley Foundation and the Manhattan Institute have both been very generous in supporting Murray, giving him grants to write books and funding efforts to aggressively promote them. It has been estimated that conservative organizations have spent well over a million dollars promoting Murray's anti-government writings.[17]

Pro-government intellectuals and their projects deserve similar encouragement and assistance from centrist and leftist foundations. If someone writes a book supporting government and its vital programs, these foundations should do exactly what the right-wing funders would do: they should buy thousands of copies and distribute them to policymakers, journalists, and libraries; they should provide generous funds for the author to go on a nation-wide promotional tour; and they should arrange for numerous glowing reviews of the book by liberal pundits and op-ed writers. Your side can't win an intellectual battle unless you are willing to vigorously promote your ideas.

A number of public intellectuals have already come to the defense of government. Benjamin Barber of Rutgers University has written extensively about the need for active government and "strong democracy." Paul Krugman, a columnist for *The New York Times*, has commented often on the right-wing attacks on government and their deleterious effects on many Americans. Reporter and author William Greider has also been writing about the radical agenda of the anti-state conservatives.[18] Even Garrison Keillor has written about how Americans need to support "government as a necessary force for good."[19] But we need many more where they came from if we want to encourage a substantial change in the public's opinion about government. This pro-government message needs to be repeated constantly in a variety of media if it is to have any effect.

Public Officials. Attacks on government are also attacks on public officials – and policymakers and administrators should see it this way. Those who work in the public sector have an obvious and strong interest in supporting it. But surprisingly, this isn't always the case. Politicians, even those who are moderates or liberals, often actively participate in irresponsible government bashing. It is fashionable for politicians of all stripes to "run against Washington" in their campaigns – to complain how government officials are out of touch and corrupt. But they are shooting themselves in the foot. They are actually contributing to the delegitimation of government and thus undermining their own power and their ability to promote the programs they value.

Public officials should be doing exactly the opposite: explaining to the public the important role that government is playing in their lives. Most of them certainly believe this, otherwise they would not have chosen a life of public service. But many seem to shirk the role of being a vocal public advocate of government. One exception has been U.S. Representative Tom Allen (D-Maine) – who could serve as a good role model in this regard. In 2001, he quickly responded to President George W. Bush's efforts to slash taxes and cut back many government programs by penning an article called "The Government: Doing What We Can't Do Alone" for his weekly column to his constituents in Maine. He started by mentioning some of the major achievements of the federal government, including reducing workplace discrimination, increasing access to health care by the elderly, expanding the right to vote, reducing disease, constructing a national highway system, promoting retirement security, etc. Then he observed:

> What is remarkable is that we take so many of those things for granted today. When we drive on I-95, we don't think of the massive federal investment it took to create a national highway system. Most of us can't remember a time, before Social Security and Medicare, when half of our seniors lived (and died) in poverty. None of these achievements could have been done by individuals, or by the private sector alone. Only the federal government could afford the risk, and get it done for the benefit of America. ...It is our civic duty to remind ourselves and our neighbors that so much of what makes our nation great has come from our collective action through government. As Lincoln wrote, "The legitimate object of government is to do for the people what needs to be done, but which they cannot, by individual effort, do at all, or do well, for themselves. ...That is why it is disturbing to hear some politicians attempt to drive a wedge between all of us and our government. They portray the government not as an institution "we" constitute, but as a disconnected "they" designed to intrude on "us." ... The more politicians make government an "us versus them" proposition, the more a malevolent and intrusive government becomes a self-fulfilling prophecy. The more we make the federal government, warts and all, "our" investment in our common future, the brighter the future will be for the next generations of Americans.[20]

When was the last time you heard a politician speak so positively and eloquently about the achievements of our democratic government? Probably not often. This has to change.

Making Support for Government a Populist Issue

While much of the support and energy for a pro-government coalition must come from interest groups, public officials, and political activists, we should not ignore the role that can be played by average Americans. Support for government needs to become a populist issue. Conservatives and libertarians have succeeded in hijacking populism and redefining it as a right-wing cause. They claim to speak for the common person against an intrusive government. This is one of the main appeals of the Tea Party movement.

We need to reestablish a left-wing form of populism: the kind of movement that was popular during the Franklin Roosevelt's administration and the activist era of the 1960s. This version of populism embraces government as a way of empowering average Americans. We need to more effectively make the case that the advantage of democratic government is that it enables us to band together collectively to generate enough power to address those issues that are normally beyond our control. For example, as Benjamin Barber points out, government can put us on a par with large powerful corporations and discourage them from exploiting us through faulty products, low wages, unsafe investments, dangerous workplaces, etc. "Big government – or let's call it strong democracy – is for the little guy; it's how he and his neighbors can take on the big bullies in the private sector."[21]

We need to stress the point that most of us by ourselves do not have the power to address the many problems that are afflicting our lives. Individual health-care savings accounts will not provide affordable medical for most of us, we all can't afford private schools to ensure a decent education for our children, the market will not provide retirement security, businesses will not always provide safe working conditions or livable wages, charities cannot possibly take care of all the needy, "let the buyer beware" is not going to protect us from dangerous products, and we can't clean up the environment simply by recycling our cans and bottles. No – to achieve these goals and to create a decent and humane society, we must have an active and well-funded public sector.

A populist vision that includes a large and active government is not something that will just appeal to those on the political left. We need to remember that Americans of all political stripes already support many government programs. When over 60% of Americans say that they want the government to spend more on education and health, 69% favor more generous government aid to the poor, 77% say the government should do all it takes to protect the environment, and 83% favor raising the federal minimum wage, these are not just liberals and progressives speaking – they include many moderates and even conservatives. Remarkably, a poll by the Center for American Progress found that 40% of conservatives and libertarians support a *larger* federal government role in areas like improving public schools, reducing poverty, and developing new energy sources.[22] So pro-government activists would be making a mistake to ignore those in the political middle or even on the right.

It is tempting for those on the left to think that all Americans who vote Republican or express contempt for government are hardhearted people who don't care about education, the environment, the poor, etc. In fact, most of these people do care, but many have been led to believe that government is bad and a poor way to promote their concerns. What they need to see is that there is often no good substitute for government – that we simply cannot rely on the ourselves as individuals, or the invisible hand of the market, to address the many serious problems and concerns that face us as a society.

The problem, of course, is that most average Americans are unlikely to get excited by an appeal to support "government" in the abstract. So we need to connect what people *are* passionate about – specific values and goals – to government itself. Thus if people want to protect their family from risks – and they do – then they should be supporting a well-funded and active government that can shield them from environmental toxins, dangerous products, deadly diseases, and financial crises. In the same way, most Americans care deeply about having a fair and just society, but they need to be reminded that we can create this kind of world only by acting collectively through government. As Diana Aviv once observed, "We all seek justice, and the path to justice leads inevitably to the halls of government. That is where this great community we call America, in its wisdom or in its folly, chooses the policies and programs that bring justice nearer or keep it at bay."[23] This is true of many other things besides justice – most efforts to promote the common good lead to the halls of government.

A broad-based effort to revitalize our public sector must be rooted in broadly shared values. And it must recognize that when government is fully democratic, it can embody the best in us. Right-wing anti-statists want us to believe that government represents only the worst in us – our corruptness, incompetence, and selfishness. But as this book has shown, government programs most often represent our finest and most humane qualities: our compassion for those in need, our desire to care for each other, our pursuit of a just society, our commitment to solve problems that cause human suffering. Most Americans are not simply out for themselves; they also want to make the world a better place for everyone. They just need to better recognize the inherent connection between their desire to promote the common good and the need for government. Government is often one of our best tools for transforming our world in a positive way.

Fortunately, there are some indications that average Americans are beginning to rally in support of government. Large numbers of Americans supported successful efforts to reform health care and to re-regulate an out of control financial industry. In many communities around the United States, citizens have begun to organize to fight tax cuts, prevent reductions of vital government services, and pressure government to expand its efforts to solve the many serious problems we continue to face as a society. In 2010, voters in Colorado defeated by a two-to-one margin three ballot initiatives that would have drastically cut funding for state and local services and banned the use of debt by the state government. The vote represented a victory for a widespread coalition that included grassroots groups and even parts of the business community. The Colorado Progressive Coalition pointed out that the defeat of these measures meant that:

> We value equal opportunities, a strong infrastructure, safety, and efficient government. We care about the services that are available and provided to EVERYONE in our state. We understand that we are stronger when we put our tax dollars together. We sent this message out to the anti-tax and anti-government faction loud and clear. Colorado is worth it!

People are getting tired of the conservative assault on important government services – tired of school budgets being cut, firefighters being laid off, environmental problems being ignored, roads falling into disrepair, and Social Security being threatened. They are beginning to realize that government is not always some remote "them," but that government often is "us." So when conservatives are able to defund and hamstring government, they are limiting our ability to protect our families from harm and to improve all of our lives. More and more people are starting to recognize that the attack on government is an attack on them, and so they are fighting back. We should all join them. We need government, and right now, it needs us.

---

1. Robert Kuttner, "Teachable Moments: Every Week, Celebrate a Public Hero." *The American Prospect Online Edition*, July 1, 2004. http://www.prospect.org/web/page.ww?section=root&name=ViewPrint&articleId=8120
2. "A Matter of Trust: Americans and Their Government 1958-2004," Council for Excellence in Government, 2005, p. 15.
3. "A Matter of Trust," pp. 32-33.

4. Meg Bostrum, *By, or for, the People: A Meta-Analysis of Public Opinion of Government* (New York: Demos, March 1, 2005), p. 34.
5. Steven Hill, *10 Steps to Repair American Democracy* (Sausilito, CA: PoliPoint Press, 2006) p. 181.
6. Bostrum, p. 7.
7. Bostrum, p. 7.
8. Bostrum, p. 7.
9. This project was sponsored by Public Works: the Demos Center for the Public Sector and the Council for Excellence in Government. Research was coordinated by the FrameWorks Institute and conducted by Cultural Logic and Public Knowledge.
10. Demos, "A Focus on Government" October 2005, p.2. http://www.demos.org/pubs/PB4_WithoutaMission_2005_09_14.pdf
11. Demos, "A Focus on Government" October 2005, p.2.
12. Demos, "Making It Real," October 2005, p.2. http://www.demos.org/pubs/PB3_ThinkingProductively_2005_09_14.p df
13. Demos, "Public Structures," March 2006, p.3. http://www.demos.org/pubs/PB_6_Public_Structures_2006_04.pdf
14. See, for example, Michael Shellenberger and Ted Nordhaus' essay "The Death of Environmentalism: Global Warming Politics in a Post-Environmental World," in which they argue that environmentalists must move beyond ineffective single-issue politics and join with labor and other groups to create a broad-based grassroots social movement. http://www.thebreakthrough.org/images/Death_of_Environmentalism.pdf
15. Barbara M. Blank, *It Takes a Nation* (Princeton, NJ: Princeton University Press, 1997), p. 203.
16. Dianne Stewart, "Add Another Job to Your List: Be an Advocate for Government," *SPARC Change*, Winter 2004, p. 5.
17. Eric Alterman, *What Liberal Media* (New York: Basic Books, 2003), pp. 92-93.
18. William Greider, "The Right's Grand Ambition: Rolling Back the 20th Century" May, 12, 2003, *The Nation.*
19. Garrison Keillor, *Homegrown Democrat* (New York: Viking Press, 2005).
20. Tom Allen, "The Government: Doing What We Can't Do Alone," Message to Maine, January 20, 2001. http://tomallen.house.gove/printer.asp?contentID=108
21. Benjamin Barber, "A Civics Lesson," *The Nation*, November 4, 1996, p. 21.

22. Guy Molyneux and Ruy Teixeira, with John Whaley, "Better, Not Smaller: What Americans Want from their Federal Government," July 2010. http://www.americanprogress.org/issues/2010/07/what_americans_want.html
23. Diana Aviv, "We the People: Our Collective Work." Speech at the Independent Sector Annual Conference, Chicago, November 8, 2004. p. 6.

Additional Resources

Books

David Bollier, *Silent Theft: The Private Plunder of our Common Wealth* (New York: Taylor and Francis Group, 2002).

Milton J. Esman, *Government Works: Why Americans Need the Feds* (Ithaca, NY, Cornell University Press, 2000).

Charles Goodsell, *The Case for Bureaucracy: A Public Administration Polemic, 4th ed.* (Washington, D.C.: CQ Press, 2004).

John O. Fox, *If Americans Really Understood the Income Tax* (Boulder Colorado: Westview Press, 2001).

Stephanie Greenwood (ed.), *10 Excellent Reasons Not to Hate Taxes* (New York: The New Press, 2008).

Jacob Hacker, *The Great Risk Shift* (Oxford: Oxford University Press, 2006).

Jacob Hacker and Paul Pierson, *Off Center: The Republican Revolution and the Erosion of American Democracy* (New Haven: Yale University Press, 2005).

Jacob Hacker and Paul Pierson, *Winner-Take-All-Politics: How Washington Made the Rich Richer – and Turned Its Back on the Middle Class* (New York: Simon and Schuster, 2010).

Steven Hill, *10 Steps to Repair American Democracy* (Sausilito, CA: Poli-Point Press, 2006).

William E. Hudson, *The Libertarian Illusion: Ideology, Public Policy and the Assault on the Common Good* (Washington, D.C.: CQ Press, 2008).

Lawrence Jacobs and Theda Skocpol, eds., *Inequality and American Democracy* (New York: Russell Sage F0undation, 2005).

Paul Krugman, *The Great Unraveling: Losing our Way in the New Century* (New York: Norton, 2005).

Robert Kuttner, *Everything for Sale* (. New York: Alfred A. Knopf, 1997).

Paul C. Light's, *Government's Greatest Achievements: From Civil Rights to Homeland Security* (Washington, DC: Brookings Institution, 2002).

Michael Lerner, *The Left Hand of God: Taking Back Our Country from the Religious Right* (San Francisco: HarperSanFrancisco, 2006).

David Moss, *When All Else Fails: Government as the Ultimate Risk Manager* (Cambridge, MA: Harvard University Press, 2002).

Max Neiman, *Defending Government: Why Big Government Works* (Upper Saddle River, NJ: Prentice-Hall, 2000).

Charles Noble, *The Collapse of Liberalism* (New York: Rowman and Littlefield, 2004).

David Schuman and D.W. Sid Olufs, *The War Against the Common Good* (Novato, CA: Chandler Sharp, 2007).

Herman Schwartz, *Right Wing Justice: The Conservative Campaign to Take Over the Courts* (New York: Nation Books, 2004).

Cass R. Sunstein, *Radicals in Robes: Why Extreme Right-Wing Courts are Wrong for America* (NY: Basic Books, 2006).

Jacob Weisberg, *In Defense of Government* (New York: Scribner, 1996).

Websites

Center for Budget and Policy Priorities: conducts research to inform public debates over proposed budget and tax policies. Also examines the short- and long-term impacts of proposed policies on the health of the economy and helps to ensure that the needs of low-income families are considered in budget debates. http://www.cbpp.org/

Citizens for Sensible Safeguards: a coalition of public interest groups across the country concerned with our ability to protect the public with effective regulatory policy. http://www.sensiblesafeguards.org/

Council for Excellence in Government: an organization that aims to provide best practices to government innovators, and works to improve the performance of government at all levels. http://www.excelgov.org/

Demos: A Network for Ideas & Action: one of the foremost organizations promoting a strong and effective public sector with the capacity to plan for the future and provide for the common good. Demos is the leading source of ideas and strategies for reviving public support for government. http://www.demos.org/

FairVote – the Center for Voting and Democracy: the leading organization promoting voting system reforms that would make government more representative of the electorate and more responsive the public. http://www.fairvote.org

Government is Good: the web version of this book. Visit this site for updates of chapters and additional material defending this vital institution from the attacks being waged by the right-wing. http://www.governmentisgood.com

National Priorities Project: a research organization that analyzes and clarifies federal data so that people can understand and influence how their tax dollars are spent. Also, facilitates dialogue and action between national social justice and security policy groups. http://nationalpriorities.org/

New America Foundation: a non-partisan policy institute that argues for more active government in a wide variety of policy areas, including education, retirement, environment, and health. http://www.newamerica.net/

OMB Watch: a hardworking organization dedicated to increasing government transparency and accountability; to ensuring sound, equitable regulatory and budgetary processes and policies; and to protecting and promoting active citizen participation in our democracy. http://www.ombwatch.org/

On the Commons.org: a project of the Tomales Bay Institute, this blog is dedicated to spreading the idea that "some forms of wealth belong to all of us, and that these community resources must be actively protected and managed for the good of all." http://onthecommons.org/

Public Citizen: an organization that fights for openness and democratic accountability in government. Also pushes for better consumer, energy, environmental, and drug regulations. http://www.citizen.org

CPSIA information can be obtained at www.ICGtesting.com
Printed in the USA
LVOW10s0815221213

366399LV00004B/207/P

9 781457 506581